The American Journalists

THE RICHMOND EXAMINER
DURING THE WAR

John M. Daniel

ARNO
&
The New York Times

Collection Created and Selected
by Charles Gregg of Gregg Press

Reprint edition 1970 by Arno Press Inc.

LC# 76-125690
ISBN 0-405-01667-0

The American Journalists
ISBN for complete set: 0-405-01650-6

Reprinted from a copy in
The State Historical Society of Wisconsin Library

Manufactured in the United States of America

THE

RICHMOND EXAMINER

DURING THE WAR;

OR,

THE WRITINGS OF JOHN M. DANIEL.

WITH A MEMOIR OF HIS LIFE,

BY HIS BROTHER,

FREDERICK S. DANIEL.

NEW YORK:
PRINTED FOR THE AUTHOR.
1868.

PREFACE.

The following Writings of the late John M. Daniel, Editor and Proprietor of the *Daily Richmond Examiner*, were published in that paper during the war. Preserved in the original text, they are republished at this day because of the intrinsic and durable value they possess, as expressed in the sanction with which they have already been stamped by the public—by the genuine public who are not only willing but desirous to hear the truth in regard to public men and events, whether of the past or of the present. By a critical analysis of the men and events of that memorable epoch, 1861-65—which in itself resumes American history, and which will not soon be surpassed in importance, on this continent at least—these writings present a true reflex of the spirit in which the conflict was waged.

F. S. D.

Richmond, Va., *May*, 1868.

DAILY RICHMOND EXAMINER.

MARCH 4, 1861.

This Fourth of March, the memorable day of a memorable year, will not attain a less celebrity in future history than the Roman Ides of the same month. We stand to-day between two worlds. Here a past ends, here a future begins. The Republic of the United States on this day bids farewell to the style, the policy, the principles that have borne it in the lifetime of a man from insignificance to grandeur, from the poverty of Sparta to the wealth of Ormus or of Ind, from the footing of San Marino to equality with the British Empire. To-day we take leave of our policy and our practice, of the manners and of the men who have marked and guided the career that is ended. The line of those high personages, who will hereafter be known in history, only, as the Presidents, ends to-day; and that generation who shall learn their lives and their character from the pages of the future Gibbon who will narrate the decline and fall of the United States will compare them with the despicable tyrants whose dismal roll commences on the peristyle of the Capitol under the light of the sun now shining, as the youth of our day contrast the grand succession of Roman Consuls with the Divine Tiberius, with the Neros, with the Claudes, the Caligulas who defiled their seats and prostituted their titles, when another such day of March had separated another constitutional republic from another disguised despotism.

President Buchanan is the last of the family of Presidents. He was learned in their school, looked and spoke, and endeavored to act and think as they did. The historical character which he desired to leave was one like theirs, and, whatever the failure in essentials, the style and outward mould was that of the Madisons, the Monroes, the Van Burens, Tylers, Polks. We would be uncandid to say that he has filled their measure; for though the retiring President is one of the most distinguished figures of our day; has passed a long life in the most splendid employment; and though he must always be reckoned as one of the most eminent and celebrated statesmen of this country, it is impossible to deny that his administration has been unequal to his fame; that he has left chaos where he found order, ruin where he found prosperity; or that much of this disaster may be fairly charged to his faults of character and policy.

It is difficult to say which was the most unfortunate, his foreign or his domestic system. It is certain that the former was the least American ever followed by a Democratic President. Even Mr. Buchanan himself would probably admit that his domestic policy has not been successful. Yet few who have either spirit, intelligence, or national pride, can fail to regret the retiring President while gazing on his successor. Whatever his particular faults, in person he well represented the decency, the dignity, the decorum of the country.

To replace him in the White House, Northern Federalism has sent a creature whom no one can hear with patience or look on without disgust. We have all heard of a King of Shreds and Patches; but in the first of "Free Presidents" we have the delightful combination of a western county lawyer with a Yankee barkeeper. No American of any section has read the oratory with which he has strewn his devious road to Washington, condensed lumps of imbecility, buffoonery, and vulgar malignity, without a blush of shame. It is with a bitter pang that we remember that these samples of utter blackguardism have already gone to all the earth translated into all the languages that men speak, to justify the worst representations that our worst enemies have ever made of the national degradation to which they pretend republican government must ever lead.

But all personal antipathies are lost in the deep sentiment of apprehension which must affect every thinking man when he remembers the terrible significance of this beastly figure. Whether we are to be governed by a gentleman or ruled by a baboon, would matter comparatively little were each the representative of constitutional government. But with Lincoln comes something worse than slang, rowdyism, brutality, and all moral filth; something worse than all the tag and rag of Western grog-shops and Yankee factories, headed by Bob, Prince of Rails, and that successor to Miss Lane, in diamond eardrops and with ivory fan to wave over the faces of the diplomatic corps in the East-room, while urging them "not to be too warm in the cause." With all that comes arbitrary power. With all those comes the daring and reckless leader of Abolitionists, who has long proclaimed and now is effecting his purpose of destroying every federative feature of the constitution, all the peculiar characteristics of the separate State systems, to consolidate them all by mere numerical force in one grand anti-slavery community.

The new President has climbed to his place on the fragments of a shattered Confederacy, and the mere necessity of things will force him to deluge them in blood long before the Ides of another March has come again. A citizen of this State, returning to his country after an absence of years, and alighting at daybreak in the streets of its Capital, heard the bugle's reveille, the roll of drums and the tramp of armed guards there till he fancied himself back in Venice, or arriving in Warsaw. The first of the Free Presidents gets to the seat of government in the disguise of a foreigner and by the nocturnal flight of a conscience-stricken murderer in purpose; he is inaugurated to-day as John Brown was hung, under the mouths of cannon leveled at the citizens whom he swears to protect; and with the bayonets of mercenary battalions commanding every road to the fountain of mercy and justice. What can come of all this but civil war and public ruin?

MARCH 19, 1861.

"Gli Animali Parlanti."

[Being the EXAMINER's Translation of Casti.]

ONCE upon a time, when it was the custom of the beasts and birds of the United States of North America to elect a king to reign over them, once in every four years, it so happened that an ugly and ferocious old Orang-Outang from the wilds of Illinois, who was known by the name of Old ABE, was chosen king. This election created a great disturbance and a revolution in the Southern States, for the beasts in that part of the country had imported from Africa a large number of black monkeys and had made slaves of them; and Old ABE had declared that this was an indignity offered to his family, that monkey slavery was the sum of all villainies, and that he would not allow it to be perpetrated on any account, and that when he became king he intended to abolish monkey slavery throughout all his dominions.

As soon, then, as it became known that Old ABE was elected king, the States lying on the Gulf of Mexico, where the beasts were very independent and ferocious, declared that no Orang-Outang should be king over them, and they, therefore, rebelled and seceded from the Union. When Old ABE heard that the Gulf States had revolted, and would not acknowledge him to be their king, he flourished his great war club over his head and swore by his whiskers that he would whip them back into the Union. He accordingly collected a great army of bloodhounds, jackals, vultures, and runaway monkies, and placed them under the command of a notorious old Turkey Cock named Fuss and Feathers, and ordered him to march down upon the Southern States and subdue them and free all of their slaves.

At this time the Boar of Rockbridge, (who was supposed to be a lineal descendant of David's Sow, and was notorious for the large amount of swill that he could consume,) was the Governor of the beasts of the Old Dominion. When he heard that Old ABE was raising an army to invade the Southern States, he issued a proclamation calling together the most learned and wise of the beasts of the Old Dominion to sit in council and decide upon what was best to be done under the circumstances.

The Council met on the 13th day of February in a large grove on the banks of James river. An ancient white Owl, from Loudon county, was called to preside over the meeting. Upon taking the stump, the President addressed the meeting in a few solemn and dirge-like notes. He said that he had but little experience in legislation, but that he would try and do his best. He dwelt feelingly upon the distracted state of the country, said that he could see in the dark further than most persons, but the gloom which now overhung the country was to him impenetrable. He hoped, however, that wise and prudent counsels would prevail, and, above all, that they would not be precipitate. He would try his best to keep order, and hoped that the spectators on the outskirts of the grove, and particularly the Turkey Buzzards, Shanghais, and young monkeys in the upper limbs of the trees, and the female magpies and chatterers, would keep silence, and not disturb the meeting by any demonstrations of applause, and that the Geese would not hiss. He then announced that the first business in order would be the election of officers.

A Raven was then elected secretary and two Magpies as reporters. A Mastiff and two Bull-Terriers were chosen as sergeant-at-arms and doorkeepers, a couple of Hawks appointed to keep order in the upper limbs of the trees, and three pretty little Poodles were selected as runners.

The Stump then announced that the meeting was ready to proceed to business.

A committee was then appointed to draft resolutions expressive of the sense of the council.

During the absence of the Committee, all eyes being turned upon the Lion of Princess Anne, he sprung to his feet, shook his mane, and gave a roar that made the woods resound. He said that he was not for waiting for this old Ape to invade Virginia. He was in favor of marching at once to meet the foe in his own country; that he had crushed one infamous beast by the name of SAM, who had ventured to invade Virginia, and that if he could get Old ABE by the throat he would serve him in the same way. If all would follow him, he would lead them on to victory or death. If they had elected him king, as he told them to do, all this trouble would have been avoided. For his part, he "would rather be a dog and bay the moon" than live a moment under the dominion of this Illinois Ape.

An old Spaniel from Rockbridge then rose, and said he hoped that the honorable beast who had just taken his seat did not mean, in the latter part of his speech, to cast any reflection upon him or any of his family. He thought that the distinguished beast was rather too pugnacious. He could see no necessity for resistance. For his part, he was in favor of abject submission. A little correction was a very wholesome thing. After kicks and cuffs always came favors, and he was willing to suffer the first in order that he might enjoy the last; that one master was as good as another, so you were kept warm and well fed. He was opposed to staying out in the cold. The beasts of the South had acted like traitors and fools, and he did not want to keep company with them. As to this monkey question, he did not think that it ought to divide the country. He had long been of the opinion that Virginia would be better off without monkeys than with them.

When the Spaniel took his seat, it was observed that he had a collar on his neck with the name of Orang-Outang written on it, whereupon a great hue and cry arose among the outsiders, and the Spaniel had to turn tail and run; and it was supposed that he went over to the enemy.

In consequence of this disturbance in the meeting, the Owl ordered the Mastiff and the Bull-Terriers and the Hawks to do their duty and clear the avenues and the upper limbs, which was done, and the meeting was restored to order.

The Red Fox, from Middlesex, said that Old ABE might take his brush if he could; he intended to die a-fighting, but did not like to go too far from his own hole, so he could not follow his warlike friend from Princess Anne; he, for one, was sound on the goose.

An old Horse, from Prince George, with shaggy mane and unkempt tail, very deaf, and sadly in want of oats, cut up some high capers and curvettes to show his condition. He said that they had no right to resist; that Old ABE had been elected king by a majority of all the animals in the country, and that it was their duty to submit; that he understood Illinois corn was very good, and, for his part, he would not object to trying a bushel or so; if he could only get into the public crib he would not care much who was king.

The Dormouse, from Rockbridge, said that the shock of battle had come, and we must stand firm, and all run together. He was in favor of "Virginia pawsing;" time enough to squeak when you felt the paw of the cat upon your back; when the worst came to the worst, he could run into his hole.

The Jackal, from Harrison, spoke in high terms of the Orang-Outang. He said that a good many of his kith and kin were in the invading army, and that he was certain they meant no harm; that whatever was done would be for the good of the Old Dominion. He was opposed to resistance, and agreed with the old Spaniel from Rockbridge, that submission was the best policy.

The Terrapin, from Franklin, said that he was in favor of waiting for more reliable information. "Time enough to move when you feel the fire on your back," was an old family adage, to which he was proud to allude, and illustrated the principle upon which he intended to act.

The Durham Bull, from Goochland, here raised a terrible dust, whisked his tail, and bellowed furiously. He was for going straight out of the Union; the red flag of Abolition had been flirted in his face, and he was ready for fighting; Virginia was in a dilemma that, like himself, had two horns, he was for taking the Southern horn, and that at once.

The Opossum, from Fluvanna, said that he did not approve of the hot haste of his horned friend and neighbor from Goochland; he was in favor of demanding our rights *in* the Union if we *could, out of it if we must.* (Tremendous applause.) Wherever Virginia went he would go; he would stick to the State of 'Flu' as long as there was a persimmon tree in it upon which he could swing his tail. Having spoken, he curled up.

A Jackass, from Petersburg, here interrupted the meeting with some facetious remarks, which caused considerable merriment, but little edification. He said he would be *ass-ass*-inated before he would secede.

A well-fed Ox, from the pastures of Augusta, said that he saw no necessity for precipitate action. He was sure that the intentions of His Royal Highness, the Orang-Outang, had been misinterpreted, that he had been well assured that his Highness meant peace, and not war; he had been in correspondence with those who enjoyed the unlimited confidence of the Royal Ape, and was happy to have it in his power to calm the apprehensions of this assembly. He thought that the best thing for Virginia to do would be to gracefully submit to that which she could not peacefully avoid. If the issue of North or South were presented to him, he would have to give his preference to the North. He wished to go where he could get plenty of grass, and Northern hay was sweeter to his cud than Southern fodder.

A dark, sleek, fat Pony, from Richmond, supposed to be much affected with the Botts, here lifted up his voice and neighed submission; one master would do as well for him as another; what he went in for was good feeding, and he believed that he could get that from Old ABE as well as anybody else; his position was a peculiar one, he was nearly squeezed to death by outside pressure, while within he was racked with the Botts. He would resist coercion with all his might and mane, and to every proposition for secession he would give a most unqualified neigh.

The Bat, from Bedford, said he had been flying around, first on one side and then on the other, and did not know exactly which side to favor—he was not in favor of submission, but was opposed to resistance—didn't think there would be any war. He changed his position so often that nobody knew exactly where he was, and finally he fluttered out of sight.

The Bear, from Wetzel, said that it was his duty to inform the Council that the beasts in his section of the State were not sound on the monkey question—that there was one member on the ground who had been elected on an Orang-Outang platform.

The Cat, from Wheeling, here jumped up with a tremendous squawl, and said that the Bear from Wetzel had trodden upon his tail. He would take this opportunity of putting his stamp of reprobation and denial upon some censorious and slanderous reports that had been industriously circulated in regard to his having distributed Orang-Outang pamphlets amongst the free monkeys of Virginia—nothing made him raise up his back and show his claws quicker than to have such aspersions cast upon his fealty to his native State. He believed that the safety, honor, and glory of the Old Dominion would be best preserved by submitting to the rule of King ABE. If Virginia would meet the Orang-Outang with a becoming spirit of submission, he was certain that he would treat her with Clemency. He hoped he would be excused from making a long speech, as he was just from a bed of sickness, having had a fray with one of the whelps of the Lion of Princess Anne, from which he had not yet re recovered. He was opposed to fighting—he had had enough of it.

The Tiger, from Mecklenburg, here rose with a terrible roar, and said that he put his paw upon such time-serving policy as had been advocated by the submission beasts in this assembly. He was for war to the tooth, and from the tooth to the gum. The woods resounded with his eloquence, and for a moment all appeared to be for war, but, after a little, up rose

The Rhinoceros, from Kanawha, who said that, on an occasion of so much importance, Virginia ought to act with calmness, coolness, and deliberation. He was opposed to hasty legislation; that time was the great pacificator; he did not think that this monkey question was of sufficient importance to break up this glorious Union; for his part, he thought Virginia would be better off without monkeys than with them; that he "would wade through a Red sea of blood" to abolish monkey slavery from the land, ere he would see this glorious Union destroyed; that many sneers had been cast upon the West in connection with this monkey question; he would let the beasts from the East know that none of their shafts had penetrated his hide; it was too thick for such paltry weapons. He went for the honor, glory, and dignity of his native State, and thought that those could be best preserved by the abolition of slavery and union with the North.

An old Eagle, from Charles City, said that he had once been king himself, and if the Orang-Outang only knew as well as he did what were the cares of office, he would be glad to return to his native forests. He had lately flown over the enemy's camp, had done his best to avert the calamity of war, but it was of no avail, they would listen to no compromise. He hoped that Virginia would not listen to the syren voice of the submissionists—our only hope is stern resistance—he was old, but was ready to fight, and, if necessary, to lead the van.

Here the Lion gave a playful growl, and said that that was *his* place.

The Game Cock of Albemarle rose on the spur of the moment, flapped his wings, and made a most eloquent and stirring speech. With his clarion voice he urged determined resistance. His motto was, "never say die."

The Leopard of Prince Edward also made a powerful appeal for resistance. He playfully remarked that it had been said he would not change his spots, but that was a mistake; if he did not like one spot he could go to another, and rather than submit to Old ABE he would go further South to a more congenial clime, and he urged his fellow-beasts, particularly those of the feline race (except the Cat, who, he said, was a treacherous beast), to go with him.

The Hyena, from Monongalia, said that he thought it a hard case that the beasts of the West should be taxed to protect the monkey property of the East, which was the cause of all the trouble. He thought that the best way to put a stop to this contemplated rebellion in Virginia was to make the monkey-holders pay all the expenses of the war; and he, therefore, introduced a resolution for an amendment to the Constitution, by which a heavy tax should be laid upon monkeys, particularly young monkeys, who were now exempt from taxation.

A curly-headed Poodle from Richmond, nearly overcome with dignity and fat, said that he had prepared a speech for the occasion, but, as the weather was getting warm, he did not feel like exerting himself; and, therefore, begged to be excused.

All this time, while the debate was going on, there was a Serpent, who was the chief counsellor of Old ABE, who had sneakingly insinuated himself into the midst of the council, and was gliding silently along from member to member, and whispering in the ear of each of the Submissionists, and promising them great things if they would only go for Old ABE. To the Pony he promised that he would cure him of the Botts, and give him plenty of oats and nothing to do.

To the old Horse from Prince George he promised a crib full of corn and a currycomb.

To the fat Ox from Augusta he promised that he should be translated to " green fields and pastures new;" to the Jackal a plenty of bones to pick; to the Cat an abundance of mice and cream; to the Spaniel the run of the kitchen; and to the Opossum a perpetual persimmon tree.

To the Rhinoceros he promised that his horn should be exalted, and his ambition gratified by a mission to Siberia, which he had previously intended for his friend the Skunk, of Maryland; whereupon, the Rhinoceros, in a rapture of poetic frenzy, exclaimed: " Now are the *Winters* of our discontent made glorious *Summers* by this son of *York*."

At last the Serpent sneaked up to the stump and whispered in the ear of the Owl that he had brought over Governor Boar himself by the promise of a bucket of swill, and that if he—the Owl—would only go for submission to Old ABE, he should be one of his counsellors; whereupon the old Owl winked, and cried whoo! whoo!! which in owl language signifies assent.

The Committee then made the following report :—

Whereas, His Majesty the Orang-Outang of Illinois has been duly and constitutionally elected the king of all the beasts in the United States of North America; therefore, be it

Resolved, That it becomes the duty of every beast and of every community of beasts in these United States to submit *humbly* and *cheerfully* to the authority of the said Orang-Outang, and that the honor, glory and dignity of the Old Dominion may be safely entrusted to his keeping.

Resolved, That we will resist with all our might and to the last extremity any attempt at the coercion of our Southern brethren, but that we do not consider the enforcement of the laws to be coercion; and if our Southern brethren resist the enforcement of the Federal laws, coercion then becomes simply resistance to rebellion, and must be acquiesced in by all good citizens.

Resolved, That we tender our congratulations to His Majesty, the Orang-Outang, to the beautiful Queen-Consort, to the accomplished Prince Bob-O'Link and the rest of the Royal Family upon their accession to the throne, and hope that in the distribution of their Royal favors they will not be unmindful of their humble and dutiful subjects in the Old Dominion.

The question was then put and the report of the committee was adopted by a large majority.

Three hearty cheers were then given for King ABE and the council adjourned *sine die*.

APRIL 17, 1861.

THE great event of all our lives has at last come to pass. A war of gigantic proportions, infinite consequences and indefinite duration is on us, and will affect the interests and happiness of every man, woman, or child, lofty or humble, in this country called Virginia. We cannot shun it, we cannot alleviate it, we cannot stop it. We have nothing left now but to fight our way through these troubles; and the inquiry most interesting at the moment is, What are our means of resistance?

We believe that we inform the public with considerable accuracy on this point, when we declare that the State's public means of resistance are simply *nil.* Virginia has few serviceable arms and scarcely any powder. The whole amount on hand is two hundred kegs, and two hundred and forty more ordered.

APRIL 9, 1861.

So long as Virginia was possessed with the notion that she was controlling every thing and making peace, she seemed sufficiently convenient, and was, in fact, tolerably subservient, to the designs of the Northern powers; but the day she learned that they had called out seventy-five thousand men to make her sure to them, she turned around and walked out of their Union with the step of an old QUEEN. Had they possessed the faculty of appreciating her virtues, they might have cajoled her into their schemes for a very much longer time. But the low-flung and mercenary vulgarity which pervades all the North and inspires the councils of the Yankee President has proved her salvation. Lincoln declares war against the South, and his Secretary demands from Virginia a quota of cut-throats to desolate Southern firesides.

A great difference of opinion on a point necessitating violent sentiment of opposition has prevailed in this State for many months past. But that difference was not in every case the result of a distinction either in character or patriotism. Had all the men of this State foreseen the course of events with an equality of vision, it is quite certain that there would never have been a party in Virginia to advocate submission to Black Republican rule under any guarantee whatever. But it is still a just matter of amazement that such a difference of opinion ever arose among the educated classes; and the utter incapacity to appreciate either the vote of last November or the current of events that has been running away with the country since then proves how far statesmanship has declined in Virginia. The country gentlemen and heads of the bar had been living so long in the heart of peace and prosperity, that they did not know the old demon of revolution even when he was up bodily before them, with every infernal ensign about him that he ever wore in history. They persisted in thinking him only an ordinary and evanescent imp of a spring election, whom they had often seen before. Had they ever witnessed a revolution or a war either here or elsewhere; had they ever watched the incipient steps and symptoms of those great troubles which leave indelible marks on the world; had they observed the movement of a race that finds itself in a false position even once, they would not have doubted the nature of the crisis that has existed here for these six months past. A mortal disease is not always visible to unlearned eyes. But a physician knows it at once by signs which he cannot always define to others. Having often seen the steps of dissolution on the human frame, he recognizes them in a moment where the patient seems to others suffering only from the effects of ordinary indisposition. He withdraws from a vain contest with the king of terrors, and his skill brings this sole profit that he warns the patient to put his worldly affairs in their due order.

Had the majority of the Convention consisted of statesmen who knew more than the politics of provinces and the secession of counties, it would have recognized the revolution as a great and inevitable fact from the moment of its meeting. Then the *patient* would have made a will, and we would not now have the law-suit of a war on our hands. The separation would have been peaceable and its consequences arranged by negotiation. But although it is nearly certain that the trouble of to-day is the result of their error, it is no longer the time to indulge in reproach. The Ordinance of Secession places us altogether, and every patriot will seek in the sincerity of his heart to heal all the wounds which this controversy has produced. Our triumph, if such it is, is still a sad one, and for conquered and captive there are those who have surrendered to their own conscience and honor.

MAY 8, 1861.

In the late debates of Congress of this Confederacy, Mr. Wright, of Georgia, showed a true appreciation of the crisis when he advocated the grant of power to the President that would enable him to make immediate defense of Richmond and to bring the whole force of the Confederacy to bear on the affairs of Virginia. It is here that the fate of the Confederacy is to be decided, and the time is too short to permit red tape to interfere with public safety. No power in Executive hands can be too great, no discretion too absolute, at such moments as these. We need a Dictator. Let lawyers talk when the world has time to hear them. Now let the sword do its work. Usurpations of power by the chief for the preservation of the people from robbers and murderers will be reckoned as genius and patriotism by all sensible men now and by every historian that will judge the deed hereafter.

If President Davis is the man for the times, and if the Southern Confederacy is worthy of existence, both will come at once to the front. We will not say that Virginia, like Maryland, will sink on her knees, if left alone, before the North; even to call up the hosts of the South we would not say that, for it would be a lie. Virginia has taken her stand; she will not yield it; she will never recede. Even if left to her own resources, she will certainly use them. France, after her first revolution, was not more certain for fight against all the odds of a world in arms than is the State of Virginia. If the pinch comes, we may see a few poltroon men mob the State authorities for submission, and a few selfish women will cry and wail. But if we are sure of any thing, it is of Virginia pluck. She will be cut into ten thousand pieces rather than yield. Now that the die is cast she will stand it. If traitors or cowards try to interfere, her people will hang and shoot them. Virginia will not yield, and will meet force with force even if left alone to do it.

But the Southern States are both traitors and cowards if they do not come at once to the front. All their available forces should be brought to the banks of the Potomac with the least loss of time. Especially should President Davis give Virginia the advantage of his presence. It would be worth an army of fifty thousand men. It would give confidence and authority to all the State's movements.

The people of Virginia ratified the Ordinance before the Convention passed it; the State seceded long before the Convention found it out. The ratification by the people on the 23d of May is a mere formality. There is but one opinion now in this State. The vote will be all one way. To wait for it is nothing but red tape in its worst form. The hour for action is on us, and, if the South has half the decision for which it bears the credit, that hour will not pass unemployed.

JUNE 12, 1861.

THERE is a prevailing disposition in the South to overestimate the value of European sympathy to the participants in the American struggle. This sympathy is only valuable to us so far as it may procure our recognition as a belligerent power, endowed with the sovereign rights of war. It is only valuable, in other words, so far as it secures fair play to us from neutrals. All we want from Europe is the recognition of our rights as a belligerent power. After those rights are granted, we prefer their neutrality to their friendship, or even alliance. It is important to us that we should sell our cotton and other leading staples. This we can do, to a considerable extent, during the pendency of the war, if those immunities and privileges are conceded to us which belong of right to belligerents. If we are a belligerent power, then our privateers are allowed to rove the seas. The whole importance of the sympathy of Europe in our behalf, therefore, concentrates in the single question of our acknowledgment as a belligerent power. Nor is it so much the sympathy of Europe that we desire as its affirmative opinion, its favorable judgment, upon the question of our political status. Now, it must be recollected that this question will be determined by Europe *upon facts;* it will not be settled by mere sympathies. The facts, which will decide this question in European estimation, are those only which concern our ability to maintain ourselves in the struggle in which we are engaged and which indicate our probable success or failure in accomplishing the objects of the struggle.

JUNE 15, 1861.

THE combat at Bethel is the first event of this war that gives comfort to the heart of the South. Here, it will be said in after times, soldiers of the Southern Confederacy proved that they could whip Yankees. Here it was first established that all Virginia Generals were not under the spell of Scott's genius. Here the policy of retreat was for the first time laid aside.

JULY 2, 1861.

THERE is no quality of man's character that depends so much on training, habit and education as personal courage. We see this fact exhibited and illustrated every day in the ordinary vocations and amusements of life. The greatest coward learns to stand and to work fearlessly at his trade on slender, insecure scaffolding, at the fourth story of a house. The bravest man, unused to ascend to fearful heights, trembles and recoils as he looks below, or feels a giddiness and "toss of desperation in the head" which impel him to plunge into the abyss. The landsman fears the sea; the sailor is ill at ease on horseback; the denizen of cities trembles in the dark forest; and the countryman feels scared and skittish mid thronging crowds and rattling omnibuses and whistling steam cars of the city. "Use is second nature," and men can be taught and habituated to meet danger in any form. The Yankee is afraid of guns and horses, because he has not been taught to shoot and ride in boyhood—and it is hard to learn any thing in manhood. He is afraid to fight with gunpowder, not only because he feels that his want of skill in marksmanship unduly and unequally exposes his life, but also because his whole moral nature has, from infancy, been trained and moulded to consider it the greatest of crimes to meddle with "the villanous saltpetre."

It is as easy to teach a man to be a coward as to train him to be brave. Cowardice is carefully inculcated on the Yankee from his birth; and if he be not a coward, he must be a fool who won't take education. But he is no fool; for, whilst he is taught that fighting is unprofitable, and therefore to be avoided, he is instructed, at the same time, that cunning and sharpness and cheating are very creditable and very profitable; and no one learns these latter lessons more readily and rapidly than he. He is born like other people, but becomes a coward and a knave from severe training and careful education. Every day we hear it said and see it written that the people of the North are personally as brave as the people of the South. It is wholly untrue. We are their superiors, not only because we are more accustomed to and more skillful in the use of arms, but also because their natural courage has been carefully eradicated by education, and ours as carefully encouraged, fostered, and improved.

What! that people brave whose foremost and most *admired men* have been kicked, caned and cowhided as unresistingly as spaniel dogs.

JULY 8, 1861.

THE presence of an inferior race influences and *helps* to mould the manners and the character of the white man in the South. It inspires every citizen with the feeling of pride and decent self-respect; renders him dignified in deportment and more circumspect in conduct and conservative in feeling than he would be without it. No man likes to let himself down before his inferiors—to play harlequin before his chidren, or to descend to familiarity with his servants.— White men, whether slave-owners or not, unconsciously, and without design or effort, behave with reserve, circumspection and dignity in the presence of negroes. None but the base and criminal make companions or associates of them. Half of the lives of the Southerners is passed in the presence of the blacks, and hence the manners which we have described grow into a feeling and a habit, and a high sense of self-respect coupled with aristocratic bearing become a part of character. All white men carefully avoid to fall into or practice whatever is peculiar to the morals or manners of the slave: and as he is given to theft and lying, these crimes and immoralities are less common with the whites at the South than in other Christian countries.

All history shows that slavery never did enervate national character, but has always strengthened and improved it. If, however, there were no other evidence of the influence of slavery in elevating and purifying the character of the citizen, abundant proof might be had by inditing a comparison between the Government at Washington and the Government at Richmond. The Federal President is a common sot and low buffoon; yet he represents fairly the party and the section that elected him, and is a fitting sample and exponent of Northern society. His cabinet are equally vulgar with himself, and far more bigoted and vindictive.

Universal liberty and equality, universal elections, absolute majorities, eternal demagogism and free competition, have leveled, degraded, demoralized and debased Northern society. Nobody there sees any one beneath himself—lower, meaner, or more contemptible than himself. Hence nobody there respects himself. Vain and arrogant Northerners we have seen, but have yet to see, to hear of, or read about the first one who, self-poised in his own good opinion, and respecting himself, knew always how to respect others. All Yankees are vain, arrogant and independent, and carry on their visages and in their manners a sort of "I'm-as-good-as-you" assertion simply because they feel that they are not as good as you.

JULY 22, 1861.

ALL day yesterday, under the hot sun of July, the army of the North and the army of the South wrestled over the plains of Manassas. The great fight has been fought, and it has pleased Jehovah, the Lord of battles, to crown with victory the standard of the Southern Confederacy.

At this hour, the deepest anxiety that can overwhelm the human heart is settled on this city. We know that a victory, such as never yet was won on American soil, has been gained by Southern manhood. We know that it was resolutely contested by the enemy and that a terrible loss of life has taken place. We know the names of some general officers who have fallen. But few families in this city had not some dear member in that army which fought yesterday for liberty and for country; and of our brothers, sons, husbands, friends who were not titled with such office we know nothing now.

The battle commenced at nine o'clock on yesterday morning; it was ended by the flight of the enemy at four in the evening; our troops remained masters of the field. We are happy to announce that our troops were, at the last advices, in hot pursuit of the flying enemy. Whether the pursuit will be pushed to extremities, and the batteries around Alexandria and on Arlington Heights stormed at once, while the foe is confused and dispirited and our men warmed with victory, is uncertain. But this we know, that if we have a BONAPARTE among our generals, we would enter Washington at the heels of a Federal rout.

JULY 24, 1861.

IT is practicable for the South, within six weeks from this day, to have an army of five hundred thousand men ready at a moment's notice to take up the line of march for any destination. There is no reason why our generals should be constantly kept before the enemy laboring under the grievous disadvantage of having a greatly inferior force to that opposed to them. There is no reason why a single day's hazard of disaster should have been run, or should be run, from this cause. The South can spare half a million of men; and that number will place her on an equality with the North upon every field.

The country expects its Congress to take immediate and efficient steps in providing a large and thoroughly-appointed army, able in numbers, as well as in pluck, to cope with the enemy on every field and to meet invasion by counter-invasion. The South has suffered long enough from the incursions of the Northern Vandals. It is time that she were commending the chalice from which she has drank so deeply to the lips of the enemy. It is certain that peace will never come until war is carried to their own doors.

The South can furnish men in abundance for this purpose. She need not stand one hour on the defensive. Ohio and Pennsylvania ought to feel, in less than four weeks, the terrors which agitate the cowardly and the guilty when retributive vengeance is at hand. They talk of making the South defray the expenses of their own armies. In four weeks our generals should be levying contributions in money and property from their own towns and villages. We trust that our army will be at once raised to four hundred and fifty thousand men.

AUGUST 7, 1861.

THE evident and predetermined spite toward the South which characterizes the letters of the *Times'* correspondent since he has gotten back to the soil of abolition is one of the chief reasons why we have reprinted them. These people write to please the European public, and they know, what we refuse to believe, that the entire European public is animated by the most unfriendly sentiment towards the Southern community.

The times are too serious to admit of indulgence in pleasing dreams. It is important that we should receive this truth, that our position in the late Union has degraded us in the eyes of the world, and that, in the process of time, our character has been so succesfully darkened by the representations of our Northern fellow-citizens that it is assumed to be the combination of every thing that is villainous.

We have not a friend on earth and can place no reliance on any help beyond that which we may find in our own hearts and earn with our own swords. The sentiment of the European continent towards the people and the laws of this country is exhibited in a thousand ways. We have become the stock monsters of all public showmen; the wickedness of Southern slaveholders is received as the first axiom of political truth; we point the moral and adorn the tale of every dealer in the platitudes of public remark. Our position before the world, during the last ten years of the Union, has been thoroughly and perfectly odious; and, however disagreeable to our feelings, it is right that we should know the truth and realize its extent, that we may find the reason and the remedy of this universal, baseless, but most malignant folly. If we ask the cause of it, our assailants are of course ready to allege the villainy of holding slaves as the sufficient explanation. But the world is full of slaveholding nations which are the objects of no such animosity. The Southern States only are the scapegoats of mankind and the recipients of all the abuse and falsehood that the bad hearts and foolish heads can invent.

The cause of that unenviable notoriety is not the existence of slavery in these States, but because we were, till lately, bound to another people, who hated us, and, when not too busy in cheating us, made our injury and defamation the business of their existence. In this work they were ardently assisted by the whole of England, high and low, great and small, because England recognized in the South the real America that rebelled against her and beat her. The world has only seen the South through Northern spectacles tinted with the British jaundice.

We have taken the first and best step to deliver ourselves of odium when we seceded from the Northern Union and declared the Northern people our enemies. Their tales about the South can no longer be received as the statements of the country itself, and other nations will seek and obtain information concerning us from different sources. But we will never be clear of the evil and undeserved reputation that we bear till we prove our power to make ourselves respected. We must be our own champions and write our true titles with the sword. Half the venom of our enemies has had its source in contempt. All the vituperation of the North has begun and ended with a declaration of our weakness, our cowardice, and our imbecility.

Things have come to that pass with us that the most certain means of obtaining injury, calumny, and scorn from foreign people, is to attempt their conciliation or seek their applause. Not till we prove ourselves independent of their opinions, above and beyond their help, will we obtain their amity and justice. We must return disdain for disdain, defiance for calumny, put far from us the fallacy that we have any friend in the world, or can get any, till we have placed our power to command our fate beyond cavil or doubt. On our own swords we must lean, on our own arms we must rely for help, till we shall no longer need any other.

AUGUST 14, 1861.

THIS is a sectional war. The dissolution of the Union was the result of a sectional quarrel. The war is not a civil war; it is a war of two countries divided by geographical lines and interests. It is a quarrel of patriotism and not of opinion. We saw the proof of these truths in the annihilation of all parties and principles in the Northern Union on the day when the first shot was fired. That shot killed several millions of Northern men with Southern principles. Those who had been most notorious for the advocacy of Southern rights and interests so long as we had any bribes to offer them, became equally remarkable for their virulent animosity and atrocious menaces against the people of the Southern Confederacy so soon as the real dissolution of the Union answered the question of interest. Of all our fast friends at the North, only two, Pierce and Vallandigham, were simple enough to stand by the professions of their lives. Everett, Fillmore, Cushing, Sickles, Van Buren vied with Sumner, Greeley and Giddings in the fiendish screams for a bloody subjugation of the South.

The truth is, every Yankee had hated every Southern citizen from the day of his birth. Those who know them will all bear out the assertion that the root of bitterness was deeply planted in every Northern heart. Interest and policy alone had prevented the flower and the fruit. When interest and policy no longer covered the soil, it sprang at once into life and light.

But what will not any Yankee do and say at the command of interest? What principles will he not adopt, what professions will he not make, what colors will he not wear, what skin will not grow over his bones, when they command money and when thrift will follow his fawning? When all the North was united by undisguised hatred of the South, till their nation of millions seemed one man— the South still had many Northern friends. We had not far to go should we desire to see them—they were collected around the doors of every department of the new Government.

AUGUST 23, 1861.

ALTHOUGH tuft-hunting is studied as a science and pursued as a profession in Europe, yet the Yankees have such remarkable natural talents for toadyism, flunkyism, and tuft-hunting, that they beat the professors of the art of cringing by force of sheer natural genius. In other countries tuft-hunting is followed because it is a profitable species of meanness; but the Yankee is a toady because he can no more refrain from boot-licking than a cat can keep its paws off a mouse.

Utterly destitute of self-respect and manliness, the Yankee must prostrate himself before something which he believes to be greater than himself. He loves to fawn about the feet of European monarchs and noblemen; and, like the ancient Egyptian, he is ready to worship any thing from Apis down to an onion or a grasshopper. His appetite for toadyism is omnivorous. He prefers traveling lords and princes, but in default of these legitimate victims of tuft-hunters he hunts down all sorts of small game. Dancing women, Japanese ambassadors, English authors, cabinet officers, Congressmen, Hungarian refugees, and many of Barnum's most remarkable monsters, have been in their day the gods of Yankee idolatry. Many of our readers have at "levees" and "receptions" witnessed the elaborate self-abasement of the Yankee flunky.

Something to worship and fawn upon is just as essential to the Yankee as his "help" and his counting-house. If he is rich and can go abroad, he dishonors and degrades the name of American by his coarse, low and slavish flattery of small German princes and unscrupulous French counts. He has won throughout Europe the reputation of being the most obsequious and ridiculous of flunkies.

Whilst Lincoln pretended to respect the Constitution, the Yankees manifested no especial esteem for him. They admitted that he was nothing more than a fifth-rate prairie attorney half-educated and ill-bred, whose manners were those of a village wag and whose morals were not at all in advance of his manners. They admitted that he was a sort of Presidential Soulouque or chimpanzee who owed his elevation to a strange freak of a very villanous party. As soon, however, as the Baboon throttled their liberties, trampled downright upon the said Constitution, put a bit into their mouths and manacled their hands, they began to worship and admire him. As soon as he became a military dictator and usurper, the spirit of Yankee flunkyism was aroused in his favor.

AUGUST 29, 1861.

PUBLIC opinion in the Southern Confederacy, guided by a sense of public danger, has destroyed all traces of the old party lines and does not permit of their revival. Whether a man was Whig or Democrat a year ago is no longer a pertinent question. But there is one party in Virginia that will not die, that cannot change, and is unable to disguise its identity. It is that submissionist party which ruled the State from the assemblage of the Convention till the arrival of President Davis, and which has sought to take possession of the Confederate Government, as it did of the State Executive, but has failed, because that Government had a sober Chief Magistrate. Hatred to the South and appetite for office were the animating sentiments of that party. Both still burn with undiminished fire in the bosom of every submissionist, whatever his new name may be and wherever he is now placed. Their party organization has not been abandoned. Circumstances compel them to conceal it; but they know and understand each other by a species of freemasonry that comes into immediate action the moment the great question of the offices, little or big, is touched on.

Under the old Federation this party called itself Federalist and it was ever ready to lessen the privileges of the States and strengthen the bonds of the Federal Government. In the Southern Confederacy its aim is apparently the opposite. It would weaken and destroy the power of the Confederation and set the States at war with it. But if examined, this appearance of contradiction vanishes. They are both external symptoms of a deep principle; hatred of the South and of slavery was and is the key to both positions. Under the old Federation the safety of the South depended on the strength of the sovereign States; under the new order it is identified with the power of the Confederacy to support the weight of the monstrous war. Hence the centralizing propensity of the quondam Federalists; hence also the new-born love of State Rights in the late Submissionist party of Virginia.

They are preparing this battle-horse for their political campaigns—that the Confederate government is hostile to Virginia. Such is their slogan for the fall election. The translation of it is simply this—that the Confederate government does not fill its offices with their men. Under Letcher's administration they had and have everything; and through the reprehensible custom of the Departments, which permits the heads of bureaux to fill subordinate offices under their order, they have nestled a family of vipers under the flag they malign and whose downfall they desire. There now seems to be a chance of stopping this practice.

SEPTEMBER 27, 1861.

We have been from the first fully assured that the true interest and policy of the South consists in a vigorous prosecution of the war. We are in favor of striking the enemy at every vulnerable point. The idea of waiting for blows, instead of inflicting them, is altogether unsuited to the genius of our people. The aggressive policy is the truly defensive one. A column pushed forward into Ohio or Pennsylvania is worth more to us, as a defensive measure, than a whole tier of seacoast batteries from Norfolk to the Rio Grande. If at this time Sidney Johnston were menacing Cincinnati, McCulloch threatning St. Louis, and Jo. Johnston and Beauregard pressing on to Philadelphia, our word for it, the Yankee Government would have little time to fit out its armadas to plunder and ravage the Southern coast. It is altogether unnecessary to argue the self-evident proposition that it will require three regiments to defend our extended coast where one would be required for invasion. The object of the Yankees in fitting out these expeditions is to compel the withdrawal of the Southern regiments for the purpose of defending their own homes. The Yankee tactics thus known to us, what is the obvious mode of meeting them? Plainly, by pressing the enemy's forces to the border, and over the border, until a thrill of terror at the heart of every Dutchman and Yankee in Ohio and Pennsylvania shall learn them that a war upon the South will not pay expenses.

And here it may be well to pause and notice a remark of Mr. Noodle, a gentleman for whom we entertain great personal respect, which lies immediately in our path.—Mr. Noodle says we are making the same mistake in advocating a forward movement as Greeley did in his cry of "On to Richmond," and that the experience of that celebrated white-hat philosopher should teach the common people to be silent upon matters which they can not understand. Mr. Noodle opines that the cry of "On to Washington" will end in a sort of Bull Run business. To all of which, with due deference, we reply that the cases are not at all similar. Mr. Noodle has forgotten that we are not Yankees; the Yankees are not Southerners. It does not follow because sixty thousand Yankees were unable to vanquish half that number of Southerners that the latter will necessarily be whipped when they have an equality of numbers.

The Bull Run business, with which Mr. Noodle thinks to overwhelm us (as if it did not gratify us immensely, as far as it goes), is, in fact, an argument why the army should go forward.

Prior to that memorable day of Manassas, the superiority of the Southern men over the Yankees had been demonstrated to our entire satisfaction; but there were in our midst some who questioned it and the North certainly did not recognize the assumption. It was natural for them to believe that sixty thousand Yankees could annihilate half that number of Southerners. Assuming the equality of the races, individually, all that was necessary was for Scott to equip and drill his army properly and march them on to Richmond. The first part of this work he did thoroughly—in a manner worthy of his great reputation. The error in his calculation was he did not take into sufficient account the essential difference between Northern and Southern men. It is not true that he allowed himself to be hurried forward. He never did that in his life, especially in military matters. He took from the first of May, or thereabouts, to the 20th of July to prepare, equip, and discipline his army, and if they lost the day at Manassas it was simply because, in the Providence of God, they were fashioned with different hearts from the men they had to deal with.

The battle of Manassas demonstrated, at once and forever, the superiority of the Southern soldiers, and there is not a man in the army, from the humblest private to the highest officer, who does not feel it. Now, this piece of information is extensively diffused in the camp of the enemy. They know, now, that when they go forth to the field they will encounter a master race. The consciousness of this fact will cause their knees to tremble beneath them in the day of battle. It will demoralize them. It has already done so.

The establishment of this patent fact of Southern superiority changes all the conditions of the argument. It utterly invalidates Mr. Noodle's comparison, which he esteemed so happy and conclusive. Did he but possess a tithe of that hard common sense which he despises in the people as incapable of dealing with these military questions, he would see what we have endeavored to make plain to him, viz.: that "circumstances alter cases," and that the march of our army upon Washington is altogether a different thing from McDowell's inauspicious tramp to this beautiful and attractive capital.

NOVEMBER 2, 1861.

We regard it as a matter of the highest importance that in a struggle with an enemy superior in numbers, capital, munitions of war, and having entire command of the sea, that concord and harmony should exist among ourselves. We need the hearty co-operation of every State and of all Southern people, in order to cope with our formidable adversary. But these are the lowest motives for unity. Bound together by community of institutions and race, by common wrongs, common perils, and common hopes, we ought to be drawn together closer than brothers. The remembrance of the battle-field of this war, to which each State has contributed her heroes and her martyrs for liberty, ought to inspire such a feeling of mutual charity and respect that the just susceptibilities of no State should ever be wounded by unkind and uncalled-for criticism.

We are happy to believe that these views reflect the sentiments of the great mass of the people of the South. We regret to say there are sometimes found men wearing the uniform of Southern officers and soldiers who are mean enough to enter Virginia thresholds, and, in the absence of Virginia gentlemen, to utter, before ladies, whose hospitalities they enjoy, remarks disparaging to the patriotism of this State, the devotion of her population to the Southern cause, and even reflections upon the behavior of her sons in the field. Conduct like this hardly requires comment. Such criticism comes fitly from those who are not found speaking them on the field in the line of their duty, but, perhaps enjoying sick-leave, obtained on false pretences, and leaving to those they defame the work of meeting the enemy. The number of these offenders is hardly large enough to justify any extended notice, but there is a greater number floating about in the social circle and on the streets, who contrive to insinuate a considerable amount of laudation for themselves and their respective States, winding up their orations with the declaration that they have "come here to fight the battles of Virginia." With such intolerable stupidity and insolence we have no sort of patience. We think it not amiss to devote a few words to showing how utterly false and impertinent the proposition really is.

How does it happen that Virginia is involved in this war? The history is so fresh that we wonder fool or knave could attempt to pervert it. Our sister States of the far South had flung off their connection with the Federal Government, and had, in the exercise of an undoubted right, erected for themselves a new Confederacy. The Northern Government denied their right to leave the Union, and declared that they would coerce them to remain under its yoke, whether they liked it or not. War was declared against them in Lincoln's proclamation. At this stage of affairs Virginia acted. She threw herself between her sister States of the South and their cruel, usurping foe. She took the fight on herself, knowing, full well, that she would be exposed to the Northern power, that her fields would have to endure the havoc and ravage of the war, that her soil would be ploughed up by the instruments of death, that she would have to bear the first onset of the foe. She knew the cost full well of what she was doing, but there was one voice only among her people. However she may have appeared before this to hesitate or be divided in council, now all was decisive, manly action. It was a word and a blow to the Northern tyrant. Lethargic she might have been hitherto, but when peril and subjugation threatened the South, she rose in her might and her majesty to the great work before her. She was like one of the knights of the olden time, who lay torpid under some foul spell of the enchanter. But the trumpet of war is blown—he starts from his slumbers, and, with lance in rest and soul on fire, he rushes to the post of duty and of danger.

Those who know the course of this journal will remember how earnestly we urged the early, immediate secession of Virginia because of the election of Abraham Lincoln. That was ample warrant for us to counsel revolution. We would have had Virginia leave the Union on that plea alone. But for a convention which misrepresented public sentiment, this would have been done. But could there be a loftier or more honorable motive for secession than the proclamation of coercion upon six sister Southern States? Virginia acted at once and without consultation with others. Her pledged friends and allies were far away. The enemy, with his giant strength and long-accumulated resources, lay at her very door. True, she might rely with great confidence on her noble and honored neighbors, North Carolina and Tennessee, but the delay of Missouri and Kentucky shows the risk she ran, and proves the intrepidity of her policy.

We suspect that some little of this contemptible spirit of disparagement springs from the fact that Virginia was tardy in seceding. If the real facts of the secession movements were fully known, or could be freely exposed, the reply would be easy enough. Some of the Southern States were carried for secession by small majorities. No one of them acted without the strongest assurances and conviction of co-operation by others. We are grateful to those who led off, we admire the spirit in which they acted, and at no time have been slow in vindicating their motives and their conduct, but we happen to know that this revolution was like every other that has occurred in the history of the world. It had to struggle against a powerful opposition, against the timidity of the weak and the selfish, and was finally borne through over the counsels of time-serving politicians by the untiring labors of intrepid leaders, aided by the instincts of a brave and spirited people. Had South Carolina, Georgia, and Alabama lay along-side the northern border, exposed to the ravages of war, we think it not unlikely that quite as large a number would have been found, among their people, for a pacific solution of the troubles as was found in Virginia and Tennessee.

We should do a flagrant injustice to States which we admire, if we failed to say that the style of remarks upon which we comment are repudiated as invidious and unworthy detraction by the great mass of their people, and more especially by those who on the field of strife have become endeared to their brethren in arms of every

State. On those battle-fields there is no State of the South whose sons have not done nobly and well. When we consider the odds they have had to encounter, in numbers, artillery and equipments, the short time they have had to learn the work of war, we know not how sufficiently to admire their bravery and determination. These noble qualities are the attributes of our race everywhere, whether in the sunny clime of Louisiana and Carolina, or in the descendants of those in this latitude who defied British tyranny, whether found in Virginia, Kentucky, or Missouri. There is enough glory for all without detracting from any. There is abundant room for each State to find gratification, not only in the achievements of her own sons, but in those of other States whose fame and honor form a part of her own heritage.

Virginia claims no superiority in this war, but she does claim to have done her whole duty. She has contributed largely in men, artillery, small-arms, and machinery. Her land has been desolated in parts. Families born to affluence have been stripped of all they possessed. Women of refinement, bred in the enjoyment of every luxury, have been made beggars upon the charity of the world. The fate of South Carolina during the war of 1776 has been that of a large portion of Virginia during this war. It is plain enough that other evils are in store. But there is no regret among our people, no looking back. Our path is onward to independence. Be it through blood, poverty, and toil, at the cost of all we possess, we shall tread it with unfaltering trust. And this is the firm determination of a people with whom resistance to tyrants is a watchword and a sign forever. This purpose nothing can shake; not the taunt of the ingrate, not the sneer of the braggart shirking his duty and the truth, not the fear of any accumulation of hostile forces, not any amount of calamity and disaster, or suffering which Heaven may inflict to prove the strength of a noble and firm resolve.

NOVEMBER 23, 1861.

THERE are some persons not over and above qualified to pass judgment upon the future, who take a gloomy view of our public affairs. For ourselves, we cherish no despondency, we are satisfied with the balance of defeat and success, and look forward with the confidence of a certain faith to a full and glorious triumph for our arms. But, if any thing could inspire a doubt in our minds, or suggest a fear that all was not going on well with us, it would be the cool effrontery with which persons, whom the public judgment has unmistakably stamped as false to the cause of liberty, and whom the severity of that condemnation has, for a space, forced to seek a cover, now dare to emerge from their fitly chosen retreats and once more provoke general disgust by impudent assumptions. It would appear that they, at least, must believe in the triumph of the Yankees, or they could not be thus emboldened to essay an experiment upon the patience of an outraged Commonwealth.

We are told, on the highest of all authority, that God, in his wrath, sent the Israelites a king to rule over them. Had John Letcher lived in those days he would have been taken for the purpose. By some inscrutable dispensation of Providence this man has been inflicted as a curse upon the people of Virginia. That we have erred as a people is but too true; still the punishment seems heavy. If this man would but keep quiet, avoid the impertinence of seeking newspaper puffs, and show by his silence some faint recognition of the peculiar estimation in which he is held all over the South, we, in turn, unwilling to expose the disgrace of our State, would let him alone, and be content to consider him in the same way that a devout Mussulman regards a December fall of snow—as a " cold, uncomfortable, unaccountable visitation of Divine Providence, sent, perchance, for some good purpose to be revealed hereafter." But when he undertakes to prate about the "public authorities" and what they have done for the cause, we think it not amiss to overhaul his pretensions without delay.

The Governor informs the Virginia Convention that "evil-disposed persons in our midst, claiming to be Virginians by birth, have misrepresented facts and distorted truth, with a view of injuring the public authorities [i. e., himself] in popular estimation, and disparaging the efforts made by the Commonwealth to advance the common cause." In this there is a slight modicum of truth, the residuum not being of that description, and bearing the same relation to the former as did the sack in Jack Falstaff's tavern bill to the charge for bread. And this simile we quote for its aptness rather than for any other point of similitude it may suggest to "evil-disposed persons," disposed to disparage the moral habits of the "public authorities."

Any man who would "disparage the efforts made by the Commonwealth" is base and evil-disposed, indeed, and deserves any thing rather than to be complimented by the Governor's censure. Such a one depreciates efforts of our people, which, for nobility, self-sacrificing heroism, stand out so bright and glowing upon the historic page that the daub of a tipsy painter cannot efface their beauty. Never, in all time, have a people acted better. They have made the name of Virginia ring in the ears of the world with a new glory; they have wrought a fresher fame than all the deeds of our first deliverance. And when the Muse of history shall narrate what has been done in this great war by the people, the numbers who have rushed to the field, their conduct in action, the munificence of those who have aided the soldier by money, clothing, and provisions, the generous enthusiasm of our women, their ministry of love and charity by the bed of the sick and the wounded, the rare patience with which the evils and ravages of the war have been borne by those who saw their homes made desolate by the neglect and improvidence of an imbecile Governor, it will not be requisite to augment the gratitude of those who shall come after us by stating the notorious fact that all this was accomplished not by the aid, but actually in spite, of the Executive of Virginia. And yet how much more praise deserves to be accorded to the patriotism of our people, when we consider that it rose superior to every obstacle and surmounted the opposition of John Letcher as easily as the Father of Waters would bear down an ugly, misshapen log upon its mighty current.

Yes, there is one, and only one " evil-disposed " person who would " disparage," if he could gain credence for his perverted statements, the efforts made by the people of Virginia, and that person is the man who dares to insinuate that he and the Commonwealth are one and identical, and that his action is to be taken as the measure of what Virginia has performed. It is a substitution more criminal by far than the changing of children at nurse, but happily in this case more easily detected and more readily punished. No man of common sense requires to be told that there is nothing in the character, precepts, or example of John Letcher to call upwards of sixty thousand volunteers to the tented field, or to inspire the chivalry with which they bore the onset of the foe. If we are not mistaken, the only time our doughty Governor has been near to the field, was when, like a bird of evil omen, he rode up in his carriage on the road to Rich Mountain, met the fugitives from a campaign he claimed to have planned, and, in stern accents, with pocket-pistol in hand, bade them return to their duty, and his driver to return to Staunton. And as he does not partake in the triumphs of the war, so, on the other hand, the people have no just responsibility for the shame. It was not through the neglect of the people of Virginia that we failed to capture the Lincoln Government at Washington when Baltimore stood ready to do her part of the work, or to seize Fortress Monroe before it was prepared to resist our assault and become a den of abolition thieves; nor was it the treachery of the Commonwealth that surrendered Alexandria and Arlington Heights to the Yankees, and allowed the whole of northwestern Virginia to be overrun by the foe, when it might have been saved if the reiterated and urgent entreaties to send troops to that quarter had been listened to. And if we should inquire who it was that systematically deceived the Confederate Government at Montgomery as to our military preparation in Virginia, overrating our strength, and thus lulling that Government into a false security; or who it was that discouraged the enlistments in Virginia at the outset of the war, chilling, by his serpent-like contact, the generous ardor of the people; or who it is that is so universally recognized as a clog and a hinderance upon the war as to find it necessary to falsely suggest that there is the greatest cordiality and unison between himself and the President; or who it was that, when the enemy first threatened invasion, defiled the whole system of military appointments by his rancor and hate for every true secessionist; and, lastly, who it is that has done the most to prepare us for subjugation, and who, if that bitter portion were our fate, would be the very first to ask for pardon and office from Lincoln, and to receive it; nobody would think of answering that it was the Commonwealth of Virginia. Indeed, we greatly fear that some evil-disposed person would say that it was John Letcher.

But for all this he has a triumphant answer. He has spent six millions of money. Indeed! Surely it did not take one to rise from the dead to inform us how he had squandered the public funds. And when we ask what we have got to show for all this expenditure beyond the pensioning of his favorites, parasites, and submissionists, or a weak attempt to purchase public approbation, we are told that "it is a source of infinite satisfaction" that all the accounts have been allowed. And for this, as in duty bound, the Auditing Board are by him duly thanked. And we, too, in our turn, offer thanks from the bottom of our hearts, not to the "Auditing Board," but to the Father of all Mercies, that things, bad as they are, are not worse, that only six and not sixty millions have been disbursed by one who never had a single patriotic instinct, and, more than all, that every day brings us nearer to that happy hour when "public authorities" shall retire from the Executive chair and taste once more the sweets of private life.

NOVEMBER 29, 1861.

THE campaign of 1861 may be considered as over. The enemy still menaces action; but what he may be able to do in the next fortnight cannot seriously affect the result, and, when the ground has been loosened by the frost, he will find it impossible to do any thing more. We have beaten the enemy in the field and foiled him in this campaign. The early danger of the South—that it would be overwhelmed in the first months of the war, before it could organize an army or prepare its defence, by the superior numbers and more abundant transportation of the Northern States—is definitely at an end. If we are conquered at all, now, it must be by the regular and ordinary means of war, and not by the rush of a vast mob.

On this much we may congratulate the country. But no one can fail to reflect with anxiety upon the next year, or observe without solicitude a certain unexpected feature of this struggle. It is the temper displayed by the United States. All calculations as to the extent to which the party holding the powers of that country would carry the affair, have been erroneous. Before the war began, all men of sane minds believed that they would compromise the political quarrel with the South; and had the North offered the South the poorest terms, so corrupt was public sentiment in Virginia, at least, that those terms would have been accepted. But the Northern rulers never harbored for one moment the thought of any compromise, and never offered any. When the war was begun, few persons in the civilized world thought that it would last six months. The six months have gone, the United States has endured defeat after defeat, has made sacrifice on sacrifice, and has closed an unsuccessful campaign without the slightest symptom of an approach to reason. In fact, the peace party of the North, like the Union party of the South, has entirely disappeared. The whole people are completely under the hand of the Government, and all together, people and Government, are bent on the prosecution of this war, even if the consequence should be a collision with England and a national bankruptcy such as was never before known.

Under this impulse they have steadily increased, and are still increasing, a vast regular force enlisted for an indefinite period, and equivalent in all its parts to a regular army. All the energy of the nation, and all the wealth in the country, has gradually centred on that one object. They have disciplined, and are still disciplining, that force by the same process that converts the peasant of every race into a formidable soldier. Now, when a government is willing to spend, and is able to raise money, by whatever means, it can purchase an army with the same certainty that an indvidual can purchase pairs of shoes; and all men, however vile and cowardly they may be, when subjected for a sufficient time to good military organization and severe military discipline, become dangerous when moved in the form of regiments and brigades in the operations of war.

It is a fact which the Southern Confederacy should not fail to recognize and consider, that the United States are preparing a regular army of not less than five hundred thousand disciplined men for our subjugation and destruction. This is the force we must prepare to meet next year. It will be a very different army from that we met at Bull Run. So long as volunteer was opposed to volunteer, raw troops to raw troops, it might be safely calculated that we would invariably remain the victors. Setting aside all questions of relative manhood in the Northern and Southern people, the character of the levies of the two countries and the class of society from which they were drawn, rendered that result certain. But what will we oppose to their regular army of next year? Vast numbers of our present volunteers were enlisted for twelve months, and their time of service will expire before the middle of the summer. How shall they be replaced?

By new volunteers? The necessity for troops is so urgent and the spirit of the people so good, that there is little doubt but that the Confederate Government could so raise all the men it needed. But while Southern volunteers are fully able, under favorable circumstances, of meeting regular soldiery with success on the field of battle, it is time to recognize the truth, that a force so constituted is incapable of answering to all the calls of war, when opposed to an army under the iron rule of enforced enlistment and regular discipline.

No half measures, or palliatives, of the well-known weaknesses of the volunteer system will answer the necessity of the case. We must raise a regular army, by some means resembling the conscriptions of all other nations in the world except England and America. That is the only system that is really just to all classes of the population. A certain number of men is demanded from each State. The State in turn demands them of its counties; the arms-bearing population draw lots, and those on whom the lot falls either go to the field, provide the substitute, or pay to the Government a sum of money that will enable it to provide him. Out of material thus obtained true soldiers can be made. With officers chosen and appointed by the Government on which the responsibility of the war rests, an army so constituted is a machine which does its work with the precision and energy of steam. The Southern Confederacy could put into the field a force of five hundred thousand men on this plan, without injury to any part of its internal economy; and with its appearance there, would end forever all the dangers of the State.

JANUARY 1, 1862.

THE end of the year just passed fills the mind with melancholy reflections on the vanity of human wishes, the instability of human creations, and the frivolity of all the thoughts of man. Where now is that wonderful country which realized the political dream of philosophers and patriots;—that grand temple of liberty, built for eternal duration; that perfect commonwealth, which gave the lie to all the ages, and proved the self-government of nations to be something more than the fable of a noble, but irrational, imagination? What has become of that splendid illusion which shed its lustre on the opening mind of the American youth—the lofty thought that he was born and would live in a glorious republic of heroic States and free citizens, whose title was above the royal rank and whose birthright was the envy of the world? One short year has ended both alike. The " star-pointing pyramid " has proven a tower of Babel; that noble faith in the virtue and intelligence of the soil's sons has given place to a disgust and indignation too deep for utterance in words; and on the plains where perpetual peace was supposed to have made her settled seat, war, with all its original savagery, reigns undisputed. The catastrophe brought by the year that ended yesterday leaves us not even the sombre consolation of the grandeur that has attended the ruin of other empires. The majestic fabric fell not beneath the giant hand of an invading race, or before the blazing ambition of a secular genius. Enfeebled by the cankers of inaction and gnawed by the teeth of vermin, it has gone down like a ship whose timbers have been the unsuspected prey of worms and mice. Few, who meditated yesterday on these things, have not felt the justice of that contempt for the conceited animal called man, his pursuits and his projects, which religion and philosophy inculcate, but few have realized before.

JANUARY 8, 1862.

THE policy of monotonous defence which has been perseveringly pursued by the authorities of the Confederacy, has been the subject of universal regret among the Southern people, of annoyance to our generals, and of disease and death to our armies. On the side of the enemy, it has more than repaired the damages inflicted upon them in many brilliant battles; and, among foreign nations, it has engendered more distrust of our ability to make good our independence than all other causes combined.

On the army it has had a deplorable effect; not merely producing that *ennui* which is the fruitful mother of diseases, discontents, and demoralization in the camp; but it has substituted for that buoyant confidence and resolution to do, to dare, and to die, which actuated our volunteers, a wide-spread feeling of listless hopelessness of results, with an indisposition and partial incapacity to achieve them.

The enemy have found themselves at perfect leisure, in the very presence of our legions, to devise, to mature, and make trial of campaign or assault which they have thought expedient. Nowhere have they been thrown, by any movement of ours, into a moment's alarm for the safety of any army or any district of country in their possession, except on the memorable occasion of their panic for the safety of Washington, which the same evil genius of defence prevented from being taken by our forces. Their generals and their politicians have felt at entire liberty to plan any schemes of campaign, any assaults or raids, or incursions in our territory, that their genius might suggest or their rapacity or malignity might devise. They have encountered no opposition at any stage of preparation for these operations. We have stood still and allowed all their preliminary arrangements to be perfected, attempting to nip no scheme of mischief in the bud, and never thinking for a single moment or in a solitary instance how much more easily mischief may be crushed in its inception than successfully withstood when at the head and in the full tide and momentum of execution.

To all eyes abroad our energies seem to have been palsied by a fatal paralysis. All that might have been achieved by policy and genius has been neglected; and nothing has retrieved our reputation for vigor and capacity but the boldness of our soldiers and the success of our generals in active engagement. The impression made upon the foreign mind is as if our generals had been all the time manacled by secret instructions from the closet; and our soldiers leashed like hounds, forced to slink and crawl at the heels of the hunter, though it was felt that they were noble hounds, needing but the sound of the bugle to open in full and terrible cry. For a general to put forth exertion, was to render some explanation of conduct necessary; for him to fight battles and win victories, was to encounter indirect censure, to provoke the cold shoulder, and to inaugurate a quarrel with the powers above.

The effect of this obstinate adherence to the defensive programme has been very deplorable upon the lists of mortality. While we have lost thousands by disease, we have lost only tens by the casualties of the battle-field. The noble spirits that, in volunteering for their country's defence, thought to seek glory at the cannon's mouth, have paid the debt of nature upon beds of fever in vast charnel houses of disease. The whole country is filled with mourning; and the sad lament of mother, father, wife, sister, all, is that their kinsmen died the horrid death of the hospital, and not the glorious death of the soldier on the battle-field. The policy of defence has thus cost the lives of gallant and brave spirits who chafed under inaction; it has bereft our army of ten thousand heroes, who, if led against the enemy, would have escaped the dangers of the field after winning victories that would have added lustre to our annals.

This defensive policy has not only cost us men, but it has cost us territory. Many counties of eastern Virginia, and important regions on the more southern sea-boards are now occupied by the enemy, who would never have ventured forth to such distances if they had been menaced nearer home. Nearly all of western Virginia is in the hands of an enemy who never would have gained a foot-hold in the interior, if our original plan of aggressive attack along the line of the Baltimore and Ohio Railway, and from Wytheville towards the mouth of the Kanawha and Sandy, through eastern Kentucky towards Cincinnati, had been adhered to, instead of concentrating our forces for mere defence. This moment Bowling Green and Columbus could be more effectually relieved and the Southern cause in Kentucky put more speedily on its legs, by menacing Cincinnati with a column from western Virginia, than by concentrating a hundred thousand men in the path which the enemy has chosen for his march from Louisville southward. That cannot be good generalship which leaves the enemy at perfect leisure to mature all his preparations for aggression, and then to choose the roads by which he will march and the field on which he will fight. That cannot be a glorious system of warfare which never ventures an aggressive movement or even a battle, and which, though expecting an attack every day, yet decimates its armies by inaction.

JANUARY 16, 1862.

FOR a period uncertain in duration, whether of days, weeks, or months, the season commands a truce. This is the true winter. The first campaign is ended, and a time has come when it is no longer unsafe to review results and to consider with candor the situation of our affairs.

The campaign has been strictly defensive. We have gained nothing, for we have attempted no gain. That we have lost comparatively little of actual territory during the latter six months, is due only to the difficulties of invasion in a country like this, the necessity for time to prepare half a million of soldiers, the courage of the Southern volunteers, and the individual cowardice of the Northern mercenaries. It is, however, undeniable that the defensive policy, besides the moral strain on our army that awaits repeated and endless attack, and the exhaustion of a country which is the scene of war, has given the enemy an uninterrupted opportunity to prepare a gigantic host, and to arrange it at leisure for the full trial of relative strength, when the seasons permit the resumption of hostilities.

While the political leaders of the South have been reposing in dreams of approaching peace, and while our accomplished captains of engineers have been expending their remarkable scientific ingenuity in the erection of works as wonderful, and almost as extensive, and quite as valuable, as the Chinese Wall to resist invading forces from a given direction, the enemy have gradually and at leisure gathered up their immense resources and concentrated their tremendous energies to envelop the Confederacy with their armies and fleets, and to penetrate the interior from some one of many alternative points. Although they can now do nothing, they have their general programme in perfect order for execution when the weather changes in the ordinary course of the earth round the sun; and at this moment we find ourselves in the face of superior forces wherever we look, whether to the north, the east, or the west, or the south itself. General Sidney Johnston has to strain every nerve to prevent the military as well as geographical heart of the country from slipping out of his grasp. Generals Joseph Johnston and Beauregard are held by McClellan on the Potomac as in a vice. A gigantic armament is ready to attempt the descent of the Mississippi, and their fleets on the Atlantic coast and the Gulf are too freshly before the public attention to require remembrance. Such are the fruits of a policy purely defensive. Without even the hesitancy which would come of a possible interruption, the enemy have thus surrounded the Southern Confederacy; and, if permitted to repeat as often as may be desired, their efforts to penetrate its heart, they will necessarily attain the place and the time where success awaits them. There is now but one chance of escape from the net that has been coolly drawn around us; it is to concentrate our energy on one point and cut it through; to convert our defensive into offensive war, and transfer the scene of at least a part of these hostilities to the enemy's own country.

FEBRUARY 3, 1862.

RED-TAPE has a mortal abhorrence of a free press. The boy Psyche was not more fond of secrecy than this hoary sinner. A felonious old rat, comfortably ensconced within the rind of a plethoric cheese, does not more devoutly believe in the doctrine of *laissez faire* than the aproned *habitué* of the Government bureau. Little children, building castles of cards, do not more dread the strong gust of wind than Red-tape dreads the animadversions of the press. For this Asmodeus to point its fingers at him, is to unroof his closest privacy and secrets to the peering eyes of a world. His dislike of a free press amounts to a passion, which often approaches in violence to that morbid phobia which the canine species sometimes contract towards the running water, clear, innocent, and unconscious of the antipathy.

In proportion as Red-tape abhors the free press, does he dote upon that portion of it, which, like himself, wears the harness of official service. He eagerly mounts its tripod and pours forth *con amore* his complaints against the wayward journals which wanton in criticisms and censures upon office-holders and peculators.

But these complaints are lost upon the Southern ear. There are but two regions on the earth where the press—which is the public voice itself—is free; and these are our own South and the old British land where our race was cradled. Better that we should tolerate its indiscretions and bear the injuries they may bring upon our cause, than that we should lose the priceless jewel of free speech itself. Our affairs have not fallen into so narrow a strait that a little free censure of our public servants, even though, in some cases, undeserved, must ruin our cause. And really the world at large—at least that intelligent and reflecting portion of it, whose opinion alone is worthy of respect—will entertain a better opinion of our affairs than otherwise, if, seeing that our press is outspoken, that it is disposed and courageous enough to visit censure where censure is due, shall find the integrity of individuals only impeached, and not that of classes or masses. It argues a much sounder state of public feeling when a press, dependent upon popular favor for support, makes a virtue of exposing the rascality of knaves, than if all complaints were hushed in the fear of exposing concealed weakness and rottenness to the enemy and the outer public.

What if these complaints should be caught up by the enemy, exaggerated and officiously thrust under the eyes of the European public as proof of divisions and distrust in our community, of discord and unfaithfulness in our public administration? Has not the intelligence of Europe long grown familiar with the extravagances of free speech in free government, and learned that the fabric of republican society may sit firmly on a foundation of rock, although the winds may blow ever so boisterously about its roof and towers?

The public must have observed the vigorous effort being made for some time to shackle the independent press of the Confederacy. It commenced with a few officers from the old army, now in the Confederate service; and it has been seconded by officers in the civil Government, all, more or less debauched in their opinions by too long a connection with the repudiated Government at Washington—a Government which has muzzled its press, and set the example its off-shoots among us would have us to copy. The period of war is above all others that in which the most dangerous abuses and corruptions are likely to arise in official circles. Unless a free and fearless press stood ready to denounce the first symptoms of delinquency, and to nip the rising crop of abuses in the bud, the return of peace would be sure to reveal a rottenness in the public administration which would disgust the people with the ruin of public morality, at the expense of which their independence had been achieved. Even if the revelations of the press should give some aid and comfort to the enemy; yet, better this than that silence should veil official knavery and corruption and hedge it with impunity.

All danger to the public liberty comes from military usurpation, all danger to the public morals springs from official immunity from censure; and official corruption is the usual incentive to military usurpation. Is the press, that faithful sentinel on the watch-tower of liberty, to be gagged and manacled at a time when all power is in the army and all authority in Government?

The most lamentable self-abnegation of which the press can be guilty, is committed, when it undertakes to complain of the exposure of abuses and corruptions. We hold that it is at all times commendable and expedient to make this exposure; and we can acknowledge no argument valid which would condemn the practice; for the simple reason, if no other, that every plea against the exposure of corruption protects and extenuates the corruption itself. Even the heathen had a maxim "let justice be done, though the heavens fall;" and the counterpart of it may certainly be asserted in this Christian age: Let knavery be rebuked, though government stagger under the blow. The Confederate States could much better afford to suffer damage from the enemy, and to forego recognition from Europe for a while, than, by gagging her press, to give immunity to corruption for the same length of time.

The objections to free speech now urged are, if narrowly examined, found to be the same that have been urged by tyrants and their minions through all ages. The enemies of the free press lay hold of excuses furnished by the war and the public peril, to put forth pleas which deserve from these circumstances a temporary plausibility; but which, if stripped of these surroundings, their authors would be ashamed to adduce. No man can point out a single disaster to the Southern arms, or a single injury befalling the Southern cause, which is traceable to our independent press; and yet who will undertake to say that untold good has not resulted to the public service from that wholesome dread of exposure with which the press has constantly inspired our whole body of the public servants. But are we not insulting the intelligence of the age in thus repeating *seriatim* the sophistries of those who would, by means of law or public frowns, suppress the free utterances of the press?

FEBRUARY 4, 1862.

WE have a thousand proofs that the Southern people are not sufficiently alive to the necessity of exertion in the struggle they are involved in. Our very victories have brought injury upon the cause by teaching us to despise the public adversary. The immense magnitude of his preparations for our subjugation has excited no apprehension, and had little effect in rousing us to exertion. We repose quietly in the lap of security when every faculty of our nature should be roused to action.

The evidences of the prevailing sentiment are manifold. They are proved by the set of men who are elected to responsible positions. Men of palliative expedients and partial measures control in our public councils. Men who could not perceive the coming storm that is now upon us, and who continued to cry peace, peace, when peace had ceased to be possible, are those who receive the largest support for controlling stations. The government is almost turned over already to these passive characters, who look upon confiscation as barbarous, aggression as impolitic, and vigorous war as a policy to be avoided because tending to incense the enemy against us.

The men who descried the cloud of war when it was no larger than a man's hand, and who now can see no peace but as the result of vigorous measures, and renewed and repeated victories, are relegated to subordinate positions; and their views being a burning rebuke to the statesmen in position, they are laboring under the weight of implied censure. To win a battle by an aggressive movement is to incur a sort of obloquy; and to lose a battle in a brave push upon the foe is to provoke a chuckle of satisfaction and the taunt, "I told you so!"

Better to fight even at the risk of losing battles than remain inactive to fill up inglorious graves. Better that government and people should be roused to duty by defeat than that the army should go to sleep, the government doze and the people grow drowsy in the very jaws of destruction. To fill our public councils with men of passive measures, who would administer war on homœopathic principles, who would whip the enemy by cowardice and sloth, is to paralyze the government and enervate the people. They are alive to the demands of the crisis, but if Congress snows upon them they grow tame and crouching.

In the midst of revolution no greater calamity can befall a people than for their affairs to pass into the control of men who could not understand it in the beginning, and are incapable of appreciating the demands of the crisis as they arise. The French, in their revolution, had an easy way of getting rid of such characters,—they chopped off their heads. They felt it necessary, as all subsequent opinion has acknowledged, to push their revolution through to a climax, at any cost; and, though often with tears and sorrow, they guillotined the public men who leaned back against the harness. Their revolution succeeded, and owed its success solely to their excesses. They passed to the promised land through a red sea of blood. Old institutions, abuses, and enormities were swept away, with every relic of opinion that upheld them. France became a *tabula rasa*, upon which a new destiny was to be written.

All Europe moved against her more formidably than the Northern hordes are beleaguering our own country; but, such was the fiery earnestness of her leaders and her people, that the gathering hosts of invasion were scattered to the four winds. At last, it must be confessed, that the subjugation of a nation is not to be defeated so much by armies and guns as by the fierce resolution of its rulers and people. An unconquerable will, and fierce, combative purpose are more effective than invincible arms. Does such a fiery purpose blaze in our Government, imparting its hot flame to the hearts of our people?

There are two things needful for the early extinction of this war. We must first banish from the country every stranger in it who cannot give a satisfactory account of his purposes and objects here. This riddance of spies is a measure of importance, but comparatively of minor importance. The next thing requisite is for the whole community to throw themselves heart and soul into the war, and practise all the self-denial that the crisis demands. Why should the country be taxed with the support of the hundreds of hack teams employed in Richmond, when, if each *gentleman* would consent to walk a few squares, horses enough for a dozen or two batteries, well-broken and well-conditioned, with a complement of teamsters, could be thus secured to the army. This is but a single instance to show what might be accomplished by a generous spirit of patriotic self-denial. What a vast system of expenditure, now exhausted upon mere luxuries, might be turned to advantage in the war, if the pampered classes of society would but consent to a temporary sacrifice of useless pleasures? He who will take the pains to run through the whole catalogue of items which could thus be turned to valuable account in the war, will be astonished at the extent and value of latent resources which the country affords. The most efficient class to bring out the men and resources of the country in this war, has been its women. In the great struggles of nations, like that in which we are engaged, they should have queens for their rulers; for it is woman alone who is proof against the persuasions of time-servers and the sin of backsliding. There has been but one Lot's wife in all the tide of time.

FEBRUARY 19, 1862.

Days of adversity prove the worth of men and of nations. It is easy to shout for success in the hour of victory, and be full of courage, if there is naught to fear. But when the tide of fortune sets strongly against the hope, and the stories of misfortune and disaster thicken, then the brave man is known, and the brave nation rouses its strength.

We have to encounter one of those periods which tests the mettle of a people. If we are weak of mind and body, faint and cowardly of spirit, the current will presently overwhelm us; we shall sink under it, be subjugated by Lincoln, and ruled forevermore by foreigners, after having been insulted, plundered, and reduced to misery by Yankee generals and soldiers. We shall be conquered, because we deserve to be conquered, are unfit to defend our rights and property and liberty, and therefore unfit to have rights, possess property, or to lift up our heads in the presence of superior races.

But if the inhabitants of the South have any real manhood, these reverses will inspire them with determination. They will cease to palter between the laws of peace and the measures of war. They will enrol their names, and compel the enrolment of all over whom they have any control. They will silence traitors with the halter or the pistol; they will force their Government and their generals to energy, their troops to fight; devote to resistance the last man, the last dollar, the last gun; support defeat after defeat without murmurs; ravage their fields and burn their crops on the advance of the foe; pluck victory from despair, and deserve the future prosperity and security with which Providence has never yet failed to reward a downright endeavor for independence.

No powerful nation has ever been lost except by its cowardice All nations that have fought for an independent existence have had to sustain terrible defeats, live through deep, though temporary, distress, and endure hours of profound discouragement. But no nation was ever subdued that really determined to fight while there was an inch of ground or a solitary soldier left to defend it. Have we not sufficient motive to make up our minds to that sort of resolution? Have our people yet reflected on the certain condition of this country if the North should succeed in establishing its dominion over us? Confiscation, brutality, military domination, insult, universal poverty, the beggary of millions, the triumph of the vilest individuals in these communities, the abasement of the honest and the industrious, the outlawry of the slaves, the destruction of agriculture and commerce, the emigration of all thriving citizens, farewell to the hopes of future wealth, the scorn of the world, the sullen sense of wrong and infamy—these are the consequences of subjugation. Would we avoid them? Would we have this a rich and great country, governed by our own men according to our own votes, with an open market for our produce, cheap supplies of all our wants, general ease prevailing, and ample fortunes arising on every side? We can have these goods, we can avoid those evils—by fighting for them! Let us then rise; let us be soldiers in earnest.

Very little fighting has been done yet. Never was there so much victory and defeat with such pitiful returns of killed and wounded. Fine words and angry words will not alter stubborn facts; and when we see battles in which eight men are killed, thirty wounded, and twenty-five hundred men are taken prisoners with arms in their hands, it is useless to talk of glorious resistance, for it is impossible to think that those who were captured had fought well. There must be an end now of this species of fighting. All that we have is at stake; every thing that makes life worth keeping is in jeopardy. Our soldiers and our generals must be inspired with a different view of their duty in action, or they will be eternally defeated, continually captured, and the country will be lost.

The fighting at Fort Donelson, we are happy to believe, has been an exception to the general rule of our battles. So far as we know, the Confederate troops made a determined struggle over those hastily-constructed and exposed works. The loss of life was great on both sides. The battle lasted five days, and assault after assault was desperately made and desperately driven back. The do-nothing policy of defence enabled the United States to organize and precipitate on that one point its whole Western army; and it has been very well understood that we contend in unequal terms with the enemy whenever he can approach by water. We must expect to bear with equanimity much heavier reverses than we have yet seen if we would indeed be free. The game we are in is no child's play. We must fight our best; we must persist in the struggle to the last, or consent to a fate too miserable to contemplate. We must go to the work with greater earnestness than we have yet shown. We must discard luxury and ease. We must put down incompetence; cease to put our trust in pigmies, and listen no longer to pedants.

FEBRUARY 24, 1862.

The Inaugural Address is a well-written document, but does not require or invite much comment. It throws no light on the real condition of the country, and gives no indication of the President's probable policy. It might, in fact, have been omitted from the ceremony, had not custom required that the President should say something on such an occasion.

The public expected a much more important communication from the President than this. It is the fervent hope of every rational man and disinterested patriot that he will with all speed create a cabinet of the ablest, best informed, most experienced, and especially of the most active and energetic men. It is hoped that the President will now see the necessity of real counsel and assistance in the discharge of his difficult and overwhelming work. Men of strong characters, men who know the affairs of the nation at large, men who have the motive power of steam engines are needed here now. Under the present regimen the so-called Secretaries are mere clerks. They are fit to be nothing else. They are men of business in their various private professions; they may be tolerably familiar and adroit in the local politics of their cities and neighborhoods. But not one of them is a statesman of calibre equal to these times or any other times. They seem to have been selected with a view to the geographical sections of the Confederacy. Now, we cannot afford that species of gratification to office-seekers. The life and fortune of the whole country depend upon the ability of the central government to direct its forces to success. Nothing but intellectual capacity, general public information, patriotism, activity, and courage should be the tests to the selection for the cabinet, and if the greatest men of the country were all inhabitants of one county, that circumstance should not weigh a feather in the choice.

The President has hitherto been the Departments. But it is clearly impossible that this system should go on. A little Joseph in the house of Pharoah might have been all-sufficient for peaceful Egypt; but in modern governments even the Napoleons have seen the necessity of dividing their power with the first men they could get, and in a Government constituted like ours it is useless to expect that one head can suffice, for the design and execution of its complicated affairs.

If any candid observer is asked for the cause of our present tide of misfortune, he will be compelled to give the mortifying answer: that the Yankees have outwitted us, that they have managed their power with much more judgment; and that on just the point where the South was supposed superior to the North; that is to say, in the art of government, the Yankees have beaten us. If this great revolution should come to naught and the country be lost, it will not be because it was not full of money and men, because the people were not willing, the soldiers brave, their officers competent, their territory great and difficult to conquer, their slaves obedient, their supplies sufficient, their resources inexhaustible; it will not be because their cause was not just, their motives noble, their spirit high; still less will it be because they had not luck and chance on their side, that Fortune did not favor them, or Providence smile upon their endeavors. Never was the chance of war so remarkably on one side as in last summer; never did a government or generals enjoy such opportunities to win the greatest prizes of war with the least trouble; never were free people more obedient and docile in deportment towards their rulers; never were politicians so impotent to disturb a government; never in any war was money so plentiful, bread so abundant, levies so easy. The Confederacy has had everything that was required for success but one; and that one thing it was and it is supposed to possess more than anything else, namely, *talent*. But the Confederacy has not shown ability in conduct. We have refused fortune when it was thrust upon us, and permitted the magnificent armies that rushed forward last year to dwindle into insignificance. Yet no State refuses its quota; every quota that the Government would ask of any State would be ordered without a murmur. No firmness has been shown towards the troops in hand. The War Department has snowed furloughs and discharges; and when the three-months' men, the six-months' men, the nine-months' men, have arrived at the end of their terms, they have been sent home without the slightest stigma. The most puerile partiality has been displayed in the treatment of individual officers; little lieutenants and colonels have been erected into major-generals without achievement or justice, and it would almost seem that the Government was afraid of genius and will, so sedulously has it kept at a distance individuals of lofty intellect, wide knowledge and enduring energy.

Much might be said, if it were useful to do so, on this unhappy theme, which would be confirmed by the inner sense of every reader acquainted with actual politics. In common with all conscientious Southern men, we have long kept silence upon it, being doubtful whether good or harm would come of such discussion and if anything necessarily to be said in it should create acrimony, or opposition between the Government and people it is regretable. But there is no longer room to doubt the propriety of saying and doing all that can be said and done to surround the President with the first men in the land. We must get more talent in that Confederate Government or be ruined. The Naval and War Departments must be filled with real men, who can comprehend the state of affairs, know the resources and character of this country and of the adversary, who have the vigor to call into full action the powers and resources of the Southern Republic! Unless we can get such persons to do the head-work of the nation our great means are as useless as the gold that is buried. All party hates, all personal feuds, all popular delusions should be kicked out of the way in the search for the strongest and ablest men. If any thing will turn the tide that has lately set in, it will be the advent of intellectual superiority to the control of the departments. How often does history show nations redeemed from the most difficult positions by the appearance of a few sufficient leaders, who have changed in a few weeks the relations of contending forces?

FEBRUARY 26, 1862.

WHAT we have a claim to expect and demand from the President is this, that his measures and orders shall be prompt, full, stern, and more than equal to the dangers we have to meet. The patriotism of the people is very real; but popular feeling never was to be counted on at the pinch of pain. The undisciplined multitude, with the women, the children, the rich and comfortable persons, always shrink and cry when the trial comes. Then it is that the Government, into whose hands the people, when in their right minds, have intrusted all their power, should use it like a bar of iron. No country or city was ever defended in any other way. We talk of Saragossa, but Saragossa would have been a Nashville but for its *Junta*, its half dozen rulers who made no more of the lives of friends or foe than of rain drops. The Government, not the people, must order the things that are to be done, and see that they are done at whatever cost. To burn the cotton and tobacco, wherever the enemy comes, is of self-evident propriety. But who can expect the owners to do it on any large or effectual scale? Though they know from past experience that the Yankees will take every shred that they find they will no more consent to burn it than the dying miser to give away his gold. The Government must do all these things by military order, and without consulting anybody. The President is looked to for the call to arms, to order the mounting of batteries, the blockading of channels and the enforcement of necessary though disagreeable laws. To the dogs with Constitutional questions and moderation! What we want is an effectual resistance.

MARCH 6, 1862.

THE new office now proposed in Congress appears to be dictated by the actual wants of the service. A Secretary of War is found insufficient for all the duties of the Department at the present period. But there are secretaries, and secretaries. Twenty secretaries of one kind would not suffice for the little army of San Marino; but one Louvois, one Carnot, one Chatham, has been found all that was necessary for some of the greatest complication of military affairs that this world has seen.

At present it may be found advisable to separate the duties of the War Department, and confide a portion of them to a general competent to understand and direct the campaign at large. But if any good is to come out of the new office, it must be filled by an able, and especially by an energetic man, who will make war in a style different from that which has hitherto characterized the operations of the Southern Confederacy. All will depend on the choice of the man. If the commanding general is only another minnow in the pond, another dummy, a respectable bubble, an echo, an amiable courtier, the position of the country will not be altered by the creation of a new office, the employment of a new set of clerks, and the verbiage of a new set of official documents.

What the Confederate Government needs is not more officers, but more brains. Whether brains come to it under the label of a Commanding-General, a reorganized Cabinet, or simply a new Secretary of War, does not matter at all. The foresight that perceives, but is not appalled by coming misfortunes, the hard sense, the vigorous command, the courage that flames up from defeat and rebounds unhurt from disaster, the manly confidence in others, the strength of body as well as of mind, which supports and renews them all,—these are the qualities that are necessary to the leaders of a cause like ours, in dangers like those that press hard upon us. The men, or man, who possesses them is the fit companion, counsellor, and agent of the President now; and whether he is called commanding-general, or something else, will not matter.

MARCH 6, 1862.

WE must become the arbiters of our national fortunes. If the same common-place line of policy which has governed our actions for the past year is continued, this war will be a long one—long as the famous Peloponnesian. Yet this even should not discourage us. Jehovah kept Moses and the people of His love wandering forty years in the desert ere He gave them a country and independence. We should be prepared for trials and privations equally great, rather than become a people of political Helots—compelled to bend before, and obey the behests of, Yankee mongrels.

MARCH 20, 1862.

THE Cabinet which we announced yesterday has been confirmed by the Senate. Mr. Davis has sacrificed to popular clamor without yielding to public opinion. He has made so small a change, that Mr. Toots would say it is of "no consequence." All of the old members were retained, except those who wanted to get out of it. Benjamin is transferred, and Mallory left *in statu quo*. The representation of the Synagogue is not diminished; it remains full. The administration has now an opportunity of making some reputation; for, nothing being expected of it, of course every success will be a clear gain.

There have been three successful Presidents on this continent—George Washington, James Monroe, and Andrew Jackson. The explanation of this success is found in the fact that neither of them was jealous of intellect that had already been marked by the public judgment. Public opinion is rarely in error as to the abilities of the public man in active management of public affairs, and he who endeavors to find great men without reputations will stumble and fail in all great undertakings. James Monroe was, in all the more dazzling mental attributes, inferior to most of the Presidents. But he had the judgment to follow public opinion in his estimate of men, and to surround himself with those whom public opinion had indicated as able men. This was the cause of his success. He never attempted to know more of the intellect of the country than the country knew. He never sought to play the political virtuoso, storing away in his cabinet articles of value to him only, because no one else could be induced to think them valuable. The Cabinet of George Washington, James Monroe, and Andrew Jackson embraced the largest reputation of their day, and therefore, contained the largest amount of intellect.

MARCH 29, 1862.

A NATIONAL coat of arms, like a national flag, is not, as some suppose, a superfluous ornament. One is a necessary of war, the other of civil relations, both with foreign governments and our own people. Every nation now in the world, or recorded in history, has been known by an emblem or significant device. The armorial insignia of the tribes of Israel are clearly given in the oldest of books: the asp of Egypt, the royal archer of Persia, the horse of Carthage, the owl of Athens, the eagle of Rome, the dragon of China, served their purpose two thousand years before the earliest inventions of modern heraldry; and the universal fact abundantly proves the actual utility and imperative need of a fixed national type or signal for many of the most ordinary acts of every organized government.

The Southern Confederacy will find itself compelled to choose an emblem and arrange it in the heraldic form now common to other nations. It is important that an object which must appear on many solemn occasions, and around which will cluster the dearest associations of patriotism, should be creditable to the country and fitting to its purposes. If such a choice could be well executed at once, it would be a convenience to the Government and a pleasure to the people. In a country where the heraldic science is generally understood by educated men, and where there are able professors of the art in every large city, the work of that Congressional Committee on Flag and Seal, which so often reappears in the reports, could be done in a morning. But this is not the case in any part of North America. Few, very few persons here, have any other than the most vague ideas on the laws and spirit of blazonry; and even those few have learned their smattering knowledge from the books of English heraldry, which is the worst in taste, the most complicated and ignoble, as it is also the least esteemed in the civilized world. Hence, the coats of arms adopted by the States of the late Union are nearly all bad, and, from their artificial and complicated character, have entirely failed to attract popular affection. Indeed the figures on their various seals scarcely deserve the name of blazon. Not only are they destitute of heraldic arrangement, but instead of the figures of heraldry, which are arbitrary types, not intended to be representations of real things, but having a beauty peculiar to themselves, they have delineated a number of familiar objects entirely unsuitable to that science, which might look well in a painting, if executed by the hand of a great artist, but which make a poor and paltry show in the form of a coat of arms. Some have an allegory on their shield, others, a landscape; some have fancy pictures relating to some story or theory. Hence they are condemned alike by the taste of those who have studied such subjects, and by the indifference of the multitude, who are oblivious of what makes no single and easily recollected image on the memory.

Yet the Eagle of the Union has made a deep and powerful impression on our people, as the Bears of Berne, the Lion of England, on the inhabitants of those countries; for that device was well chosen, probably by those who had taken the pains to get good information on the matter intrusted to them, or who perhaps employed the assistance of some professional hand.

Considering the numberless failures already made by American States in their ignorant and premature attempts to devise proper insignia, it is hoped that the Congressional Committee will not be in too great a hurry to fix another abortion on us. Especially is it desirable that they should make the plan which they think most appropriate known to the public before it is established by law. The fate of the flag invented at Montgomery should be a warning to them against secrecy and haste.

Public taste cannot be compelled, and the flag has been found so objectionable to it, and is opposed by so many solid arguments, that it has become necessary to change it. It would be unfortunate if the Congress should adopt a coat of arms with a like result; and the only means of avoiding such mishaps is to subject its project to general examination before it is finally decided on.

The scheme said to be at present most in favor with the committee, is a shield bearing representations of cotton, corn, tobacco and wheat, would better serve for the vignette of a counterfeit note on a rural bank than the escutcheon of a nation. Without entering into technicalities, we may remind its inventor that there are certain plain principles of common sense, as well as heraldry, against which it offends:—1st. That simplicity and unity are the first requisites of a device that is intended to impress itself on the eye of a multitude; and that one figure on a shield is better than several. 2d. That the national device is part of a *coat of arms*; its signification should be warlike, and should express the power and courage, some capacity for offence or defence of a nation, rather than any other class of ideas. 3d. That the objects chosen should be such as can be easily and clearly represented in the style or mannerism usual in blazonry, without which only can armorial insignia be long tolerable to the eye and taste. The vegetables which are proposed for the shield of the Southern Confederacy are undoubtedly valuable; so are carrots and turnips; but they are not the figures likely to recur in imagination excited by patriotism, nor to be associated with the dignity of the country or its power of defence or punishment.

APRIL 4, 1862.

IF King Cotton has lost his sceptre for a time, it has been from the incapacity of his ministers. The fact of the loss is admitted even by Mr. Yancey, one of his staunchest subjects; and that gentleman, if report be true, does not hesitate to ascribe it to the cause we have indicated. This opinion of Mr. Yancey is not merely shared by the border States, but by the States of the Gulf. His case presents another melancholy instance of a great prospect blasted by imbecility.

The fortunes of the cotton dynasty depended upon bold action and great and energetic measures. Its policy should have been a continual assertion of power and majesty, not a continual depreciation of war, a perpetual protestation for peace, a constant appeal to Providence, or the European Hercules, for help. There was nothing within the range of public action too great for its energy and enterprise to compass; but whether this was so or not, its ministers should never have confessed to have "undertaken more than they could perform."

King Cotton began his reign under many auspices. He had been furnished with a hundred and fifty thousand stands of arms, which belonged to him of right, but of which he had been wrongly kept out of possession for fifty years. While the ports were open he should have added a hundred and fifty thousand more, which twice he did not do.

Since the first day of last May there have existed in the Confederacy seven hundred and fifty thousand men, between the ages of eighteen and thirty-five, who, by the operation of conscription, could have been embodied and drilled in an invincible army, competent, not only to oppose invasion at every point of our frontier, and to preserve the sanctity of every foot of our soil, but to conquer peace in the dominions of the enemy. Instead of this force being at once called into requisition, in accordance with the advice of men of brains and forecast, the wretched shift of twelve months' volunteers and raw militia was preferred, in the vain delusion that European interference was certain and peace was near at hand. It is only now that the measures that should have been adopted ten months ago is put into requisition.

There are two requisites to a great Government in a crisis like this in which ours is involved. The men who administer it must have a thorough knowledge of the means and resources of the country for offence and defence; which, in our case, are ample and unbounded; and, knowing these resources, they must have the capacity to call them forth and employ them. The misfortune of our Government has been that it has been both ignorant of the great resources of our country, and incapable of managing and employing even those of which it knew.

APRIL 8, 1862.

A VICTORY on a large scale, and with results more splendid than that which made the plains of Manassas forever famous, has crowned our hopes on the highlands of Mississippi. Although no Washington is within a day's march of Shiloh, to remain uncaptured, and though Fortune gives no second opportunity of striking such a blow as we could then have struck to pass unimproved, yet the prizes of the victory now won, though less dramatic than what those of Manassas might have been, are not less valuable.

These prizes are not the prisoners taken, though they are many; nor the cannon captured, though their number is unusual; nor the stores, nor the wagons, nor even the territory which may be recovered, if the victory is improved with half the celerity and enterprise which may now be expected. The great results of this battle are its moral effects on the Southern Confederacy, the United States, and the European continent.

It lifts the South from dejection not the less deep and painful because covered with silent fortitude. It will dispel from the popular mind of the United States the hallucinations of arrogance which have sustained the unparalleled exactions of their leaders. It will give new light to the undecided cabinets and vacillating public sentiment of Europe.

General Beauregard has given to his victory a sounding and triumphant name. The event is forever associated with the grand title selected, and will, also, be eternally connected with his own name. What part his conduct may have had in the result, cannot now be justly said. But popular feeling, right or wrong, will hereafter think him and luck synonymous. Many competent persons, while admitting his talents and acquirements as an engineer, deny that he possesses the qualities of a field officer, and declare that he has not evinced the capacity for strategy. But it will, at least, be hereafter admitted that he possesses the one. thing for which the great Sylla felt the most satisfaction. That man of genius made no account of the praises he received for his skill, his valor, his combinations, and his power—but was deeply pleased when the public voice styled him SYLLA THE FORTUNATE.

APRIL 15, 1862.

It is feared that those worthy persons who have packed up their spoons and prepared their souls for the storm, sack, and conflagration of Richmond, as foretold by McClellan, and who attend that unpleasant event like the followers of Father Miller, when they dressed in their grave-clothes and ascended the tops of their houses in readiness for Gabriel and his trumpet at the predicted minute, will have to provide themselves with a considerable stock of patience. For every day increases the probability of the report that McClellan has betaken himself to the *spade*. With a hundred and twenty thousand men under his hand, he proposes to attack Magruder's fortifications by "regular approaches." As the Confederate generals never attack anybody, it is presumed that he will be met with regular defences. In that case there will be a grand display of engineering science in strict accordance with the school-books of the military academy, concluding with a masterly retreat, or evacuation, by one party or the other,—all of which will take time—a great deal of time—so that immediate fears for Richmond may be postponed, if not abandoned.

The war has now lasted a year. Twelve months ago the Government at Montgomery had ordered eight thousand rifles as about the proper estimate for the army that it believed adequate to the crisis. Twelve months ago, in the fine weather of another breezy April, Fort Sumter fell, after a most tremendous and most bloodless bombardment. Lincoln thundered out a call for seventy-five thousand volunteers to squelch the Confederacy; and Davis answered with a demand for one hundred and fifty thousand men to meet them. Such large armies were yet unknown to Americans. Both proclamations were regarded by most people as mere *brutum fulmen*, and few believed that half those numbers of troops would ever come to the field, or that either Government could maintain them for six months. Yet they came, and many more after them; and the war has not only lasted its year, but, in the hands of West Point, promises to last another, and another.

Unless a great change in the manner of conducting civil and military affairs takes place in the Confederacy, not only may the war last seven years, but all who read these lines may die a natural death and be buried by their children without seeing that degree of law and order restored to this country in which they grew up. Indeed, nothing will ever bring peace and security to any part of this land but the extinction of the dynasty of ignorant and imbecile politicians who have long monopolized place and power here. When misfortune and suffering have forced the people of the South to think seriously and act earnestly, they will rid themselves of the whole Washington school of politics and inaugurate a new system of public measures.

APRIL 21, 1862.

VICTORY on the peninsula would give us time to reorganize our defences on water, and to create an army large enough to set the North at defiance. With the creation of a new army might come a change of our plan of campaign. The profound strategy of the back track, of withdrawing everywhere, fighting nowhere, suspending fighting generals, and promoting non-combatant generals to supreme control, might then be changed. The enthusiasm which originally burned in the breasts of soldiers would then be rekindled, and the country would not have to mourn any more the loss of commanding officers from indiscreet exposure in urging their troops into action. A spark of enthusiasm is worth more than a dozen cartridges; and it is useless for Government to waste its money on powder and ball if it pursues a policy to chill the spirit of the soldier.

It is impossible to overestimate the crisis on the peninsula. It has ever been the habit of great generals to expose all the dangers and all the advantages of defeat or victory to their troops on the eve of great battles. It is the timid policy of our own day to conceal the significance of contemplated engagements from the troops and the country. The country should know the full extent of its reverses as well as of its success. The spirit of the people will rise with the occasion. This land is not inhabited by the effeminate followers of a court. Our race can look fate in the face, and will prove equal to every danger that it is allowed to understand. With a patriotic people, candor is the most judicious, safest, and wisest course.

APRIL 21, 1862.

THE dispersion of Congress to-day cannot be regarded otherwise than as a most untoward event. It is an odious example to all classes. It is done by the votes of the Senators of those very States which have been loudest in their professions of patriotism and valor. Many of them now think Richmond insecure, talk about the probability of evacuating Virginia ("temporarily") in case of a defeat, and wish to be safe on their cotton plantations when that event takes place. They exhibit in this way of thinking a very narrow vision, a most imperfect idea of what is passing here, and are completely in error as to the future that lies before them.

The loss of Virginia is a thought which should not be admitted into the head of any person of authority in the Confederate States.

If the Confederacy loses Virginia it loses the backbone and right arm of the war. If they indulge the pleasing speculation that the Yankees will be content to make peace with the original Southern Confederacy when they have been appeased with a sacrifice of Virginia, they trust to a delusion, and are caught in a snare by which goslings would not be entrapped.

Possession of the Border States is only a means to the end of the Northern horde. If we were the only South, they would never put forth the gigantic effort they are making. They would be well content to let us go. It is the cotton of the Gulf that they want and must have. If they can conquer Virginia, the destruction of that strong bulwark will only fill them with hope and confidence; and the decisive battles will be fought a few weeks later on the plantations of the fugitives, with what difference of chances let reflection say.

To leave Richmond at the very moment of the hazard is not the way to encourage the army or help a cause in peril. Far wiser, and, indeed, more prudent, too, would be the noble and more courageous course of remaining in the capital till it is certain that it can no longer be defended. It will be time enough to go when it is no longer possible to stay, and at least the disgrace will be avoided of premeditated flight.

APRIL 28, 1862.

THE fall of New Orleans will swell the Yankee heart with a certainty of triumph too big for utterance. Now, indeed, they believe the revolution near its close, and expect the collapse of the Confederacy and the prostration of the South.

It will be some time before either party will know the causes, or rightly appreciate the consequences of this event; but it is certain that those who suppose the courage of the Southern people and armies will sink into despair under the blow, are doomed to disappointment. So far from insuring our subjugation, it concentrates our energies in a more limited circle and the Confederacy is now capable of a more dangerous and tremendous exertion than before. All that is needed to turn it into an advantage is a change in the spirit and counsels which direct at Richmond the employment of power. But little is yet known of the fall of New Orleans, except that when the British were cut to pieces before that city, Jackson was there; and when it fell, without resistance, before the Northern gun-boats, the commander was not Jackson. It would appear that no defence was attempted except the cannonade from the forts; yet what a reminiscence is suggested with the name of Chalmette!

MAY 1, 1862.

IN the vain hope of replenishing their Treasury the Yankee Congress are sorely exercising their ingenuity upon the subject of confiscation. They are endeavoring to find some legal means of accomplishing a general condemnation of the property of the South, and liquidating their debt from the proceeds of its sale. They are engaged in this fruitless attempt to relieve themselves from the odium that must befall the authors of the war among their own taxpayers. There are two modes of confiscation which they have before them under discussion, namely, by military seizure and legal process.

The difficulty of the military method consists in the impossibility of holding all parts of the South with a military force. It is simply impossible for the North to occupy the South throughout with a force strong enough to carry out so brutal and high-handed a policy. It might, in detached localities, succeed in enforcing its measures; but it would require a standing army of a million of men to enforce it throughout the country, and that number of men, and even less, would cost more than the value of the confiscations many times over.

Turn the subject over in any way, there is little prospect of revenue for the Federal treasury from confiscations even in the impossible event of conquest. If the United States should by any chance or mischance, succeed in subduing the Southern States and bringing them again into the Union, their true financial policy would be the proclamation of a general amnesty, the restoration, if possible, of fraternal feeling, and the imposition only of such taxes on the refractory section as they impose on the other. Even if the policy of robbery and wholesale confiscation could be carried into effect, it would be no other than a repetition of the folly of the clown who ripped open the goose for the golden egg. On the whole, it is plain that in no form or shape will the South, by any possibility, ever contribute, either willingly or unwillingly, to the liquidation of the Yankee war debt.

MAY 1, 1862.

It cannot be denied that the position of the Confederacy is anything rather than desirable. Indeed, if any country ever had a gloomy day, it is ours now. How the great opportunities of the past have been improved, how the immense power of the South has been frittered and squandered away, and whither a persistence in the policy and principles which have brought misfortune on us will eventually lead, are the thoughts that recur frequently to every mind. If any good could be done by showing the origin of these evils, and demonstrating the certain source of these calamities, the task would be easy. But it would be useless in every sense. Opinion is unanimous upon the character and conduct of the Government. Except the hangers-on of the Departments, and other holders or expectants of place and personal benefit, there is not one person of a sane mind in the Confederacy that approves the one or justifies the other. All think alike on these points, and it is, therefore, useless to argue them; nor is there any hope that an expression of the public voice will have the least effect for good.

On the conduct of the Government we cease to have any hopeful calculation. It has lost the popular confidence and heart, never to regain them. But it does not follow that the cause is lost or that the Southern Confederacy will not triumph in this war. The force of circumstances has compelled the concentration and consolidation of our armies; great battles, some of them at least beyond the enemy's vessels, will now be fought; and in these there is rational ground to think that the superior energy and courage of the Southern soldiery will inevitably tell.

MAY 16, 1862.

VIRGINIA is not dead yet! The ancient spirit is still in the land. If the steady valor displayed by that great army she has given to the cause of liberty did not sufficiently prove the truth, the action of her legislature would be sufficient to put some backbone into the feeblest nation and the weakest government.

It is encouraging that the legislature has found its communication with the President, on the subject of the defence of Richmond, satisfactory. It is to be hoped that when the President speaks of twenty years' combat on Virginia soil, he does not omit to calculate the demoralizing effect if Richmond should fall. It would be very great. If he listens to the voice of Virginia, her authorities, and the true people of Richmond, he will never permit this city to be taken, or leave it while one brick remains on another.

When we speak of the people of Richmond, however, we do not include the Rats. We do not include the contemptible sneaks who care more about their ornamental dwellings and fashionable churches, and their own rickety carcasses, than for the independence, the destiny, the existence of the Confederacy.. Some of these whitened sepulchres, who were, too, early preachers of secession, are now palavering the legislature about women and children, and bed-ridden persons, and will, no doubt, manipulate the Government into imbecility if they can. But let all persons in authority be warned in time. The counsels of these reptiles in broadcloth are the counsels of cowardice; they are liars and hypocrites in their words as in their lives. If the Confederacy hopes to exist, it must fight for Richmond,—fight over it, too, if necessary. Its possession would give renewed energy to the whole North; after this possession, nothing would be sufficient to discourage the United States Government and its armies. Its evacuation and loss would be a mortal wound to the Southern cause. If the authorities have not the energy, decision, firmness and resource to keep their grip on Richmond, then may God help the South!

MAY 19, 1862.

THE President proclaimed last Friday to be a day of official prayer and religious ceremony, and it was so observed. The Departments were closed, and the necessary work of this trying period was brought to a stand-still for twenty-four hours. Never has any one year seen so many of these affairs. It is hoped that the latest is the last. The country has had quite enough of them. Religion is the sentiment of individuals, not a matter of military order or formal injunction; and though it is well that a government should pay proper respect to the religious ceremony, that has been done, and overdone by the Confederacy. In truth, these devotional proclamations of Mr. Davis have lost all good effect from their repetition, are regarded by the people as either cant or evidences mental weakness, and have become the topic of unpleasant reflection with intelligent men. Piety is estimable, but energy, common sense, impartial justice, courage, and industry are also qualities very useful to rulers and to nations. It is to the diligent employment of the faculties God has given us that we obtain His blessing, and not by vain and affected supplications. When we find the President standing in a corner telling his beads, and relying on a miracle to save the country, instead of mounting his horse and putting forth every power of the Government to defeat the enemy, the effect is depressing in the extreme. When the ship springs a leak, the efficient captain does not order all hands to prayers, but to the pumps. The same newspapers that are burdened with the news of the evacuation of Norfolk announce that President Davis has just been "confirmed" in the Episcopal Church. Perhaps the authority of an eminent divine in that church may have weight with him. His name was Muhlenburg, and one Sunday, in 1774, he closed his last sermon with the words, that there was "*a time for all things;* a time to fight and that time had now come." Having pronounced a benediction, he deliberately pulled off his gown and appeared before his astonished congregation in complete uniform. Then, descending the pulpit, he ordered the drums at the church door to beat for recruits. His regiment was the first organized for the Continental service; and both his example and his doctrine, that "there is a time for all things," may be well recommended to the consideration of all considerate persons.

MAY 21, 1862.

The atrocious order issued by the Federal General Butler at New Orleans is characteristic and worthy of that proven coward. He who turned white and trembled all over at the Charleston Convention before the menaces of personal chastisement, which his roguery provoked from a gentlemen in this State, is brave as Nero, or a eunuch ruling the seraglio of a Turk, to the women of Louisiana. The *General* issues an order to this effect. That the Federal troops having in vain offered their compliments to the ladies of New Orleans, and having been "rudely" treated by them, the commanding general declares that in future, should any Southern woman express her aversion to Yankee soldiers or treat them "rudely," she shall be considered by authority as a wench of the town, and treated accordingly by the troops.

Butler has improved upon the Austrian generals. None but a coward of his stamp and race could have imagined or issued such an order, none ever have sunk into equal libidinous filthiness and depravity. But let us not reproach Butler. Let us wait to see the consequences of his order before we blame him. We have now to learn whether Southern men love any thing better than whole skins and ignominious lives; for if any thing will arm the hand of the male population of New Orleans, it will be this order and the first attempt to execute it. Then will come the end of the practice of tame submission to military occupation. Up to the present time, all resistance and trouble has ceased with the entrance of Yankee troops into Confederate towns and territories. They have taken what they pleased and done what they pleased; the people have done nothing. Declaring themselves unarmed and unable to fight any longer, they have folded their arms and submitted to fate; consoling their pride with *looks* of defiance and the tongues of the women. But they are soon to find that all cannot be so ended. The invader will shortly render death more tolerable than life. They submit to save their families; their families will not be saved by submission, and then they will rise, one by one, content to die if they can send a single Yankee devil back to hell before they quit the world themselves.

JUNE 10, 1862.

The Northern journals, from which the military news was yesterday extracted into this paper, call on us to explain what they are delighted to believe and call "Jackson's retreat." Old Stonewall has himself already given them an explanation, which is clear, if not altogether satisfactory. "The toils are skilfully laid," exclaims the Northern spectator of the chase after Jackson. It appears to have been quite time; the "toils" were so skilfully laid that they have actually caught him. Fremont caught Ewell, and Shields caught Jackson, with what results the public is this morning informed.

A wild boar taken in a net arranged for capturing quails; a lion started in the brush that was beaten for a deer, probably would act upon the fowler, as Ewell and Jackson on Fremont and Shields. But with regard to Jackson's retreats, we will lend our Yankee contemporaries a word of light.

In countries where cock-fighting is considered a civilized amusement, there is a well-known species of the game chicken, known by a Spanish name, which signifies *the wheeler*. He is much prized, because he scarcely ever fails to kill an ordinary adversary. When he is put down for battle, and has exchanged a blow or two, he seems to fly, and the inexperienced spectator regards him as craven. So, too, does the other cock, which rushes after, fluttering with pride and confidence. But suddenly, with the rapidity of a bomb-shell, he wheels—there is a crashing collision—and the pursuing cock drops dead with a spur in his brain-pan.

Jackson, at the head of his small force, has often retreated—his opponents say fled—yet his retreats, unlike those of other generals, have never affected the estimation placed on him by his own troops or the country; for the people and soldiers instinctively perceived the military truth. Jackson never made a real retreat or evacuation—his retrograde movements are only his style of fight; he is, in fact, a *wheeler*, the most dangerous of antagonists in the cock-pit or in the field.

On the power of Jackson's army to inflict a vital wound upon the body of the enemy, and render necessary a recall of their forces for the defence of their own territory, are staked the best hopes of Richmond and the Confederacy. As for this city, if its fate depends on a game in which "*spades are trumps*," played by two eminent hands of the old army, each knowing every thing that the other knows, there is no doubt but that the Confederate Government will, sooner or later, be spaded out of Richmond.

SEPTEMBER 2, 1862.

RETALIATION is the principle at the foundation of criminal law. No other effectual means has yet been discovered by human experience or intelligence, to prevent the atrocities of the cruel and vile. In peaceful times and organized societies, it is possible to envelop this principle in modes of procedure which will direct its effect upon the head of the guilty individual alone. In wars between nations, retaliation is still the only means known in the history of human transactions, as sufficient to compel a cruel and a bad nation to conform its conduct of war to the laws and usages of Christian civilization.

The United States are conducting this war in a style which can only be characterized as diabolical. The Government of the Confederate States seems to have fully recognized this truth, if we may judge from the declarations repeatedly made by the President in his State papers. But, while it has promised, preached, denounced, and vapored, we are yet to hear of one single practical act of that nature on the part of the Confederate authorities, military or civil.

What will people say? What will the civilized world think of us? Why shouldn't we be thought better than the Yankees? Why should not we be reckoned chivalrous knights, while they are bloody barbarians? These and the like puerile conceits constitute the key to much of our conduct in this war. The Confederate Government has been *attitudinizing* throughout. The President's State papers are all pitched in that key. Every line of them suggests self-conscious vanity. How do I look in this position? How does this sound? Does not this surpass the *Pater Patriæ?* These are thoughts which seem to be present in the composition of those documents. Vanity, and not humanity, prevents an immediate resort, in this country, to retaliation of the sternest and most decisive species. Our case demands, and our common sense commands it. We have only to wait awhile longer, and the individual sufferings of those who are now amusing themselves with a parade of lofty chivalry will cause them many an hour of bitter repentance for their childish folly.

SEPTEMBER 6, 1862.

A PAINFUL rumor throws a gloom over the spirit of the Southern public in the hour of victory. It is feared that General Pope has been mortally wounded. We sincerely hope that this disastrous report is destitute of the least foundation in truth; indeed, it is so improbable that this noble friend of the South should have got within the reach of a bullet, we may still flatter ourselves that his services will long be enjoyed by the Southern Confederacy. It is our earnest prayer that God may protect that precious life; that he may preserve his head, his heels, his tongue, his hand, and all the members of that valuable body, from bullets, steel, and rope.

Among the officers of the late United States Army, an acquaintance existed which enabled them to gauge the characters of each other with great accuracy; and when the news arrived that the Yankees were about to pull down McClellan and set up Pope, there is not one of those officers now serving in the Confederate armies, who did not ejaculate a fervent prayer that the hosts of the enemy might soon be under the command of Pope. Lincoln's estimate of Pope, it is said, is "great brains, great indolence, and great unveracity;" but an associate in the old army has characterized him more simply as "the biggest fool, the most arrant coward, and the biggest liar that ever disgraced epaulets."

Pope is a Yankee compound of Bobadil and Munchausen. He won his baton of marshal by bragging to the Yankee fill. On what monstrous principles he commenced it, and what orders he issued, are still fresh in the public memory.

"I desire you to dismiss from your minds certain phrases," said Pope to his army, "which I am sorry to find much in vogue among you. I hear constantly of taking strong positions and holding them; of lines of retreat and bases of supplies. Let us discard such ideas. The strongest position a soldier should desire to occupy is the one from which he can most easily advance upon the enemy. Let us study the probable line of retreat of our opponents, and leave our own to take care of itself. Let us look before, and not behind. Disaster and shame lurk in the rear."

With such notes as these, commenced the shortest and most disastrous campaign to be found in history. Never did a cock that crowed so loud lose his comb so quickly. No event has been more auspicious for the South than the accession of Pope to the command of the Yankee armies, and there is scarcely any loss which we could support with greater difficulty than that which his death would occasion. Let us trust that the Goddess of Cowardice enveloped him in a cloud, like one of Homer's heroes, and bore him to a place of safety, so far ahead of his flying followers, that he has been reported dead, only because he has not yet been overtaken.

SEPTEMBER 11, 1862.

The principle now in contest between North and South is simply that of State sovereignty. The war has embraced some of the features and elements common to all wars, and is, for the time being, a trial of physical strength; but the original, fundamental principle in dispute is the right of a State to resist the power of the Federal Government, in attempting to coerce it to submission to unconstitutional measures.

It has become fashionable to ignore States Rights. These valuable attributes of our Southern commonwealths are habitually whistled down the wind by sanctum men. The plea of public necessity is held to justify every usurpation, and officers of government, solemnly sworn to respect and observe the Constitution, are amongst those most glib in urging this sorry plea of expediency in justification of acts which, on their part, are no less than acts of perjury and fratricide.

It will not do for the Confederacy to lose sight of the principle of free government, for which it is now contending. We are not struggling to establish a national republic; but we are defending the right of independent sovereign commonwealths to resist unto blood the usurpation of their rights by federal power. For the better success of this effort, these sovereign commonwealths have formed another Confederation, based upon the same written Constitution on which the first had been founded.

It is time there should be a pause in this career of usurpation. It has become a most pertinent inquiry whether there is any such thing left at all as State authority, or State sovereignty. The answer might be, that there is now practically no such thing in existence among us.

The department of government chiefly responsible for this course of things has been Congress; but it is a subject of the most serious regret that this body should sometimes seem to ignore the most vital principles of the Constitution.

SEPTEMBER 11, 1862.

The public will have observed with some curiosity, a recent proposition, made in Congress, to depute an ambassador to the Yankee Government, to treat with it on the manner of conducting the war.

The proposition is simply absurd, in view of the experience which this Government has had of the hardihood and imperviousness of the Yankee rulers; it is derogatory to our dignity, when we recollect the insolence and contempt with which agents, deputed by this Government heretofore to visit Washington on missions common to the usages of belligerents, have been turned away from the Yankee capital. The South wants no more ministers or agents smuggled into Washington, to be insulted there and dismissed.

The people have, before this, been disgusted with weak and ridiculous attempts to enter upon diplomatic intercourse with the North. They have invariably exposed us to the coarsest insults and the most undisguised derision of our claims for recognition at Washington, in the persons of ambassadors or deputies. A persistence in these attempts is wounding to the pride and self-respect of our people, however the Government may reconcile it with its own notions of dignity.

It would not have been worth while to discuss this proposition, but that we detect in it a sentimentality which has been manifested in other measures; which has been disguised under pleasing forms of humanity; and which should be severely checked before it develops itself in some weak and fatal policy.

The proposition to mitigate the horrors and severities of the war is curiously introduced into Congress at the very moment our armies are passing into the enemy's territory. It proposes a sentimental appeal to the people of the North, calls them "our brethren," and declares that we would still make them our friends. The time for this stuff about brotherly love is past. The idea of conquering the North by sending armies into her borders, which are to respect the rights of private property, maintain guards around Yankee houses, give protection to abolition non-combatants, treat Yankees as "brethren," and extend to them the embraces of fraternal reconciliation, is supremely absurd.

Our armies have passed into the territory of the North, and it is now too late for us to talk about mitigating the severities of war and sparing that truculent country the scourge of invasion. As they have done to us, we must do to them; measure for measure must be returned, and on their heads must rest the crime of the fearful works of carnage and desolation in which we shall be rightful avengers and instruments of justice. If peace is ever conquered from the North, it will be only when the horrors of invasion are felt by it, and the scenes by which scars of desolation have been left on Virginia soil are repeated in Pennsylvania and Ohio. The sentiment that would tame our armies on the soil of the North, that would have them fight against the detested Yankees only as a misguided "brother," and that hopes for a conclusion of this war by mitigating its severities to the enemy, will be fatal to our cause if it is ever adopted in the policy of the Government. Such counsels of humanity are fine for sermons and sophomorical speeches. They are good in the abstract; they would be unimpeachable under different circumstances. But when they are advocated in favor of an enemy who has filled our country with mourning and distress; who has violated on our soil every law of humanity and every custom of decency; who, it is mockery to suppose, can ever be subdued by any generosity on our part, and who, at this very moment, after abandoning Virginia, is enacting in a more distant State of the Confederacy—brave, unhappy Missouri—atrocities unheard of before; who is still crying out for more blood, more torture, more pillage of "rebels,"—they are sentiments unnatural, unjust, weak, cruel, and absurd.

SEPTEMBER 22, 1862.

THERE will, of course, be great vaunting in the North over the retreat of General Lee from Maryland; but there is no doubt that his conduct has been very judicious under the circumstances, and that the Yankees have gained nothing by that retreat. On our part, this attempt at invasion, brief as it has been, is a great gain. It has learned our troops and officers what they can do, and taught the North that war can be waged at its own doors.

SEPTEMBER 29, 1862.

THE Government of the United States has shot its bolt. The proclamation of Abraham Lincoln, which we publish this morning, decreeing the unconditional abolition of slavery in all the States which shall not submit to his power by the first of January next, is the fulfilment of a menace made ever since the commencement of the war. Enormous results have been, and are, calculated as its consequences. It is scarcely necessary to say to any one who knows the public mind in the South, that it will have absolutely no effect at all, either one way or the other, on the conduct of the States. The only serious importance which it possesses consists in the indubitable indication that the Northern Government is resolved to pursue the affair to its extremity—intends to stop at nothing in the prosecution of this war. What we have hitherto seen is but the prelude of the war which will now begin—the war of extermination. Let us at least hope that one effect of this proclamation will bring the Confederate Government to a realization of the business in which we are engaged. But a short time since Mr. Davis came out with a solemn publication of his intention to punish the violation of the rules of civilized war by Pope and his officers. Our brave troops having taken a number of these officers prisoners, they were brought here to Richmond and placed in confinement. Only last week the resolution of the President melted down. Pope's officers were all sent home on the cartel. It was insinuated that the United States disapproved of Pope's proclamation; at least it had recalled Pope, and relieved him of his command. Now comes the proclamation of Lincoln!—

A fitting commentary upon the contemptible back-out at Richmond —the call for the insurrection of four millions of slaves, and the inauguration of a reign of hell upon earth!

NOVEMBER 25, 1862.

THE history of the world shows that the art of war, in its highest and most brilliant sense, as distinguished from the dull routine of military operations, is peculiarly the product of revolutions. This difficult and grand art requires the presence of genius, and is naturally developed amidst revolutionary agitations. A revolution demands quick and daring action; it rejects the " prudence of mediocrity;" it kindles whatever there is of mind in a country; it depends for its success in military matters not on routine or circumspection, but on the adventure and masterly rapidity of genius. Its art of war is essentially different from the conduct of hostilities between old established powers.

The historian Thiers happily seizes this distinction, and illustrates it in a comparison of the tactics of the old powers of Europe with the art of war as practised by Napoleon. The distinction runs through the whole history of the French revolution. The tacticians of the coalition fought Napoleon with unimpeachable skill and wonderful elaboration. To each battalion they opposed another; they guarded all the routes threatened by the enemy, and they made but few advance movements which might possibly uncover them or risk a disadvantage in ground.

It remained for Napoleon to regenerate the art of war. To form a compact body of men, to fill them with confidence and daring, to carry it rapidly beyond a river or chain of mountains, to strike an enemy unawares by dividing his forces, by separating his resources, by taking his capital, were his grand and novel illustrations of warfare. The genius that accomplished these wonders was developed in the midst of a revolution, and stimulated by its sympathies and excitements. In any other circumstances than those in which he lived, Napoleon might never have been heard of.

The memorable examples furnished by history of the genius and enterprise natural to all struggles originating revolutions are sadly contradicted by our experience in this war. The terse criticism of Thiers applied by him to that art of war in which the fire of revolution is lacking, seems, by singular controversion, to describe exactly the military operations of the revolution we are now fighting. The only modification necessary to suit his language to us is that " the man of genius " has never yet appeared in our revolution, nor is likely to come but by tribulation as long as every promising commander in our army is repressed, as Herod did the babes of Bethlehem. " The prudence of mediocrity sacrifices more blood than the temerity of genius, for it consumes men without producing adequate results," says Thiers; and this sentence is surcharged with truth and emphasis as descriptive of the war in which we are engaged.

It is difficult to find an adequate explanation for this anomaly. The war we are waging is essentially a revolutionary one. In the mental excitement with which it was inaugurated; the upheaving of the masses; the close sympathy between the army and the people; and the desperate spirit, it has all the elements which make up the historical idea of a revolution. And yet, in its practical conduct, it has been emphatically a war of "routine and circumspection," and is chiefly remarkable for a fruitless consumption of life in stationary camps and on indecisive battle-fields. The courage and endurance of our soldiers, and not the genius of our commanders, gives it the only adornment it has in the eyes of the world.

It may be, however, that we are hasty in remarking upon the low state of the art of war and mediocrity of mind, as characteristics of the Southern revolution. Military talent may now be painfully working its way up through executive disfavor, and the restraints and snares of official jealousy. It is a quality of genius that the arts of meaner men cannot repress it. It may be thwarted to some extent by jealousies, and kept under the shadow of names great in authority; but it asserts itself at last. It is yet possible that some great and adorning name now mounting to the vision, or still beneath the horizon, may arise to overshadow the mediocre reputations of this war, and to give to the Southern revolution its true position in history.

DECEMBER 17, 1862.

GENERAL LEE's account, and very moderate estimate of his victory on the heights of Fredericksburg is published this morning. It contains no new fact, and is chiefly remarkable for claiming less than the public naturally expected. The battle is defined to have been simply a signal repulse of the enemy. There was no rout or pursuit. The Confederate general's plan was purely defensive, and was perfectly supported in all its parts. The chief strategic results are the discomfiture of the enemy's scheme for an advance on Richmond by the railroad,—the loss of men, dead and wounded—and the demoralization of a defeat sustained by his army. What that loss was is not estimated in any manner by the Confederate general. He puts his own loss at eighteen hundred—killed, wounded, and missing. This is an exceedingly small number, considering the large force engaged, the fierce conflict, and its long duration, but it can be easily credited by those who know the admirable position occupied by the Confederate troops; while the havoc in the lines of an enemy who attempted to carry it by an advance from the plain of Fredericksburg, could not have been otherwise than disproportionally great.

General Lee, in another short, but significant dispatch, announces that the enemy has recrossed the Rappahannock with his whole force, withdrawn his bridges, and appears to be in motion for some other point unknown. We sincerely hope to find unfounded the statement volunteered that the enemy will not probably attempt another advance on Richmond by their late line of march. Nothing would be more agreeable than to hear that their columns had again formed for the ascent of those hills still firmly held by the Confederate army. Would that all the war was a repetition of that assault.

The retreat across the Rappahannock is the confession, absolute, of defeat. No flag of truce, or petition for burial of the dead, tells the tale so positively as such movement under such circumstances. An army that does this, in the eyes of all the world, and in its own eyes, is certainly a defeated army; literally and ignominiously defeated.

We shall await the next arrival of Northern news with great curiosity. Yet, we should not be at all surprised to find the Yankee press in full conflagration of triumph over the splendid and decisive success of the invincible Burnside, and the immortal army of the Potomac. The world has not forgotten that this same army, after gaining a signal victory at Mechanicsville, in view of the housetops of Richmond, was conducted through five more victories, yet more glorious and complete in all their parts, across the Chickahominy to Harrison's Landing, thirty miles off, on the James River. After this miracle of Yankee cuteness, the late mysterious event on the Rappahannock can be consistently and clearly explained without difficulty.

DECEMBER 31, 1862.

AT length the last day of a terrible year has come. Few persons now living can point to another period of their existence in which fortitude has been more severely tried. He who casts a retrospective glance upon the dangers all have risked, the privations and ruin many have suffered, the dear friends most have lost by a violent death, will have reason to be grateful for the insensibility of his heart, if he is not oppressed by painful and sombre emotions. While many hundred thousands, accustomed to independence and comfort, have been reduced to abject poverty and distress, those who have escaped must reflect that they have been nearer to utter destruction than they were ever before this year began, or are like to be again when it is ended.

But this year is not without glorious consolations. The unaided strength and unbacked courage of the nation redeemed its fortunes from the dust, plucked up its drowning honor by the locks, and tore from the very jaws of death the right to live forever. History will hereafter show no page illuminated with more enduring glory than those which record the heroic events of the circle of months which end with this day. In those months a forlorn republic, a people covered with the opprobrium and prejudice of the world, have secured a place in the Pantheon of remembered nations far above the most famous.

Neither the story of Greece, or of Rome, or of France, or of England, can bear a fair parallel with our own brief but eventful narrative. Is not this triumphant crown of victory worth the awful price? The question will be answered according to the temperament of the reader. Many think, with Sir John, that honor cannot cure a broken leg, and that all the national glory that has been won in battle since Greeks fought Trojans, will not compensate the loss of a beef or a dollar. But the young, the brave, the generous will everywhere judge that the exercise and exhibition in this year of the noblest virtues has been more than worth the misfortunes which have marked its progress:

> "Sound the clarion, fill the fife;
> To a sensual world proclaim,
> One crowded hour of glorious life
> Is worth an age without a name."

JANUARY 21, 1863.

It little concerns the South on what grounds the Democrats of the North may choose to base their political action. It is solely a matter for their own decision. But as they desire to make the South a party to their proposed line of action, it is certainly proper that they should be informed of our own feelings and determinations in that behalf.

The Northern Democrats are conducting their controversy with the Abolitionists in power upon three several propositions, to wit: first, that arbitrary arrests at home of "loyal" citizens must cease, and domestic liberty at least be preserved; second, that the war must be conducted with reference to crushing the rebellion, and no longer merely for the aggrandizement of favorites—with the object, moreover, of restoring and harmonizing the Union, and not for the insane purpose of Abolition propagandism; and, third, as a preliminary to peace, that a convention of delegates from all the States of the two hostile powers shall be called, charged with the duty of adjusting on a constitutional basis, and with constitutional guaranties, terms of re-union.

With the two first propositions the South has no concern. The Yankees will carry on the war vigorously or not, and deal with each other roughly or smoothly, without any reference to the wishes of the South, and without any interference from her in their intestine squabbles. But, when one of the rival factions proposes to call the South into council with a view to restoring the Union, they may as well be told promptly and solemnly that that part of their programme cannot be carried into effect.

What cold and heartless people are these Yankees, even these Northern Conservatives. How can any one with a particle of human sympathy actuating his bosom suppose, after the malignant, appalling brutalities of this war, that the South could consent to unite in amicable conference with such an enemy as hers? If the living could consent to bury and forget their resentments, what would be done with the dead, whose blood cries out against the murderers with a voice which no apostacy could stifle? The dead of this war met their fate in performing the duty of heroes; and by a base re-association with the enemy we would consent to dishonor their names, and to brand with infamy their conduct.

The advocates of peace at the North may as well dismiss from their programme the preposterous proposition for a joint convention with the South. The South cannot by any moral possibility consent to a re-union.

It is not for us to give advice to any party at the North, but in this case the maxim is certainly true, which holds that it may be wise for them to learn from an enemy. The lesson which we would teach the Northern conservatives is simply this, that *honesty is the best policy*. Let them not go before their people with a delusive and false programme. Let them not deceive their people into the belief that the South will unite in the convention which they propose. The Union is broken, and broken forever. Like the beautiful bubble blown from a pipe, once broken, it can never be restored. The blood which has been shed can never be washed out. The grievous wrongs which have been inflicted upon us can never be repaired, forgotten, or forgiven. The South, even if she could consent to dishonor herself, could never consent to defame her dead, or turn a deaf ear to the voices appealing from fifty thousand graves against the enemy of their country and their race. She cannot consent to reconstruction; and the Northern conservatives, if they have hearts and feelings, know it. Their hands, no less than those of the Abolitionists, are stained with Southern blood; their consciences are equally loaded with the guilt of this wholesale and wanton bloodshed; and we will not, we cannot grasp them in friendship. It is a fraud and falsehood to teach the Northern people that we will unite with them in convention.

JANUARY 26, 1863.

THE custom of denouncing the Yankees is becoming common. Under the soft influences of a serenade, President Davis likens them to hyenas; Governor Letcher, in his mild way, insists that they are a heaven-defying, hell-deserving race, and pleasantly consigns their chief magistrate to a doom more fearful than that of Devergoil. Is it to be wondered that Mr. Lincoln has had a trouble on his mind ever since this fearful doom was pronounced upon him—that he is getting gray, and finds it difficult to tell a dirty anecdote every ten minutes during the day?

The practice of vilifying the Yankees has gotten into the newspapers. Editors spend most of their time in concocting diatribes against a contemptible race, whose only defect is a proneness to all that is foul and every thing that is evil. Why should a people so despicable be aspersed? Even this newspaper, careful as it is, never to say a word that would disturb the most placid tea-party, has been known to speak disrespectfully of a race which the civilized world, with one consent, acknowledges to be its last and vilest product. One would suppose that creatures so abounding in the stenches of moral decomposition would never be alluded to in decent society. But somehow the habit of expectorating upon the vermin that swarm in the Northern dunghill has gotten the better of gentle natures; and time drags heavily on the Southerner who refuses to indulge himself some twenty times a day in a volley of direful anathemas against the Yankees.

Reflecting persons tell us that this is altogether wrong. We should restrain ourselves, and be scrupulously polite when speaking of these abominable villains. We should recollect that these infernal scoundrels are human beings, and bear in mind the fact that they never lose an opportunity of heaping the most outrageous abuse upon ourselves. Nor should it be forgotten that they have attained an almost inconceivable perfection and dexterity in lying; so that if it were possible for us to match them in Billingsgate, we would still be at their mercy in the trifling matter of falsehood. We are told by our philosophic friends that it should serve to cool the intensity of our hatred to remember that they are hourly committing every crime known to man, and some with which even the fiends are not familiar; that a thrill of delight should pass through us when we recall the pleasing circumstance, that upwards of a million of these incarnate demons are hired by the year for the sole purpose of murdering us, burning our houses, killing our cattle, stealing our slaves, destroying our crops, and driving our wives and helpless children into the waste, howling wilderness in midwinter; that a genial glow of the purest love should pervade our hearts at the thought that they candidly avow their purpose to exterminate us, to kill every one of us—men, women, and children—to take our possessions by violence—in a word, to annihilate us, to destroy us from the face of the earth, so that our names shall no more be heard among men.

There is another view which should encourage us in the purpose henceforth to cherish an affectionate regard for the accursed beings at war with us. To the well-regulated mind, the beastly practices of beasts excite no disagreeable emotion; and it is said that the scientific intellect finds a world of enjoyment in the contemplation of the disgusting utility of the lowest order of creatures. Surely the feast of the vulture upon carrion is not reprehensible, and occasions in the beholder no special wonder, and never any animosity against the bird for gratifying his peculiar tastes. So the tiger that laps blood, and the beetle that gorges excrement, are but Yankees of the animal kingdom, accommodating the wants of nature; and it were folly to impute to them improper motives in partaking of their ghastly and sickening repasts. It follows that our feelings towards the people of the North, the scarabæi and vipers of humanity, should be characterized neither by rage nor by nausea, but by a fixed, cheerful Christian determination to interpose sufficient obstacles between them and ourselves; to curb their inordinate and bloody lusts by such adequate means as natural wit suggests; and, as a general thing, to kill them wherever we find them, without idle questions as to whether they are reptiles or vermin. A certain calmness of mind is requisite to their successful slaughter. The convulsions of passion are out of place when one is merely scalding chinches to death.

The foregoing reflections are suggested, naturally enough, by the accounts in Yankee newspapers of Butler's triumphal progression from New York to Washington, and back again to Boston. A great hue and cry has been raised at the South because the spawn of Northern cities saw fit to prostrate themselves before this new Haynau, this modern Verres, returned from his conquests—this Beast, emerging from his cave filled with dead men's bones. Why this outcry? Wherefore assail the Brute, clotted with gore, or the chimpanzees that danced and chattered at his coming, and beslobbered him with praise? What had this hog-hyena done contrary to his instincts, that we should so berate him and his worshippers? He had hanged Mumford. That was true Yankee courage. He had issued a hellish order against the ladies of New Orleans. That was unaffected Yankee gallantry. He had put the mayor and hundreds of others into dungeons. That was the Yankee conception of the proper method of administering the laws of the "best government the world ever saw." He had banished from the city more than twenty thousand people who refused to perjure themselves by taking the oath of allegiance to the United States. That was the Yankee idea of justice. He drove those people off without a change of clothing, and with only fifty dollars in money. This was the Yankee idea of humanity. He confiscated property by millions. This was Yankee honesty. He supplied the rebels in Texas with munitions of war, and pocketed the proceeds of the cotton received in exchange. This was a smart Yankee trick. His troops were whipped at Baton Rouge, while he was in New Orleans; he was never under fire, and never smelt gunpowder, except at Hatteras, when the long-range guns of his fleet opened upon a mud fort, which had no ordnance that could reach him two miles off; and on the strength of this he issued an address as pompous as Satan's speech to his legions in the bottomless pit. This was making material for Yankee history. After inflicting innumerable tortures upon an innocent and unarmed people, after outraging the sensibilities of civilized humanity by his brutal treatment of women and children, after placing bayonets in the hands of slaves, after peculations the most prodigious and lies the most infamous, he returns, reeking with crime, to his own people, and they receive him with acclamations of joy, in a manner that befits him and becomes themselves. Nothing is out of keeping; his whole career and its reward are strictly artistic in conception and in execution.

He was a thief. A sword that he had stolen from a woman—the niece of the brave Twiggs—was presented to him as a reward of valor. He had violated the laws of God and man. The lawmakers of the United States voted him thanks, and the preachers of the Yankee gospel of blood came to him and worshipped him. He had broken into the safes and strong-boxes of merchants. The New York Chamber of Commerce gave him a dinner. He had insulted women. Things in female attire lavished harlot smiles upon him. He was a murderer. And a nation of assassins have deified him. He is at this time the REPRESENTATIVE MAN of a people lost to all shame, to all humanity, all justice, all honor, all virtue, all manhood. Cowards by nature, thieves upon principle, and assassins at heart, it would be marvellous indeed if the people of the North refused to render homage to Benjamin Butler, the beastliest, bloodiest poltroon and pickpocket the world ever saw.

JANUARY 31, 1863.

WHAT would have been the governmental policy of the Republicans had there been no war? Many people at the North fancy that it was not their original purpose to subvert the Constitution and change the whole structure and policy of the Government, but that they have been driven by the war into excesses which they never contemplated. The suspension of the *habeas corpus*, the suppression of free speech, the muzzling of the press and of the telegraph, arbitrary arrests, and all other outrages are due, it is said by these apologists, to military necessities which override all law. Granting, what can be proven false, that the Republicans did not bring on the war—that the nine governors who went to Washington, did not decide Lincoln in favor of bloodshed—granting this, the question arises, what did they intend to do, how did they propose to carry on the Government, what were their plans and their ultimate aims? If this question could be answered satisfactorily, the soberer portion of the North would have some idea of what is in store for them, in case the South is not subjugated, and the Republican party is permitted to retain power.

The Chicago platform, disdaining concealments, announced flatly that free soil was for free men, and that the South had no rights in the Territories. Lincoln was no sooner elected than he declared boldly that he "intended to place the Government actively on the side of freedom." He added, that he was "utterly opposed to any concession or compromise that shall yield one inch of the position occupied by the Republican party on the subject of slavery in the Territories." If these declarations be studied attentively, they will show that it was the purpose of the Republicans, from the beginning, to throw the whole weight of the Government against slavery, and in favor of free-soilism—in other words, the essence of the Republican platform was abolition. For it is not possible to use the influence of a powerful government against slavery without destroying it—unless war intervenes—and the destruction of slavery is abolitionism.

A thousand other proofs might be adduced to show that the Republican party was originally what it has been since it came into power, and what it is at this moment, a party of one idea, and that idea one which is at variance with the Constitution and the whole past policy of the United States. In plain terms, it is a revolutionary party, based upon a theory as visionary as any of the French revolutionists, without any conception of the spirit or the form of true government, and without the least familiarity with its administration. Is it to be wondered that its leaders have exhibited the extravagance, the corruption, the mendacity, the unscrupulousness, the violent passions, the ignorance, the endless crimes, the thirst for blood, that have in all times characterized fanatical men while in power?

The Republican party was formed, then, for the purpose of overthrowing the Government of the United States. Its aim was so to change the Constitution as to make it inimical to slavery. Beyond this it had no fixed policy. But in carrying out this new policy, in putting into practice the dogma of abolitionism, it has been found that an entirely new system of government must be adopted : a dictatorship which is fully upheld by the Republican party. A Union without State lines is the only Union they care to save; a consolidated, abolitionized "nation" is the result of the feast of blood to which Lincoln's guide, Wendell Phillips, invites the people of the West.

FEBRUARY 4, 1863.

Mr. DAVIS has his favorites to whom he gives opportunities denied to all others. He persists in maintaining in chief command one Lee, although Lee has had that position for nearly a year, and won glory enough for three men. He appears unable to divest himself of the idea that Joe Johnston must never be denied the place he so much covets, the front of battle, where he may accumulate lead in his tissues, and adorn himself with a few more dozen of honorable scars. He is infatuated with Beauregard, dotes on Bragg, and, in fact, seems disinclined to give up any one to whom he has ever taken a fancy. Not so with Lincoln. He has no prepossessions in favor of anybody, or, if he has, they are not allowed to interfere with the good of the country. With an abundance of military talent at his command, he wisely determines to avail himself of the whole, and not of a part. Prompted by a love of justice, he retains a commander only long enough for him to make a reputation, then relieves him and calls for another, who else had languished in obscurity. No wonder that his armies are always successful, that his soldiers fight so well, that their military councils are so harmonious.

He began with Winfield (or Wingfield) Scott, a man famous in two hemispheres, full of strange oaths to support the Constitution of the United States, of infinite hatred to Jeff. Davis, piqued against Virginia for not voting for him for President, trained in war and confident of crushing the rebellion—the man of all others that an ordinary President would have kept as generalissimo during the whole war. Scott chose as his Lieutenant and Executive Officer, Irwin McDowell, a sturdy, soldierly person, who shared the confidence of his gigantic patron. On his way to Manassas, Irwin told an old lady, who had been molested by his soldiers, that she need give herself no uneasiness as to the future, for his army would be in Richmond in a few days, and would return to Washington by a different route. Sometime on the afternoon of Sunday, the 21st of July, 1861, he appears to have changed his mind and the direction of his army. He returned to Washington by the very road that he came. A number of people, none of them disposed to lounge by the wayside, were in the road that afternoon, and it has never been known how McDowell contrived to pass them, or at what precise hour and in what frame of mind he reached Washington.

Scott and McDowell had a fair chance at Manassas. Wingfield swore he was the greatest coward in the world, and Lincoln took him at his word. He sent him to West Point to nurse his gout, gave McDowell command of a division, and called from the mountains of Virginia an avaricious railroad President, of doubtful loyalty, who had stumbled on a success over a handful of Confederates, whose leader had been slain—Lincoln's choice was approved by his subjects. If any of them had been inclined to murmur at the removal of men so great as Scott, they soon became silent, or filled the papers with hosannas to the new chieftain—thus evincing that heavenly harmony which is the soul of patriotism and the glory of the North American nation.

Accustomed in peace to the indecent haste of railroad travelling, McClellan adopted in war the sedate tactics of the mud-turtle. He manifested no fondness for former pursuits, except a passionate affection for spades and pickaxes, a reverence for trenches, and a sublime fervor for embankments. He developed the strangest liking for mud and marshes, and no muskrat ever delighted in ditches half so much as he. Some accused him of letting out the war to his old friends, the contractors, at so much the cubic foot, but Lincoln paid no heed to these satirists, believing with McClellan, that the best way to extricate the nation from a difficulty was to excavate, or exhume it. Accordingly, McClellan continued to excavate for nearly a year,—and at the expiration of that time was found by Lincoln at Harrison's Landing, still digging with unabated ardor. Abraham was well pleased, but concluded that George had had his day.

His next selection was John Pope, who was called to the supreme command, not because his master had any particular confidence in him, but because his turn was come, and because of a singular optical inability under which he professed to labor. He had never been able to see any thing but the backs of the rebels. As this incapacity had never been experienced by the former leaders of the Grand Army of the Potomac, it was thought desirable by Lincoln to test its advantages. The experiment was thorough, but of brief duration. McClellan having exhausted the tactics of the turtle,

Pope adopted the manœuvres of the crab, an animal whose gait is a sort of uncertain retrograde flank movement, not very clear to itself, and entirely incomprehensible to beholders. Pope carried out his crustacean theory with wonderful accuracy and alacrity, arriving in Washington at the expiration of a few weeks without loss. About two-thirds of his army remained behind for the purpose of studying his theory at leisure, and a few thousands applied themselves to study with such ardor, that they perished, martyrs to the new science of war.

Gratified with Pope's performances, Lincoln sent him on a pleasure trip among the Indians of the Northwest. Being somewhat doubtful as to whose turn came next, he reinstated McClellan until he could make up his mind. Unwilling a second time to imitate the turtle, McClellan announced the ram as his model and engaged in a great butting match at Antietam, whence he retired with an addled brain, which, in the opinion of Lincoln, demanded a protracted leave of absence. Little Burnside was then called up to the head of the military class, and in spite of his protestations of mental disability and general worthlessness, was commanded to carry on the war in what fashion he pleased, provided always that it was vigorous. Burnside obeyed. He had been victorious at Roanoke Island, and in the fens and pools of that scene of triumph had discovered an instructor in the art of war whose method he deemed invincible. Rejecting with scorn the turtle, the crab, and the ram, Burnside elected the snake-doctor as his tactician. This shrewd insect exhibited to Burnside movements the most masterly, combined with strategy the most profound—his method consisting in a sudden and unexpected sideways dodge, followed by a bold pause, and then another dodge, more rapid and unforeseen than the first—in fact, a surprise which it is impossible to anticipate, and still more impossible to foil. Long study over the pools and puddles of Roanoke Island had made him so familiar with this system, that in less than a month after he assumed command of the army, he executed the snake-doctor dodge down to Falmouth, and then paused. He then snake-doctored his army across the river, and paused. Afterwards he dodged it against some obstructions that happened accidentally to be upon the hills outside the town, paused for a day or two, and then, being convinced that he came very near achieving an impossibility, quietly snake-doctored his decimated legions back to Stafford again. Still another snake-doctor dodge he attempted lately, but becoming entangled in McClellan's favorite cement, mud, threw up his commission and retreated to Washington.

Nothing could have been more acceptable to Lincoln, not that he was dissatisfied with Burnside, but that he felt it was a fitting opportunity to put a fresh general on trial. The new man is Joseph Hooker, or "Fighting Joe," as his friends are pleased to style him— a personage destined to perform the most extraordinary feats, as soon as the mud gets dry. It is fair to infer that his science of warfare will be borrowed from none of the aquatic or amphibious tribes, but from some purely terrestrial and unmoistened creature or class of creatures. He tells us that his army is superior to our own in "equipments, intelligence, and valor," and his friends assure us that he is "Fighting Joe," that is to say, an old-fashioned, plain, honest, straightforward fist and skull fellow, who goes in for "fair play and no gouging." He will adopt none of the new-fangled practices of his predecessors. He will disdain the "big Indian" method of FUSS and FEATHERS, the turtle tactics of McClellan, the crab practice of Pope, the snake-doctor dodges of Burnside. We are curious to know in what category of fighting animals he will find his exemplars. After much reflection upon so important a subject, we have narrowed his choice down to two dry-land specimens of the animal kingdom—one, a pugnacious quadruped, the yearling bull, the other a belligerent insect known to school-boys as the doodle-bug. One of the two "Fighting Joe" must elect, and we are inclined to think that he will choose the latter. The custom of the doodle-bug is to come out of his hole, attack his enemy wherever he finds him, and never to let him go until one or both are dead. This is the style, we should say, that would suit a "fighting Joe." And when Joe, the great Yankee doodle-bug, does pounce upon the poor fellows on the Rappahannock, who have no "equipments," no "intelligence," and no "valor," we tremble for the result. But if they do whip him, Lincoln, having tried everybody else, will be compelled to take command in person of the Army of the Potomac, and then the fate of the Confederacy will be sealed. One joke from the Gorilla will do the business. An army convulsed with laughter can't fight; it is whipped before the battle begins. And that, we seriously fear, will be the end of Lee's army.

FEBRUARY 9, 1863.

CHRISTENDOM is about to be regaled with a most savage, ridiculous, ineffectual and odoriferous novelty. Dispatches of Friday last announced that the "negro soldiers' bill" had passed the Yankee House of Representatives by a vote of 88 to 54. "The slaves of loyal persons," says the dispatch, "are not to be received, and no recruiting officers are to be sent into the Border States without the permission of their governors. Mr. Stevens said three hundred thousand men would leave the army in May. We could not raise fifty thousand white men. Conscription was impossible."

What a confession is here! More than twenty millions of white people, educated in common schools, accustomed from childhood to those practical exercises by which the wits are supposed to be sharpened, and the body invigorated, and priding themselves upon their endowments, make war upon less than one-third of their number of semi-barbarian Southerners, slothful, ignorant, enervated, depraved; and after two years of war such as no people ever waged and none ever endured (so vast is its magnitude and so vehement and malignant its energy), the stronger power is forced by the stern necessity of constant defeat and the inherent wickedness of the cause, to appeal from its own race and section to African slaves for help. How shameful the admission of weakness—how ridiculous the appeal for aid! Three hundred thousand white men, trained in the art of modern warfare, throw down their arms in disgust in May, and their places are to be filled with negroes who scarcely know the muzzle from the butt of a musket, and who, there is every reason to believe, can never be taught the simplest evolutions of the line. Could the absurd folly of the Abolition crusade be more glaringly manifest than in this preposterous substitution of muscle and ignorance for education, inexperience for training, clumsiness for skill, blind brute force for patriotism and intelligence? It is the insane malignity of fanaticism whipped, beaten, driven to desperation.

Enlightened Europe may turn from the threatened sickening horrors of a servile insurrection invoked at Washington to a phase of this war, as it will be waged next summer, which, when depicted with historical accuracy and physiological fidelity, can scarcely fail to relieve its fears as to the future of the white race at the South, and conduce, in no small degree, to the alleviation of any epigastric uneasiness that Exeter Hall may experience in regard to the corporal welfare of the colored brethren. To be sure, some Southern families may be massacred, and some thousands of the dusky fraternity may be extinguished by way of mild admonition to the remainder; but to suppose that the masters of Cuffee will be generally abated at the point of the John Brown pike, or that Cuffee himself will be slaughtered by wholesale, as swine are at Cincinnati, is to indulge a nightmare which only weak tea, admixed with unadulterated fanaticism, can engender.

The fate of the negro, of the white population at the South, and of the Northern army, respectively, will be decided in a brief contest which will occur about the middle of next June, and which we will describe as gravely and succinctly as possible. On the first of April, fifty thousand negroes, who have been previously drilled in various camps of instruction, will be debarked at Aquia Creek. Pugnacious Joseph Hooker, foaming at the mouth from long delay, will organize them into brigades and divisions with the velocity of frenzied impatience. But it will require six weeks of incessant toil to perform this simple feat. It is at last accomplished. The pontoons are laid safely and crossed without opposition. To prevent accident, the Grand Colored Division is put in the van. Greeley, its commander, remains at Aquia Creek "with a powerful glass," after the manner of Burnside. The skirmishers of the Grand Colored Division are thrown out. They deploy.

The voice of an overseer calling hogs, is heard in a distant field. They rally on the reserve. No rebels being visible, they are again thrown forward. They feel for the enemy, but he is not to be felt. They fire at nothing, fifty feet in the air, and hit it every time. The rebels being thus driven to their earth-works, the Grand Colored Division advances at the *pas de charge*, singing a Methodist refrain, to storm the enemy's position and to " carry the crest " at all hazards. Of a sudden, the artillery of A. P. Hill's command belches forth a hurricane of shell and shrapnel. There is a rising of wool, as of quills upon the fretful porcupine, under the caps of dusky brigadiers and sooty major-generals; there is a simultaneous effusion of mellifluous perspiration from fifty thousand tarry hides; there is a display of ivory like fifty thousand flashes of lightning; fifty thousand pairs of charcoal knees are knocking together, and one hundred thousand Ethiopian eyeballs are rolling madly in their sockets, like so many drunken and distracted moons dancing in an ebon sky; the Grand Colored Division trembles like a mighty pointer dog on an icy pavement—there is an universal squall, as if all Africa had been kicked upon its shins, and, at the self-same moment, a scattering, as if all the blackbirds, crows, and buzzards in creation had taken wings at once. To a man, the Northern army lies prostrate in the field, asphyxiated by the insufferable odor bequeathed to the atmosphere by the dark departed host. For a like cause, the rebel army is in full retreat to Richmond. Solitary and alone, with his nose in his hand, A. P. Hill surveys the silent scene.

MARCH 14, 1863.

LET the South be warned by the spectacle which the North has presented during these years. What has happened there has not happened here; but it might have done so, and it may yet happen. The elastic plea of public necessity deluded the North. The people there were told that all the power of the country must be concentrated in the hands of one man that he might crush a rebellion; that private suffering and injustice must be inflicted to prevent the destruction of the nation. The same overpowering argument has been often urged on the floor of the Southern Congress and in the Southern press. The nation has refused to listen to it, and, up to the present point in the war, has preserved its Constitution intact. But when the tug of trial comes, and the weak are alarmed, we shall hear it again, and if the representatives of the nation then listen, the Constitution and the cause will die together.

For never was sophism more fallacious than this. The strength of the Confederacy will depart from it the moment it becomes a pale reflex of the Northern empire. The North possesses greater numbers, and all the physical advantages in a greater degree, than the South. Yet the South resists with success, and why? Because of its superior moral force. This is still a free republic. Our armies fight with courage for their property and liberty. Our people endure the ills of war with fortitude, that their laws and privileges may be secured. The North is governed by a despotism; its soldiers and its people are enslaved. But if we do as the North has done, and surrender all the powers of the State into the hands of one man, the South will be governed also by arbitrary power, and its people, too, will be slaves. Then the struggle will resolve itself into a struggle between two despotisms, each possessing a certain amount of brute force. As the

South has far less of this than the North, the conclusion is inevitable that the South must succumb. The only hope of this country rests on a strict adherence to its republican principles. The restoration of the Union becomes a possible thing the moment it is presented in the form of this question: Shall we belong to a great country governed by arbitrary and despotic power, or belong to a little country also governed by arbitrary and despotic power?

MARCH 14, 1863.

SECOND only to finance is the vital subject of impressments. Indeed, the question of food ranks before that of money; and impressments affect the supply of food more than any other action of Government. These impressments are the uppermost subjects at this time with the agricultural population; and if this business is not regulated on some satisfactory basis, the food of the country will be diminished in all the grain producing portion of the Confederacy by one-third. Congress and the Executive may as well accept and recognize this fact at once; for if they postpone their action until the season of seeding is over, they will then act in vain.

Laws have been passed to restrict the culture of tobacco, and others will be made to prohibit the production of cotton; but inasmuch as these are staples which the Government does not impress, they are likely to be, if some guarantees are not furnished against unjust impressments, more encouraged by that omission than if a bounty of twenty-five cents a pound each were offered for their cultivation. Let Congress pass a law authorizing impressments without what is a real and just compensation, establishing a high commission to fix the prices of supplies; and more cotton and tobacco will be cultivated in the South than was ever known before.

The temper of our people revolts at injustice and arbitrary violence. They are accustomed to the enjoyment of their rights unimpeached; and until recently they have been strangers to wrong and insult from Government officials. If they are properly compensated, and equally dealt with, they will give all their labor and savings to Government, and give them cheerfully, but if these are exacted arbitrarily, and with insolence and insult, they will not only give nothing at all, but they will take effectual measures to prevent the minions of Government from obtaining what they prowl through the country to seize for a mockery of payment. There is a feeling of resentment, deep seated, and widely pervading the best class of the community, against Government, which is held responsible for these mad and reckless impressments; and there are high officers in this goodly city who fancy that they are popular in the land, but whose names are held in execration by the staunch classes which control public opinion.

Official, legalized robberies never answered a good purpose in any country or any age of the world; and of all countries and ages they suit ours the least. Strange, that, when the people are willing to contribute to public service with cheerfulness and alacrity all that they have, on liberal terms, Government should insist upon exacting their substance under multiplied circumstances of gratuitous wrong. Strange, that, when so much depends upon augmenting the supplies of food, so much should be done by Government to diminish them; that, at a time when bounties should be offered for the encouragement of agriculture, the most effective measures for discouraging it should be resorted to!

These arbitrary impressments of Government touch the people's pride and sense of justice; and they have effected a great and natural change in their sentiments towards the cause. Men, who, in a romantic and pious enthusiasm for their country, have cheerfully given up their sons to the battle, and have assisted with a sort of mournful pride in the burial of their offspring slain on the field, have had their feelings and temper towards the Government suddenly changed by the rude and rapacious action of Government press-gangs. They make this natural reflection, whether a good cause, administered in wrong and rapacity, can succeed; and these impressments have done more to shake the confidence of the country in the capacity of its public men in civil office for administering affairs, than any other cause and all causes combined.

Whether regard be had to a supply of food sufficient to sustain the people and their armies; or to securing the continued cordial support of a valuable class of citizens to the Government and the country; or to preserving the sanctity of private rights, the integrity of the property and the immunity of the people on their own homesteads, it behooves Congress to redress the present wrongful practice and establish a proper system of impressment without delay. No one denies that impressment is frequently necessary to supply the army in active service the requisite food; but it should be fully compensated, and the powers of the agents making it should be strictly limited. It does not seem difficult to provide by law proper regulations for impressment.

APRIL 2, 1863.

FEW doubt, even in a faint degree, the ultimate triumph of the Confederacy. It is gloom, not fear, that clouds the face of the people, and it is caused by the extinction of all the delusions and illusions which shed a false, flattering light on the road ahead. They have been forced to the stern conclusion that their country is alone on the earth; that they have no friend but God, who is afar off, and no hope but in their own swords. With these they can do what many other nations have done in similar circumstances. They can defend themselves. They can so cut and hew the hordes of robbers and murderers coming down upon them that they will one day be glad to cry quits. But the work will be long.

Many do truly believe that the cause is in danger from an insufficiency of food. But those apprehensions are certainly much exaggerated. The scarcity of food is but temporary, and is artificial rather than real. A vast supply exists. It has not been put in market, nor has the Government been able to find it, simply because the Commissariat of the Confederate States, whether from folly or a worse cause, has been palpably mismanaged. It has failed to get what it wanted because it would not pay just compensation. But this difficulty, we hope, is past. Whenever the Government is willing to pay just compensation for property, it can get all it wants. Soon the very remembrance of this portion of our trouble will be forgotten.

Of the final results of this war there can be no doubt, if the spirit of the people can be maintained at the height which it has held hitherto. All depends on that. Ours is the inferior party in numbers and material power, and the only hope of the Confederate cause rests on the superior pride, fortitude, and constancy, not of the army only, but of the country, which creates, supports, and inspires the army. Hitherto the sentiment of the country has been truly heroic. Nothing that the enemy has done or can do will destroy it. But it is possible for the Government of the Confederacy to do what the enemy has failed to do: to discourage and disgust the Southern people. Hitherto they have been very patient, even under the provocations of the many jacks-in-office, thieves, renegade Yankees, and nondescript parasites who have fastened on our Government. Unfortunately, this class wishes to do more than plunder the legitimate sovereigns of the soil. They wish the Confederate Government to become a pinchbeck imitation of the Lincoln Usurpation. Until now they have met with small success. But from this source comes the true danger of the Southern cause. It is the duty of the people's representatives to check the Government in its follies, and support earnestly its measures when they are sensible. The people themselves have now the opportunity to select for their representatives men who have the firmness necessary to repulse every attack upon the rights of States and the rights of individuals, and the wisdom to do so without falling, even under the most aggravated provocation, into factious opposition to an administration which has its merits as well as its demerits, and with which the cause of the country is now identified in many points.

MAY 4, 1863.

NEVER, probably, was there a deliberative assembly intrusted with the high responsibilities of legislation in a momentous crisis less gifted with commanding talent, or signalized by initiative power, than the Confederate Congress. The business of the country has been creditably performed; important measures have been adopted from time to time; not, perhaps, the best that could have been devised, nor free from grave errors of detail, but still aiming to accomplish important objects, utilizing the resources of the country for the support of the army and conduct of the war. All these measures, however, have been urged and forced by the people upon their representatives.

The necessities of the situation, coming home to the most sacred feelings of every man in the Confederacy, have aroused thought, stimulated discussion, and concentrated the whole intellectual power of the people upon the few vital points essential to their existence. In the collision of opposing sentiments, and from the suggestive power of discussion, certain general conclusions became fixed in the popular mind, which Congress was only called upon to elaborate and perfect. They have been satisfied with the humble part of giving expression to the popular will, and have not aspired to the loftier position of the chosen intellects of a nation, from whom originality of thought and fruitfulness of expedient is expected; who tower above the general mediocrity, and, like lofty mountains, catch the first beams of the rising sun before it irradiates the plain below.

That great genius should not have been evoked by the creative power of the stirring epoch through which we are passing is somewhat remarkable. It may detract, apparently, from the poetical character of the contest, that no individual should stand prominently forward to receive that hero-worship to which human nature is so prone; but, in real grandeur, as well as in solid hope of future prosperity, the spectacle of a nation, sustained by generally diffused intelligence and patriotism, far transcends the fitful display of individual genius. The dazzling exploits of an Alexander or a Napoleon command the admiration of mankind and change the fate of a generation, but the solid virtues of a Scipio or a Washington, springing from and harmonizing with the deep-seated and widely-disseminated love of country, afford a surer guarantee of national greatness.

The Confederacy may well dispense with the shining talents that stamp their impress upon a nation's history, provided the intelligent requirements of the people are executed with reasonable zeal and fidelity. History will find no more instructive theme than the spectacle of a nation in which the martial virtues were happily conjoined with pure patriotism and political intelligence; whose independence should be secured and institutions consolidated, not by the transcendent abilities or controlling influence of a few dominant minds, but by the general devotion and intelligent co-operation of the whole community. In such a country, the talents of the soldier and the statesman will never be wanting in sufficient measure to serve the State usefully; they will never so completely overshadow the country as to become dangerous to liberty.

MAY 7, 1863.

THE depravity of Northern sentiment could not be more forcibly exhibited than in the expectations which that people had formed from such a mountebank and braggart as the now beaten and disgraced Joseph Hooker. That he is a man without faith, truth, honor, or any of the distinguishing qualities of a gentleman, is established by the fact that in the old army he was held in contempt by his fellow officers, who refused to tolerate his society, and that when he was appointed to the supreme direction of the Federal forces at Fredericksburg, men of respectability, like Generals Sumner and Franklin, retired in disgust from their commands.

He owed his elevation to the responsible position in which he has just so signally failed to the most dishonorable and disgusting conduct of which it is possible to conceive an officer can be guilty. He owes it to the fact that he was capable of appearing before a secret committee of the Federal Congress, and, in testimony filling many documental pages, indulging in most offensive, criminatory, and flippant criticism upon the conduct of his superiors in command, and his associate officers in the field. Full of vanity, and self-conceit, and assurance, he represented to the committee the perfect possibility of capturing Richmond at any day of McClellan's campaign from Yorktown to Harrison's Landing, vaunting that he alone could have accomplished the achievement on several occasions, if he had not been constantly restrained from the work by his General-in-Chief. Indulging that capital blunder in generalship of underrating an adversary, and as voluble as conceited, he made the committee understand, by vociferous and minute explanations, how open the Confederate capital was to capture at every moment of the siege, and with what ease and expedition General Joseph Hooker could have clutched the glittering prize, if his arm had not been held by the evil genius who commanded the investing forces. That a dishonored ingrate, capable of giving such testimony, should have been selected by the Washington administration for the responsible task of directing the movements of a great army, is a fact which displays, with striking force, the utter absence of moral tone in the men who rule the most corrupt and demoralized people on the globe. Reason should have taught them that a fool so puffed up with his own consequence, a brain so bloated and blinded with conceit, a general so oblivious of all merit in an enemy, should not be intrusted with a campaign designed to repair and redeem the overwhelming misfortunes of no less than four successive campaigns of disaster. The narrowness of this conceited General's mind, and the intensity of his conceit, have just been exhibited in conspicuous relief. Thoughtless of what his adversaries might do, he undertook the critical task of flanking a formidable army after crossing a considerable river. Absorbed in his own plans, this adventurer and blusterer was incapable of bestowing any thought upon what must be the palpable strategy of his adversary; and the result is, a defeat at Chancellorsville more signal than that which was sustained by Burnside, and more disgraceful, because lost by more clearly stupid generalship in command of a far larger army.

In contrast with the calamitous denouement of this adventurer's career, and to afford an insight into the character of a Yankee General-in-Chief, we shall allow this irrepressible fighter to relate his own exploits, in a few random extracts taken from his evidence before the committee above mentioned. We shall permit him to begin his adventures at Yorktown. It will be seen that the committee in question was very willing to draw him out to the full length of his tether.

"Q. To what do you attribute the failure of the Peninsula Campaign?

A. I do not hesitate to say that it is to be attributed to the want of generalship on the part of our commander.

Q. What course would you have advised at the time of the landing on the Peninsula, under the circumstances?

A. What I subsequently did, will, I think, convey an answer to the question. I attacked with my single division a line of works at Williamsburg, stronger than the line across the Peninsula at Yorktown. I never could understand why I was required to send one-half of my number on duty, day and night, to dig, so as to invest the place. I felt that the enemy's lines could be pierced without any considerable loss. We could have gone right through, and gone to the rear of the enemy. They would have run the moment we got to their rear, and we could have picked up the prisoners.

Q. You were there when the enemy retreated from Yorktown?

A. I was within a mile and a half of there.

Q. Will you state briefly and succinctly what took place upon their retreat?

A. Had General Sumner advanced at the proper moment, the rebellion would have been buried at Williamsburg. He did not advance at all.

Q. Where was General McClellan all this time?

A. At Yorktown.

Q. You stood your ground?

A. Yes, sir. I have since learned, from the most reliable sources, that when the news of that battle reached Richmond, Jefferson Davis and Governor Letcher moved their families out of Richmond, removed the archives and their libraries, and every citizen who could command a vehicle, had his goods piled on wagons, and prepared to abandon the city. They only returned (those who had left) when they found that the pursuit ceased—I almost say, was abandoned." [When they heard Hooker was coming, they packed up to run; when they heard that Hooker was forbidden to come, they unpacked their trunks, restored their books to the shelves, and went to bed in security.]

"Q. Is it your judgment that you could have gone into Richmond then?

A. I think we could have moved right on, and got into Richmond by the second day after that battle, without another gun being fired.

Q. What was done?

A. We moved on in a manner I never did understand, losing time."

On the first day of the battle of Fair Oaks, or Seven Pines, every thing went wrong. Hooker was not in it; his division was posted six miles from the battle-field. Late in the day, however, he was ordered forward, got fairly down to the work next day, and, as will be seen from his own testimony, soon sent the rebels into the woods.

" When reaching within about a mile of what was called Savage's Station, the head of my column became impeded by the fugitives, trains of wagons, and fragments of batteries upon the road, and was prevented from advancing, except with their bayonets at a charge. From this cause my column could make but little headway, and at the time I left them, to ride to the front, I doubted if they could advance at all. When I reached there, the battle of Fair Oaks for that night was nearly over. About dark my troops came up. We bivouacked on the ground, the firing having been suspended. The next morning, about seven o'clock, the firing was renewed. I started with the half of my division I had with me, to meet the enemy. The enemy was firing on Sumner's command, which was occupying the railroad at that time. I made towards the heaviest fire, and came up in the rear of the enemy, and in half an hour after my men became engaged, the enemy was routed, throwing away their arms, clothing, and haversacks, and broke for the woods in the direction of Richmond.

Q. That was the second day of the fight?

A. Yes, sir; and that was the ending of the fight at that battle."

Hooker had done the business up in the right style, and made a finish of the fight.

" Q. Suppose that the next day after this repulse of the enemy at Fair Oaks, General McClellan had brought his whole army across the Chickahominy, and made a vigorous movement upon Richmond, in your judgment, as a military man, what would have been the effect of the movement?

A. In answer to that, I would say, that at no time during the whole of that campaign, did I feel that we could not go to Richmond."

In fact, there was no time at which Hooker (in Hooker's opinion) could not have gone into Richmond.

" Q. Were you in the battle of Malvern?

A. Yes, sir; and at that place we won a great battle.

Q. Could you have gone into Richmond after the fight?

A. I have no doubt we could."

The fighting of this redoubtable man was as decisive at Antietam as on the Chickahominy. He fought and actually won that battle, if his own narration is to be credited, with his own division alone, but swooned from a wound received in the act of consummating his victory. Since waking from his swoon, he has never been able to understand how the rebels got away in good order, and how it came to be a drawn battle.

It is unnecessary to follow this irrepressible conqueror through the campaign of the Rappahannock. There was too little fighting in that affair to afford full scope to his genius. Enough was said by him before the committee to convince Mr. Lincoln that that campaign was lost in consequence of inattention to the counsels of General Hooker. He opposed the direct attack upon Fredericksburg, and advocated the crossing and flank movement above, the merit of which has just been so signally illustrated in the sanguinary engagements of last Friday and Saturday. The result of that battle affords the most eloquent and crushing commentary upon the braggadocio whom we have set forth at such length. In his language to the authorities of his Government, he seems to have improved with great diligence that text in the first chapter of the Book of Judas, which declareth: "Whosoever bloweth not his own horn, verily the same shall not be blown for him." But when charged with the duty of performing the task he professed so much anxiety to undertake, and so much confidence of achieving, he has afforded the most deplorable instance on record of the folly of intrusting a blusterer and pretender with grave and great responsibilities.

MAY 9, 1863.

The Rappahannock has been passed probably for the last time by the Grand Army of the Potomac. It is scarcely possible that the successor of General Judas Hooker will again attempt to carry it on to Richmond by the mail route. Where the Army of the Potomac will next turn its dismal steps, and where it will next be beaten, is yet unknown. It is certain, however, that it must move somewhere. From the beginning of the war to this hour it has led the life of that famous Joe, whose name and fate have been rendered familiar to the world by the most popular of living writers.

"This boy," says the constable, "though he has been repeatedly told to, *won't move on.*"

"I'm always movin' on, sir," cries the boy, wiping away his grimy tears with his arm, "I've always been a-movin' and a-movin' on ever since I was born. Where can I possibly move to, sir, more nor I do move?"

"He won't move on," says the constable, calmly, "although he has been repeatedly cautioned, and therefore I am obliged to take him into custody. He's as obstinate a young gonoph as I know. He won't move on."

"Oh my eye! Where can I move to?" cries the boy quite desperately, clutching at his hair.

This interrogatory cry of poor Joe might be adopted and uttered with heartfelt earnestness by the Grand Army of the Potomac, when next it is taken into custody by the *Herald* or the *Times*, and sternly told to Move On by Lincoln. Where, indeed! No army ever made such a variety of movements; all have been equally unsatisfactory. Whenever it has moved on, no matter where or which way, it has moved to a beating. No sooner had it come into existence, than it heard, in tones of thunder, the order On to Rich-

MOND! It moved on—to Manassas. It has been "a-movin' on" continually since, and to similar purpose.

The Grand Army of the Potomac has never achieved a success. It has been periodically defeated for two years, and cannot, without such lying as would hurt the conscience of a prostitute, claim a single victory. The annals of history may be searched in vain for another military organization which has been paid more, supplied more, recruited more, deserted more, moved-on more, been more whipped, or which has run away such a monstrous number of times. On all of these points it may proudly claim a pre-eminence over the most famous failures of recorded memory. What will become of it now? Must it be thrashed any more? Are its legs equal yet to another race? Can 2.40 be gotten out of it again?

What, too, will become of Judas Hooker? He betrayed his master, like the other Judas, and, like him, the only thing the "reward of iniquity" has gained for him, has been this new Aceldama, this modern Field of Blood. Will he go out like his prototype and hang himself there? The prisoners say they saw him falling from his horse. Did he, too, there "burst asunder in the midst, all his bowels gushing out?" Fortunate is he if it was so. No form of sudden death would not be preferable to the infamous depth of disgrace into which he will now tumble. In what condition does he return to those who hearkened to his brag!

MAY 11, 1863.

THE hero of the war, that great genius, that noble patriot, the support and hope of this country, STONEWALL JACKSON, is no more. He died yesterday at three o'clock in the afternoon. The immediate cause of his death was pneumonia, against which his constitution, shaken by the sore wounds received in the glorious victory at Chancellors, was unable to struggle. This announcement will draw many a tear in the South, and many a shout of malignant exultation in the North. Whatever difference of opinion may have existed among the semi-intelligent, the instinct of the people was fixed in the belief that this silent Virginian was one of the first of living men. In the popular estimate we most sincerely concur. There was the stuff of Cromwell in Jackson. Hannibal might have been proud of his campaign in the Valley, and the shades of the mightiest warriors should rise to welcome his stern ghost.

MAY 12, 1863.

WE have had recently some remarkable returns for the pretty civilities showered by Stuart and Hampton on the Dutch farmers of Pennsylvania during their raid to Chambersburg. That souvenir of chivalry is forcibly brought to mind by the sharp contrast of recent occurrences. It has long been a laughing-stock for the North; and the narrative which was published by Colonel McClure, the Yankee commander at Chambersburg, of the polite phrases and punctilios of the "soft-mannered rebels" who invaded his military dominions, still survives among the Yankee humors of the war. We still have the picture before us of the sleek Yankee watching from the cover of his porch the wet, weary, and hungry "rebels" exposing themselves to a drenching rain, rather than invade the sanctity of the homes of the citizens of Chambersburg; "begging" a few coals to light their fires, and humbly asking permission to buy food from the negro wenches in the kitchens; while the officers made their salaams to Colonel McClure, and "thanked him for his candor" when he informed them that he was a red-hot abolitionist. It never seemed to have occurred to these damp knights that it was their duty to their men to take from an enemy what they wanted of food and shelter; they were too intent on pruning their manners, practising the knighthood of the middle ages in Pennsylvania, and establishing a chivalric fraternity with the Dutch civilization they had invaded.

We have had enough, in the recent Yankee raids, to put to the blush these recollections of "chivalry," and to teach us that the gentle knight-errantry of rose-water is but a poor way of opposing an enemy whose mission is that of savage warfare.

From our Southern exchanges we gather some accounts of the conduct of the Yankees on their recent raid in Mississippi. We might prolong the frightful tissue of these barbarities; but it is not necessary to exhibit the brutal and despicable character of the enemy whom we are so courteously fighting.

During the excursion of Stoneman's bandits in this State, no opportunity was lost by them to insult females, to search the chambers of ladies, and to steal jewelry, chickens, and whatever articles of merchandise they could conveniently pocket.

In Kentucky, the conduct of the Yankee marauders, who are constantly spying out the land, is licensed and uninterrupted outrage.

The contrast which these recent Yankee raids have afforded between the savage conduct of the enemy and the false tenderness of such knights as those who made the cavalcade to Chambersburg, not only disgusts and offends the true patriotism of the South, but it presents a case of rank injustice to our own people, who are debarred from retaliation, and whose interests are subordinated to the ambition of some officer to make a reputation for "chivalry" in the North, and earn a compliment in the *New York Tribune*. Again and again have Southern people had occasion to know the ridiculous figure they make, the contempt they bring upon themselves, and the positive injury they invite, by their sentimental tenderness for Yankees and their monkey chivalry to their enemy. But court to Yankees is a fashion that seems to be ingrained in the Southern mind. An opportunity never seems to be lost, whether they invade districts occupied by the enemy, or come in contact with him, or take prisoners, for some vain Confederate commander to make a display of stilted wanderer, and dance some ridiculous jig of politeness, to the edification of the varlets who surround him.

Chivalry is a very noble quality. But we do not get our idea of it from the mincings of dandy preachers and parlor geldings. We do not derive our interpretation of the codes of war from sprigs dressed up in Confederate uniform of uncertain moral gender. We know that we are in a dreadful war; that we are fighting a base and deadly enemy. While it is not for the South to fight with any mean advantage, it is time for her to abandon those polite notions of war which she has got from the Waverley novels, and to fight with fire and sword. If any retaliation is to be made for the recent Yankee raids (and present opportunities invite it), its history should be written in broad tracks of blood and destruction. There should be no re-enactment of the scenes at Chambersburg. We must pay the enemy back in the savage coin of vengeance, and settle our accounts in blood.

MAY 14, 1863.

ON one point the North feels the weight of the war. Strange that precisely where the Southern Government assumed from the first that it could make no show—on the sea—it inflicts the only blows which have touched the vitals of the enemy. Our victories on land have saved us from destruction, but have not hurt the North. Dead Yankees are cheap. Lost guns and consumed stores make room for more, and the contractors, who are the whole Northern people, grow rich by replacing them. But on the sea they feel what is the misery of war. A half dozen forlorn privateers have done more towards rendering peace possible than all our great generals, brave armies, and prodigious triumphs. The vessels burnt are dead losses; losses without insurance; and Rachel weeping for her children was never more inconsolable than wealthy owners. A glance at the Northern press is sufficient to gauge the savage violence of the sentiment which the Southern success at sea creates in the Northern heart.

It appears that the ocean is the only field, at present, on which the South can attempt or perform aggressive war. Let us hope that it will not always be thus. So long as Northern armies can batten on Southern soil, while their own towns and farms flourish, untouched and secure; so long as we can do nothing but defend ourselves, while the foe feels not the sharpness of the sword, and sees not the torch of war on his own roof; we may anticipate the continued duration of the present situation. The treaty of peace, if such a writing shall exist, will be signed only on the soil of the enemy.

MAY 20, 1863.

WHAT is the meaning of this cuckoo-cry of the North, that they are waging war to save the "life of the nation?" Is there no life for them except in a union with the South? The Confederate States can support a national existence very well by themselves; why cannot the North do likewise? And how unworthy of any nation is the plea, that it must die a political death if they lose their association with another, which desires to get rid of the fellowship! Besides, even if the plea were ever so well grounded, if the North were, indeed, a mere parasite incapable of self-existence, does that circumstance confer upon it any moral right to yoke another people, alien and hostile, to an abhorrent association? The rule in the natural world is, that parasites may be destroyed; not that the self-existing plant, or animal, must support the parasite. Is the South not entitled to "live" as well as her enemy.

But the abject meanness and the moral worthlessness of the plea is only equalled by its falsity. The "national life" will not perish by the loss of the South. The Yankees can still maintain a respectable nationality, if only they are capable of pursuing a virtuous course of conduct. They have a splendid country, a vast and unoccupied domain, a propitious climate, immense capital, unlimited resources of minerals, and forest wealth, skill in the mechanical arts, and great experience and enterprise on the waters. They are the best masters in the world of steam. What, indeed, have they not in material resources? Why, then, must they lose their national existence by separation from the South? The moral rottenness of their social fabric? But the Yankees do not acknowledge this: their excuse for the war is based on some other theory; it is the true reason nevertheless.

It is precisely on account of their want of national and individual virtue, an imperative motive, why the South should flee from the modern Sodom. The South is forced by the most cogent reasons to make good her separation, and the North has no right to inflict her moral corruption upon her neighbor. The victim of the small-pox is bound to keep himself aloof from other people; and he may be shot down in his tracks, if he persist in thrusting this mortal contagion upon the public.

MAY 30, 1863.

THE Grand Army of the Potomac is said to be "moving on" once more. Where it is going is a matter of surmise. Perhaps it is somewhat at a loss to know where it had best turn its steps. It has tried every known route to Richmond, and has come to grief on them all, and may be now quite uncertain whither it can go to avoid misfortune.

The Federal Government itself might well be as much perplexed with its huge, magnificent, but most expensive and useless Army of the Potomac, as the happy purchaser of the elephant at auction. No army ever cost so much in men and money, or ever accomplished so little; certainly none has ever been beaten so many times without being destroyed. If its proprietors are tired of it, we are too.

Though easily and regularly whipped, it has at least kept out of useful employment the best army of the Confederacy, including nearly all the Virginia troops.

If this war was a tournament, we might desire nothing better than the manner in which it has been conducted by these two hosts up to the present time. The six months they have passed between Falmouth and Fredericksburg furnishes a fair specimen of their extensive intercourse. After long and careful preparation, the Grand Army crosses over, a hundred thousand strong; fifty or sixty thousand Confederates, well posted, fight with them; the Grand Army is prodigiously whipped—loses twenty thousand—and then marches back to camp. After a month or more of recruiting, it comes again—finds the same Confederates reposing in the same fields—is whipped again, loses more men, and marches back to camp in the same order. On the occurrence of these events, great praise is given to General Lee, and several Yankee Generals are dismissed the service, relieved of their commands, or sent away to torture old men, or fight women and little children, in some unfortunate district of the country subject to the striped flag. If we could import shiploads of Irish and Dutch, after each of these "victories," no way of carrying on this war more favorable could be desired. But, while our army kills a great many Yankees, Dutch, and Irish, on one of these splendid field days, it also loses a considerable number of brave men. One of these is a greater loss to us than three of the others to the enemy. If that loss were counterbalanced by some military advantage which might serve as the foundation for future hopes, it would not be a loss at all, but a wise expenditure. Unfortunately, such victories change nothing. The United States and the Confederacy preserve their proportions and attitudes. The war will last forty years on these terms. Take the last of them, Chancellorsville. What have we gained by that glorious battle? The poor lands of Spottsylvania have received a costly manure, and that is all. After the fight, the general order for both armies might have been the musician's command at the conclusion of a quadrille—"as you were!" Hooker, in Stafford, Lee in Spottsylvania, the Rappahannock between. If they go down to the Chickahominy, or the James, what will be the difference?

We should be rejoiced, however, if Lincoln is the first to tire of this monotonous dance; as for Old Virginia, "she never tire." In the present moment nothing seems more likely than that the discomfited and heart-broken Army of the Potomac should be taken home to Washington and broken up.

JUNE 2, 1863.

THE war has proved the degeneracy of Virginia horse-flesh. We still have as fine horses in Virginia as ever; but they are few. At one time in the history of our Commonwealth, first-rate horses only were bred; but the general practice has long ago ceased, and our stock of horses has become mixed almost universally with base blood.

Accordingly, that which should be the strong arm of the Southern service, the cavalry, is the weakest and most contemptible. A band of Yankee buggy drivers and teamsters, mounted on Pennsylvania Conestogas, intermingled with cold-blooded Morgans and trotters, have swept leisurely through that part of the Confederacy which should have been alive with fleet, ubiquitous, and irresistible cavalry. Chase was made in one instance, and the enemy overtaken and chastised, but he rode away after his beating, and our cavalry were unable to follow, the horses being broken down and broken-winded. The celerity of Lee's legion and the partisan corps of Sumter, Marion, and Hampton, in the Southern campaigns of the Revolution, was due in great part to the excellence of their thorough-bred steeds, which were very fleet, had great bottom, and possessed withal, in some degree, the gift of Fortunio's horse, which fed but once a week.

JULY 1, 1863.

No fact yet indicates the plan of General Lee, and, however curious the public may be, it must continue to wait. He is steadily pouring his troops into Pennsylvania, and it cannot be supposed that his only object is to show himself to the Dutch, or to satisfy the Yankees that they may devastate the South with impunity. Retribution is the law of nature, the law of God, the law of man, the law of nations. Punishment of crime is a necessity of society, and, when communities are guilty, the same justice which is meted to individuals, is also fitting for them.

JULY, 1, 1863.

THE country has learned with pain the particulars of the *Atlanta's* loss. The general fact had been briefly stated by the telegram; but what we lost, and how we lost it, was unknown outside of the Naval Department. The Yankee press, however, tells us the least detail with unsparing care. This ship, the *Atlanta*, was an ironclad of the first class, some three hundred feet long, constructed in our own waters. The Northern captors declare it to be superior to any other vessel of that character now afloat. She was so much swifter than any of their monitors that she could easily have walked away from them. Her walls consisted of four inches wrought iron, four of live oak, and four of pine, which last material, as always appears, was proven by the result to have been an error in the construction. Her guns were all on the Brooke pattern; and her armament was gigantic. A long beak of twenty feet in solid iron was a feature of the model. Her provisions, coal, and ammunition were ample for a two-months' cruise without a visit to port. She had just steered out of harbor; was attacked by the Weehawken and Nahant; was grounded on a mud bank; and, after having hauled off it, grounded again almost immediately. Only nine shots were fired before she struck her flag. The last was a fifteen-inch shell, which failed to pierce her mail, but shattered the pine lining, killing one or two persons with its splinters, and shocking the rest of the crew with the concussion so much as to have led to surrender. The Yankees got the vessel in a condition nearly perfect, hauled her off the bank in a few minutes, and found that she passed all their steamers on the way to New York. It is painful to hear such a tale; nor is the pain alleviated by learning that the unhappy commander, after making a brief address to his crew of Georgians, in which he advised them to be resigned, fainted away on his quarter-deck. The surrender was probably made in due accord with the laws of the naval art; certainly any court-martial would absolve the captain; but it is to be regretted that the vessel fell into the enemy's hands in a perfect condition. We have built this magnificent machine for the enemy. The *Atlanta* has gone the way of all Mr. Mallory's ironclads. Indeed, their way has gone from bad to worse. Hitherto they have only been burnt or blown up within a few weeks of their completion. Now they have learned the trick of dropping into the enemy's hands as soon as they get out of port. If history lacked proof that there is such a thing as an evil fortune, a bad luck, attendant on all the steps of particular men, the chapter of Mallory will hereafter furnish those proofs, to confirm the conviction of the greatest minds, and the superstition of the simplest, upon that point. So long as Mallory reigns, all that he touches,

"*quamvis Pontica pinus*
Sylvæ filius nobilis,"

will explode or sink. Never yet has he turned out of hand one good thing. The curse is on him, not on the Confederate sea-flag, as the exploits of the Alabama, Florida, Tacony, which he *did not* make, furnish a daily and glorious evidence!

JULY 7, 1863.

THE invasion of the North will demonstrate a fact long insisted on by that portion of the Southern press which exercises an independent judgment, and indulges in a free expression of opinion; namely, that no country on the earth is so susceptible of being overrun by a hostile force as that of what the French would call " our friends, the enemy."

The ridiculous imbecility of the Pennsylvanians affords a faithful example of what would be exhibited throughout the North. There is no country in the world abounding so richly as the North in the materials needful for the subsistence and use of an army of invasion; and not even the Chinese are less prepared by previous habits of life and education for martial resistance than the Yankees.

From the very beginning the true policy of the South has been invasion; and yet from the very beginning this policy has been so rejected and denounced by the authorities, that it is even now incredible that they should have given their cordial sanction to the movement of General Lee. The future historian of this war will stand amazed at the inexplicable fact, that the South, for two years, stood with her arms folded, stolid, sluggish, and impassible, waiting for the enemy to mature all his preparations for attack, choosing his times, modes, and places of assault, overrunning one-half the country, retiring, advancing, and destroying as he pleased.

The present movement of General Lee will be of vast importance in its immediate military results; but it will be of infinite value as disclosing the great fact of the easy susceptibility of the North to invasion. The marvellous success of Bonaparte was due to the fact that he constantly maintained the aggressive, carried the war into the enemy's country, and made his adversaries subsist his army as well as their own. An army of a hundred thousand men, held under strict discipline, may march from Chambersburg to Boston, finding provisions, animals, and transportation wherever it goes.

The South is so sparsely inhabited, and its wealth is so little concentrated, that rapid raids through its territory can do little else than temporarily break up lines of railroad and devastate narrow belts of territory. We can well afford to risk this species of injury, and to carry our armies far into the enemy's country; exacting peace by blows levelled at his vitals. Invasion ruins him, while it only cripples us. It is cheaper to suffer from raids while subsisting our armies upon his substance, than to stand at bay on our own soil, supporting with its produce both his army and our own.

JULY 9, 1863.

THE news of the Vicksburg surrender is not less astonishing than unpleasant. It is the most unexpected announcement which has been made in this war. So astoundingly contradictory is it to every particle of intelligence lately received from that quarter, either from our own people or through the enemy, that there is a strong disposition to doubt the authenticity of the dispatch sent to the Secretary of War over the signature of General Joseph E. Johnston. The last dispatches of Grant made public by the Washington Government did not foreshadow an immediate fall of the place. Thus it was the moment of all others when a capitulation seems most inopportune and unlooked for. We have reason to believe that the Confederate Government was not less unprepared for the reception of such news than the public. The circumstances that the surrender was made on the "Fourth of July," that the whole garrison are returned home as paroled prisoners, that the officers carry off their personal effects, that there was no fighting, and has been none for many weeks past to authorize such a step, do not assist its probability or intelligibility.

There were 27,000 men in Vicksburg. It was announced, on good authority, that the town, when the siege commenced, some five weeks ago, was provisioned with rations for two months, and could hold out on half rations for five months. Strong expressions of a determination to hold out while a man remained alive were attributed to the general in command. The place was impregnable by assault. This sudden surrender cannot be explained at present without resort to theories, all unpleasant, and none justified by known facts. Some will say the garrison was mutinous; others, that Pemberton was traitorous; others, that Johnston was remiss or cowardly in the performance of his duty. But we must be slow to believe that the troops which exhibited so much courage in the assaults have suddenly become recreant. We are equally disinclined to think that General Pemberton, though a lieutenant-general without fighting, and though a Pennsylvanian, has incurred the infamy of Arnold. Nor can we think Johnston, after fighting bravely, and acting with wisdom and energy in so many circumstances; after having been eleven times shot down in battle; after Manassas and Seven Pines,—has suddenly become a coward or a fool.

It is quite impossible for any just or sensible man to form an opinion upon the merits of this affair with the present light, or rather, no light. Let us rather consider the consequences of the event. We do not hesitate to repeat, what we have often said before, that the public of the North and the South both rate the importance of Vicksburg far too highly. So much blood and treasure have been poured out on that place, the unthinking have come to the conclusion that the possession of Vicksburg must mean the possession of the Mississippi River. Yet nothing is more certain than that this belief is an error. When Columbus fell, the wise public will recollect, it was satisfied that all was over; that the river was subject to the enemy, and that nothing could prevent its immediate navigation and employment by his steamboats and transports even to the Gulf. But it was a mistake then; it is a mistake now.

JULY 10, 1863.

THE crew of mercenaries, the hangers-on and parasites of power, are joined in an outcry against General Johnston. He is responsible for the fall of Vicksburg. He did it. He ought to be hung, shot, cashiered at least. Here is a disastrous event, which is supposed to involve a fault. If there is a fault, two men are implicated in it. One is a young man, without a past, whose first battle was Champion Hill, who owes his commission to favor; the other is an old war-dog, of long experience in his trade, with a body seamed with scars, who is held in the highest esteem by the military profession, but who never had anybody's favor; who is disliked by Mr. Davis. No one here is yet acquainted with the circumstances which attended and preceded the fall of Vicksburg; but the blame is Johnston's.

He did it. Who can suppose, even for a moment, that the fortunate, victorious, heaven-born Pemberton, could have done the wrong?

We have not the pretensions to be of Johnston's friends. The writer knows him only as some hundreds of thousands of other Southern men have been compelled to know him. We have no private interest or personal desire to divert public censure from him. If Johnston had a force under him sufficient to raise the siege of Vicksburg, and if he did not do it—if he left undone any thing he ought to have done, or could have done, to relieve the garrison, let him bear the whole penalty of such guilt. But not one atom of evidence is now patent to authorize the accusation. The late events in Mississippi are imperfectly known. As to the surrender of Vicksburg, inspiration only can enable any one to judge now whether Johnston or Pemberton, or either, or neither, is culpable. What we do know is that the army which defended it, and the campaign which preceded the siege, was lost under the sole command of Pemberton; and no honest man can fail to protest with indignation against this filthy effort to shield a general by favor (for where were his battles, where the service which earned his commission?), and those who are justly responsible for him, from the consequences of his incompetence by making a brave old soldier the victim and the scapegoat.

When a steam doctor has brought a patient to death's door, his friends get scared and run off to the family physician. He comes, finds the patient in spasms, speechless, pulseless. He thinks the case to be hopeless when he sees it, but he does something that he thinks may perchance help; or perhaps he does nothing but watch for an opportunity to do something. The patient dies. The steam doctor's party in the house are triumphant. The patient died because that other doctor, that allopathist, was brought. His lancet, his drugs, his science killed DOBBINS; or if they did not, they let him die, doing nothing *secundum artem*.

The campaign of the Mississippi was settled without Johnston. He had been ordered to Kentucky, and put in charge of Bragg's army, for reasons well known in congressional circles. When the crash came, and Grant burst through the puny barriers strung about Grand Gulf and the valley, a *third* order hurried Johnston down to Jackson. If he could not redeem Vicksburg, he might at least shoulder the responsibility of its fall. If he could not prevent Vicksburg from following New Orleans, he could at least keep Pemberton out of Lovell's shoes. The situation of the parties was remarked at the time when he was sent there. And, now, when the announcement comes by telegraph that Vicksburg "capitulated on the Fourth of July," what is heard? That Johnston is a coward. Kept idle an army larger than that with which he won Manassas, while Vicksburg was starved. Johnston is a dunce and a coward; Pemberton, a hero and a genius.

The late events in Mississippi—Grand Gulf, Champion Hill, or Vicksburg—are disasters which require public examination. There are maladies so violent, and constitutions so weak, that they are beyond the reach alike of the Thompsonian practitioner and the regular physician. If Grant came to Grand Gulf with a hundred thousand men, a fleet, and re-enforcements always superior to his losses, perhaps it did not matter whether the army of Vicksburg was kept together or scattered as it was; whether Johnston or Pemberton had charge of it. The data for settling a decided opinion on the campaign are yet wanting. But on one thing it is not necessary to suspend judgment. It is the policy of appointing unknown, inexperienced men, whose services give them no title to the highest positions, to the most important trusts, to the command of the greatest armies, solely because the opinion, prejudice, or fancy of the President is favorable to them. The appointing power is a trust to be executed according to certain evident principles. If he takes into his councils the first men of the nation, puts over the troops officers of tried ability, and failure ensues, he will be absolved from blame. But if he fills such posts by the second-rate and the obscure; by men who have done nothing to secure the confidence of the country; by adventurous foreigners, who come here to " offer their swords;" even if they are fortunate, he is blamable; while, if the cause is lost in their hands, no punishment that this world or the next affords is adequate to the crime of their elevation.

JULY 11, 1863.

FEW do not heartily approve General Lee's orders forbidding pillage and marauders; few are satisfied with his determination to inflict no retaliatory punishment on the nation that has desolated the Southern country. The people of the South neither expected nor desired that our army, when it entered the territory of the enemy, should execute a wild and irregular retaliation by individual acts of outrage and revenge. Such a course would have resulted in the certain demoralization of our army, been an occasion of scandal to the world, and, although the provocation and the precedent were alike given by the Yankees, would really have been a dishonor to our arms.

It is not necessary that retaliation should be made, or that punishment of the enemy should be executed by acts similar to the atrocities he has committed on our own soil. Because the enemy is guilty of theft, murder, and rape in our own territory, we do not advise that we shall commit the same crimes in his dominions. It is neither necessary nor proper that the soldiers of General Lee's army should plunder houses, assassinate the unarmed, or invade the beds of the uxorious Dutch. But it is proper, and in the highest sense it is necessary, that the Confederate armies should inflict upon the enemy some injury commensurate, as far as possible, with the outrages he has committed and the hate he has wreaked upon our own people. The rule of retaliation for us is to be found, not in the imitation of the crimes and vices of the Yankees, but in the principle of commensurate injury or loss. This, so far from compromising our self-respect or dishonoring our arms, is the foundation of all civilized laws on the subject of punishments, and the just, and even moderate, guide of modern warfare.

It had been supposed that our armies in Pennsylvania had made at least some approach to this very moderate rule of penalties by the levy of forced contributions upon the enemy, and it was published as recently as Saturday last that General Early had made a levy of this description upon the people of York. But the pleasant intelligence now appears to be a mistake. Since its publication there have appeared the specific orders of General Lee, which show that these so-called levies are nothing more than ordinary requisitions for supplies; that "all persons complying with such requisitions shall be paid the market price for the articles furnished;" and that where they shall venture upon the insolence of refusing the money of the Confederacy, they shall be pacified by "a receipt specifying the kind and quantity of the property received or taken * * and the market price," which, as a certificate of indebtedness, may, after the close of the war, be recovered in gold and silver. The effect of these extraordinary orders is to put the Yankee in the same position as our own citizens, and to give him the same protection. They effectually close the door to all hopes of retaliation, ignore the history of the war, and authoritatively decide that the policy of our invading armies shall be the rigid protection of the enemy's private property. They compose the alarm which, it was supposed, invasions were intended to inspire, and, in fact, protect the only point where the Yankee is vulnerable—his purse. For to the destruction of public property he is by no means averse, since it occasions new expenditures and new crops of contracts, and, indeed, in this sense, assures for us a prolongation of the war.

There are a few persons in this Confederacy who boast the philosophy of milk-sops in war, and would have our armies enact the part of Uncle Toby and the fly. They do not consider that a spiritless warfare which does not intimidate the enemy is likely only to exasperate him by its small annoyances; that it thus prolongs the struggle; that its mistaken tenderness brings us only into contempt; and that its expression of justice is a thankless mercy to the enemy, a direct discouragement to our army, and an outrage upon those who, in their wasted farms and the blackened ruins of their homes, have constantly before their eyes the mementoes of their invaders.

Where in history or in ethics does it occur that a barbarous and brutal enemy entitles himself to the refinements of war, the protection of private property, and the restraint of every thing like revenge? In our wars with the Indian we fired his villages, destroyed his home, burnt his corn, and drove him into the wilderness. There were no pious ejaculations on these occasions, and nothing said about the merits of making war according to the principles of civilization. Compared with the modern Yankee, the natives of our forests were an enemy not more barbarous in deeds, and deserving far more consideration and pity on account both of the merits of their cause and the ignorance that blinded them to its perversion. The claim of the Yankee for the protection of his private property in this war is certainly not preferable to that which the Indian might have urged in his extremity. This, and all other incidents of enlightened hostilities, our present enemy forfeited by his own choice of a barbarous, bloodthirsty, and devilish warfare.

JULY 13, 1863.

THE attitude of the Southern Confederacy on one matter, is truly humiliating. The enemy has gone from one unmanly cruelty to another, encouraged by their impunity, till they are now, and have for sometime been, inflicting on the people of this country the worst horrors of barbarous, uncivilized war. They destroy the products of labor, devastate vast tracts of country, drive out the inhabitants where they do not destroy, and appropriate all their property, real and personal. They murder numbers of peaceful persons in cold blood, on the slightest pretenses. Meeting no check in these proceedings, they have begun to treat Confederate soldiers falling into their hands, in the same lawless fashion. Their imprisonment is more severe than that of felons, and every vain pretext is seized for hanging them. The enemy makes no secret whatever of doing so. Not a Northern paper falls into our hands which does not contain exultant paragraphs, telling how one, two, or three " rebels" were hung here or there, for " bushwhacking," spying, bearing dispatches, &c. Their illustrated weeklies are filled with carefully executed wood-cuts of gibbets, and "rebel officers" dangling from them. Soon the rules that they now apply to individuals, will be applied to masses of men. This will be a war of extermination, *to us*, not to them, if they are not checked in the road they have steadily pursued with speed always increasing.

Human experience has yet discovered but one means of preventing violent crime. It is by violent punishment. The only effectual preventive of murder is retaliation! Society says to its enemy, if you murder one of mine, I will murder all of you; and it does so. The only means of dealing with a nation that adopts the maxims and practices of bandits and assassins, is still an extension of this oldest law of the world. There is no alternative but sufferance and submission, which individuals may prefer for themselves, but which governments are sworn not to adopt. This truth has been fully recognized by the Confederate Government. It knows the right, and still the wrong pursues. Mr. President Davis's proclamations and pronunciamientos, his horrible threatenings and gloomy appeals, have been so often repeated that they are the sneer of the world. But never have they resulted in one solitary performance. He is very obstinate, very bitter, when he gets in a quarrel with some Southern officer, over whom the law gives him temporary control. He is very firm, indeed, in maintaining a minion or a measure, against the smothered indignation of a people who are compelled, by their present unfortunate situation, to support silently, a great deal from their officials. But, when his duty brings him in contact with the enemy, he is gentle as the sucking dove.

Lately, the question of retaliation has come up in a form singularly direct. Two Confederate recruiting officers were captured in Kentucky and hung, on the ground that Kentucky was one of the United States. As Virginia, the Carolinas, and all the other States are claimed by the Union, it is evident that this precedent, if unpunished, will hang every officer that recruits, in every State of the Confederacy. The point was too plain to be evaded, and the Government took two Yankee officers from among its prisoners, and ordered their execution. But, instead of hanging them, it commissioned a personage no less considerable than Mr. Stephens, the Vice-President of the Republic, to arrange a back door of mercy to the enemy, and of cruelty to its own people. Mr. Stephens was sent to Washington with a letter of credence to Lincoln, and another of instructions to himself from President Davis. A good deal was said in this last letter about titles, &c., which looks pitiful enough; and the rest, relating to the business on hand, amounts to this: that if the Federal Government will only vouchsafe a civil word or so; will say, for instance, that it would like to mitigate the horrors of war, the Confederate Government would be happy to indulge in boundless compassion for the two Yankees aforesaid. As to the two murdered officers in Kentucky, who feels compassion for them? The Vice-President went on his errand as far as Hampton Roads; was stopped by the enemy's admiral there, to whom he signified his desire to open communication with the Federal Government; kept two days in his steam-tug on the water; and then dismissed with this flea in his ear:

[D.]

UNITED STATES FLAG SHIP MINNESOTA, OFF NEWPORT NEWS, VIRGINIA, July 6, 1863.

SIR: The request contained in your communication of the 4th instant is considered inadmissible.

The customary agents and channels are adequate for all needful military communications and conference between the United States forces and the insurgents.

Very respectfully yours,
S. P. LEE, A. R. Admiral,
Commanding N. A. Blockading Squadron.

HON. ALEXANDER H. STEPHENS.

Now, who will deny that the Confederacy makes a sorrowful figure in this matter?

JULY 15, 1863.

EXAGGERATION is a popular vice. It is never indulged in so freely as after a battle. The battle at Gettysburg has furnished material for the usual amount of it. The most prodigious ciphers are employed by the Southern telegraph and the Northern press, to signify the simple fact that a great many people were shot within a space of six miles, near Gettysburg, and that nobody has counted them; that many more were taken prisoners by the two armies, and the reporters are perfectly ignorant of their numbers. If we attempt the estimation of the loss in combat, from the few persons in position to have, if they choose to use, the means of ascertaining the casualties sustained. the numbers dwindle singularly. What, then, is the meaning of those individuals connected with the army, who write home after every battle, that this or that brigade or division—always theirs—went into the fight two thousand or five thousand, and came out with four hundred or fifteen hundred? Did all the loss, then, fall on two or three brigades or divisions? It is not necessary to admit the supposition, nor yet to question the accuracy of such statements. The chief "loss" in such cases consists of stragglers. In plain words, many more run (a little way) from every battle and every fighting army, than are troubled with wounds or bruises. When, for instance, the commander of a Minnesota regiment writes home that he had 2,100 men at muster-roll on Friday morning, and did not need three hundred rations for his troops next day, it is to be understood that Minnesota is fleet of foot.

The losses on both sides in the fight at Gettysburg have been so exaggerated, that it is as yet not easy to ascertain the true figures. It was a battle in which the Confederates had their own way during two days, and were repulsed in an attack made during the third on certain powerful positions. They remained a day unmolested on the ground, and then retired in complete condition and order. So far as the fighting went, all that the Federal army did was to prevent its own annihilation. The Confederates were repulsed, but cannot, at present, with justice or candor be said to have suffered defeat. It may hereafter be so said with reason if the offensive campaign ends with this battle, because it will be thought by the world that the accomplishment of General Lee's intentions in Pennsylvania was prevented by the resistance made at Gettysburg. This point, however, is not yet decided. General Lee holds an impregnable position on the other side of the Potomac at this time, and has not yet given the slightest indication that he has renounced the campaign. The moral effect, at the moment, is in favor of the North, but it is so from causes wholly independent of the action itself. The troops of the United States have suffered acknowledged and most disgraceful defeat by the army of Northern Virginia during an entire twelve months. Richmond, Manassas, Fredericksburg, and Chancellorsville—the four seasons. They were not entirely beaten at Gettysburg, and the unaccustomed result has raised the spirits of their country to the point of frenzy. We were not entirely victorious at Gettysburg, and the South is impatient at the contradiction to its usual fortune. Southern men of constitutional despondence are unduly depressed, as the whole North is extravagantly elated. But can they reconcile their momentary melancholy to common sense? What is lost even if the offensive campaign should be given over for the summer? We are not worse off than before it began, nor is the North a whit stronger.

JULY 16, 1863.

Those interesting persons, whose imagination is better developed than their reasoning faculties, frequently think themselves at " the last ditch," when it is distant many a year's journey. They create a crisis out of the slightest symptoms, and propose the wildest and most dangerous remedies, on the ground that it is impossible to kill the patient more dead than he is. One of these has written an eloquent letter to the editor of this paper, which we are not able to print for him. He wants universal martial law; revolution of government; despotism: a levy *en masse* without distinction of age, occupation, or bodily health. The crops are to be left ungathered, the horse unshod, the railroads shall cease operations, the courts be closed, the jails opened. All the people, old and young, sick and well, must run into the fields to fire glory out of fictitious muskets, and live on imaginary bread for the next twelve or twenty months. Further, our friend addresses a private appeal to this newspaper; inviting it, in a most complimentary manner, to take down the horn it blew in the spring of '62, and blow, blow, blow, till we raise the country. Softly, good friend! We wish to blow that horn to a purpose, and it will serve none if we take it down too often. To scream out "wolf" when there is none, is admitted to be a bad policy. If the people are called out to die in the last ditch when no ditch has been dug, perhaps they might not come when it is really ready.

Let us look at things as they are. The conditions of the belligerents is wholly different from what it was in the days of Donelson and Yorktown, and the difference is all in our favor. Then the Confederacy was an empty egg-shell. There was no army. Handfuls of troops were thinly sprinkled along a continental frontier. Their line broken, the country was without defence. But now we have an army, a terrible army; and the existing laws, if enforced, furnish the means of maintaining and increasing it. The territory lost, however regretted, is certainly a military gain. Over every part of it, the enemy must drag supplies, march armies and keep up long lines of communication. On every foot of it he must leave some portion of his strength, or incur certain ruin when reverses come. Our contracted line is the easier defended. What military advantage have we lost by the fall of Vicksburg? The South has held that place for a year chiefly from pride. We gained nothing from the Mississippi. Its banks are ravaged. To keep an insecure possession of them, the enemy must garrison them. If he advances on the interior, he will plunge into disaster. On the other side, the Confederates have their forces consolidated on an interior line, close to their resources of provisions and men, and can make either defensive or offensive war with better chances than ever before.

The Confederacy has lately received two "facers." It has a bloody nose and a black eye—but it was never sounder in wind and limb than it is at this moment. Even if the late checks were such as to endanger the life of the nation, we are sure that its situation would not be improved by martial law and despotism. No power in this country can put in force martial law but a general of an army, and his power to do so is limited by his lines. As to arbitrary government—that is not what the people have made here. If arbitrary power should be inaugurated by the action of a clique, it is revolution, and the death of the Confederacy. How many would uphold it longer? The people are fighting for their constitutions, laws, and liberties. They will never understand the logic of surrendering them that they may keep them. When they are gone, no matter how, all is gone.

If we had the power to rouse anybody now, we would try that power on the Government that exists. The laws are sufficient for all purposes, save those of selfishness and wickedness. Nobody frustrates the operation of those laws. Enforce the laws of the Confederacy with diligence and good faith, and the most that human agencies can do to save this country will be done.

JULY 17, 1863.

GENERAL LEE has recrossed the Potomac. With this announcement, it is supposed, the second invasion of the United States is at an end. The Government and its chief General undertook this campaign on their own responsibility, and at their own time. Public opinion did not impel their action. But public opinion did, most certainly, justify, approve, and adopt it. Although it has been abruptly terminated by an unsuccessful battle, we are far from thinking that the design was injudicious.

This war can be terminated only by such a measure. It might have been gloriously terminated in a month, had Gettysburg witnessed the annihilation of the Federal Army of the Potomac. But that battle was fought in a position which rendered success impossible. Why it was fought is yet unknown. Many persons now blame General Lee for attacking the enemy there; but we shall be slow to criticise an officer of his service and capacity until the facts are better known. We would only remark, in passing, that while Lee is censured for attacking an army little superior to his own, with the advantage of position against him, Johnston is denounced for not attacking four times his number, in fortifications and position by the side of which Gettysburg was a play-ground.

But this campaign is not without gains which compensate the sacrifices made. It has filled the North with a sense of insecurity which cannot fail to suggest a different opinion of the power of the Confederacy, and a better notion of the advantages of peace.

The Confederacy has lost several thousand able officers and brave soldiers; but war cannot be made without such losses. The enemy have lost more, and the comparative strength of the parties is unchanged. We are thrown on the defensive; but since we have no longer to maintain the outposts of Mississippi and Tennessee, the work of defence can be accomplished with greater ease and certainty than before. The Confederacy can defend itself forever, if necessary. In that species of warfare, the party that will hold out longest is the party that wins. Every chance is in its favor. The South will be that party, for it cannot yield. To yield is to lose all that its citizens have on this earth.

JULY 21, 1863.

IF it has not been demonstrated that the Southern people (those of the Cotton States more especially) are without that tenacity of purpose, that indomitable obstinacy of patriotism, which have characterized many races of the earth—the Spanish, for example—it certainly has not yet been proved that they possess it. We might make an exception to this remark of the people of Virginia, who, though slow to enter upon the present conflict, and though suffering unspeakable misery, privation, loss, and calamity from the war, are yet as resolute at this moment as at the beginning, and may be said to carry the war on their shoulders; but we refrain from the subject, leaving it for candid men of other States to characterize the part she has borne in this struggle, and the qualities she has displayed in its progress.

But, speaking generally of the Southern people, and passing by the exceptions which may exist to any general declaration, it is certainly true that we have yet presented no general example of patriotic devotion to country and principle, such as was exhibited by the population of La Vendée, during the French Revolution; nor any special instance of that sublime tenacity which characterized the Spaniards in the many renowned sieges, ancient and modern, from Numantia to Saragossa, which constitute such brilliant chapters in the Spanish history and such redeeming traits in Spanish character.

On the contrary, the condition of affairs in portions of the Southwest is sufficient to make us blush for our race. Those rampant cotton and sugar planters, who were so early and furiously in the field for secession, and who, after the war had commenced, were so resolved on burning their cotton and destroying their sugar, not only did not burn and destroy in three cases out of four, but a great many of them, having taken the oath of allegiance to the Yankees, are now raising cotton in partnership with their Yankee *protectors*, and shipping it to Yankee markets. The baseness of this conduct is twofold. It not only involves the most shameless moral turpitude and personal apostasy, but it inflicts a heavy injury upon the general cause of the South, which is forsaken by these apostates. The quantity of cotton procured by the Yankees through the failure of cotton planters to burn their crops, and through these partnership arrangements for planting and selling it, is little imagined by the loyal portion of our people. Not less than ten thousand bales a week are said to be received at Memphis alone. With a receipt of cotton as large as this, and a monopoly of the stock, the stability of Yankee finances is no longer a matter of surprise. Five hundred thousand bales per annum, at present prices, will give them as large a fund to draw against abroad, as the whole Southern crop of three or four millions of bales afforded before the war. With the advantage of receipts like these, it is no longer a wonder that exchange on London continues to fall at New York, and that gold falls along with it.

The cotton planters who refused to burn their cotton, and those who have entered into these base partnership arrangements for cropping and shipping, have inflicted as heavy a blow upon the South as all the Yankee armies. They have given the Yankees the means of upholding their financial system, and of keeping on foot the large armies that are invading and desolating our country. They are the men who really recruit, pay, and subsist the troops that are laying our country waste with fire and sword. The greatest pains and care ought to be taken now by Congress, to cause an accurate list to be made of the men who refuse to burn their cotton, and who are now raising and shipping it to Northern markets. It will constitute for all time the blackest roll of shame in Southern archives.

The want of tenacity of purpose and inflexibility of patriotism in the character of a class of Southern people, is painfully conspicuous in these cotton transactions. When it is remembered that the secession movement was inaugurated by the cotton population of the South, that the Confederate Government is conducted almost exclusively under the auspices of cotton statesmen, even to the extent of proscribing other important and quite as patriotic classes, these shameful transactions of mercenary cotton planters on the flats of the Mississippi appear still more strange and reprehensible. If the secession Government is to be used as a private tart of cotton men, the infamy of the treachery of these cotton planters becomes the more black and shameless. These cotton apostates were long and loudly clamorous for principle, and the South discovers, in the agony of the crisis, that their principles are the loaves and fishes.

JULY 25, 1863.

THOSE who choose to receive their political opinions from the English press, reviews, and newspapers, the *Times* and *Punch*, look on the present master of France as the modern SPHYNX, whose riddle no man need try to read, whose future actions cannot be anticipated from his past career, and who is led by motives not to be understood by sane minds—a hidden character, an unfathomable policy. Yet, if any one will dismiss this current nonsense, this cockney gabble, and go to the natural source for information, he will soon be satisfied that there is less than the usual foundation for the popular delusion. Louis Napoleon is a political gambler, who plays *dummy* at the whist of nations. Before he began the game, he spread out his cards, faces up, on the table; now, that he is seated, he says nothing; but all who choose may see each trump before he draws it from the hand. Though "reticent" now, he was once a profuse writer. Among other things, he wrote a little book entitled *Idées Napoleoniennes*. The title is familiar to English and American readers—but chiefly so from the witticisms of *Punch*—for very few have read it. None who have done so regard the French emperor as a living enigma. The line of conduct expedient for France, the internal and foreign policy fitting its position in the nineteenth century, are described therein with singular minuteness of detail and precision of conception. The principal enterprises and all the measures of Napoleon during the last ten years were proposed in that work in the plainest language, their purpose stated, and their machinery explained. This monarch has really done nothing but pursue a consistent plan which he wrote out and printed years before he ascended the throne, but which a large portion of the civilized world have refused to consider, though their interests are deeply affected by every feature of it.

The book purports to be an attempt to deduce a number of general principles from the facts of Napoleon's history. That portion of it which relates to the aim of Napoleon's conquests, immediately interests the Southern Confederacy at this time. The writer endeavors to show that it never could have been the intention of his relative to incorporate the territory he conquered with the realm of France, but to cover Europe with kingdoms, independent in their forms and in some realities, but organized on the French system, endowed with French institutions, united to France by community of laws, coinage and commerce, so completely, that they would be compelled by their interest to accompany her in all offensive and defensive movements, and follow her steps through the future developments of civilization. France was to be the spring, the neighboring nations the wheels of the watch, which, in like manner, would cause other nations, like other parts of the machine, to revolve and mark the hour on the dial of time. Thus, France would govern the world, and govern it for its good—its French good, at least—and this, according to the nephew, was the universal empire, the only universal empire possible, at which his uncle aimed.

Whether a correct statement of the first Napoleon's design or not, it has been consistently pursued by his successor. He has reduced Europe to something very like the real dependence, under apparent independence, which he described long ago as the future confederation of civilization. If he was not too old to admit the hope that he might live to complete an enterprise so great, recent events would lead us to suppose that he had undertaken the application of his system to the American continent. His conquest of Mexico can scarcely be explained in any other way. He has, from the first, declared that he has not the slightest intention of permanently incorporating that vast country with the French empire. That, indeed, would be a dangerous, a troublesome, an impossible project. It is an Italy, not an Algiers, he is making in Mexico. But even such an organization could not long keep its connection with France under the pressure and influence of the United States, if that republic should continue to control the whole force of the North American continent. If France is to get any permanent good from Mexico, the Union must remain dissolved, and one or more new governments be established between it and the United States, which would be bound, by the principle of self-preservation, to recognize French Mexico, and seek through it the support of France. The emperor undertook the business of Mexico, only after the dissolution of the Union was an accomplished fact. Now, that the Mexican conquest is as good as finished, it may be reasonably supposed that he will not pause long before taking the further necessary step of confirming and securing the dissolution of the Union. If this Confederacy is conquered, his Mexican labor is in vain. By his usual manœuvres he has been gradually approaching the American quarrel for the past six months. The first indication was given, as customary with him, at the New Year reception, in the memorable compliment to the Yankee Minister, noted in these columns at the time. The last is the message sent by Mr. Roebuck to the British Parliament. The advance is so considerable, that the *coup d'état* may perhaps be not far off.

JULY 28, 1863.

ABOUT eight months ago, in a speech before the Legislature of Mississippi, Mr. Davis pronounced the solemn opinion that the war would soon come to an end. About twenty months ago, Mr. Benjamin, we believe, wrote to New Orleans, then a Confederate city, that within sixty days the country would be at peace. In Montgomery, at the period of the inauguration of the Confederate Government, the opinion which prevailed was that there would be no war: and, any one who had the hardihood to express a contrary sentiment, became a butt of raillery or the object of suspicion. It has been asserted repeatedly, without contradiction, so complete was this feeling of security at Montgomery, that only eight thousand stand of small-arms were ordered from Europe on Government account, during the months which intervened before the establishment of blockades. Had it not been for a Virginian statesman, then a member of Buchanan's cabinet, who entertained a very different opinion as to the character of the then approaching revolution, an opinion which he has on frequent occasions sought since to impress upon the country, the South would have been without arms with which to commence the war.

If we contrast the determination with which the North has prosecuted the war with the opinions which the Montgomery politicians held in regard to its probable character, we shall be much impressed with the prescience or sagacity of those gentlemen. We believe Mr. Stephens declared, in some public speech delivered at the beginning of the war, that it would be useless to keep great armies in the field; that when a battle was about to be fought, our people could quit home for a few days, go and fight the battle, and then return to their peaceful habitations.

Such have been the amiable and *nonchalant* sentiments which have actuated our rulers from the beginning; and it was possible, on some amiable idea, that the Lincoln Government was at last disposed to pacification, that Mr. Stephens was lately dispatched to Hampton Roads, whence he speedily returned.

That the men who obtained control of the Confederate Government have constantly entertained these fixed ideas concerning the character which the war would assume, though not creditable to their understanding, is certainly, in a moral point of view, very highly creditable to the Southern heart. Peace men throughout the world cannot fail to understand from this absolute incredulity of our public officers with respect to the war, not only that they did not desire the conflict, but did not expect it, or have any part in bringing it on. Every additional month's continuance of it has been a disappointment to them; every new development of it into larger proportions and darker colors has been a surprise. In the outset of the conflict, when we could have invaded the North, we stood on the defensive from a desire felt by our Government not to excite a war feeling in our enemies; and lately in carrying invasion to their own doors, we purchased our supplies at fair prices, in the hope, by thus heaping coals of fire on their heads, to excite some contrition for the barbarities they have committed in our own confines, and dispose them to peace.

The strange and fierce contrast to this amiable Southern feeling which the Northern Government has exhibited in its conduct of the war, presents a subject of serious reflection. Much as they have suffered, the Southern people scarcely yet realize with what ferocious determination the North originally embarked upon, have continued to carry on, and are still bent upon prosecuting this war. Refusing to learn by experience, and apparently incapable of realizing a fact demonstrated by the most potent evidence, there is a sentiment even now pervading the Southern community that the war may be mitigated by forbearance, or perhaps concluded by negotiation.

It is a vain delusion. The worst is all before us. We have not yet reached the grapple of the conflict; the fatal and deadly blows are yet to be struck; the last stage of passion, exhaustion, and painful agony is yet to be passed. The North is as full of poison as a nest of vipers. It expects to conquer and subdue us for the purpose of executing or imprisoning one portion of the people, exiling another, beggaring the rest, filling their places in the land with their own set. Riots and seditions will perhaps intensify this purpose of the majority. These disturbances do but hasten and precipitate their leading object. It gives them an excuse for inaugurating a reign of terror at home in order the better to prosecute their truculent designs upon the South. Peaceful sentiments and overtures on our side are worse than vain; they only imply a trifling imbecility in our councils.

The United States have, and do offer, one only species of peace to "rebels": lay down your arms and submit unconditionally, first to the armies, and then to the enforcement of the laws on treason and confiscation. That is to say, peace by negotiation is essentially the same thing as peace by actual conquest, with the additional cruelties which cowards never fail to inflict on those who they know to be greater cowards than themselves. The first consequence of either peace would be the division of the Yankee armies, now consolidated at certain points, into small bodies, which would be posted in every city, town, village, country seat, and rural neighborhood of all the Southern States. The States themselves would be at once converted into Territories, placed under military governors, military tribunals, and military police. These would immediately abolish the relation of master and slave, and seize the negroes to work for the profit of the Northern Government, or to build prisons and fortifications in convenient places. Then would follow the usual procedures of the Butlers and the Andy Johnsons, till the country was "pacified," and till the "courts of the United States," that is to say, the judges of New England, were ready to open their sessions and "enforce the laws." What the laws of the United States in regard to the people of the Confederate States are, we have often explained. One of their operations will be the sentence of death by hanging for a hundred or so thousand of honest men. The more prominent among them would be executed; the sentence in the majority of cases would be commuted to the penitentiary. Then the law of property strips *every* man who has aided or *countenanced* the Southern Confederacy of every dollar's worth of real and personal property he has. It would be enforced; without an exception or an omission; for the Yankees want our money, want our lands, want our houses, want our furniture, our clothes, down to the shirt of every man and the petticoat of every woman. The law gives all—they will take all, if the day comes to re-open the courts of the United States in these regions. Happy will be the man who shall have gotten in his grave before that day. These are the plain, straight, sure consequences of the only treaty of peace with the North, other than that which shall secure the independent existence of the Southern Confederacy. They will not be aggravated in the least by resistance to the last extremity. Quite the contrary. A brave, powerful, fierce man is respectfully treated even in chains; who knows but a smack too many, or an unlucky kick might make him break the chain or catch his tormentor by a limb and then ——! But a cringing, abject creature, who could fight, but preferred to poke out his wrists for the handcuffs—who's afraid to spit in his face, feel in his pockets, or make him pull off his breeches?

Negotiation with the Yankee is a delusion and a snare. Blow for blow, life for life, battle after battle on every foot of the soil, are the only good dealings between the Southern Confederacy and the United States. War, pushed to the last extremity, is the resolution of the South. By it, ultimate victory is secure. Our strength is unbroken, our force unexhausted. Territory occupied by the enemy signifies nothing while our armies keep the field.

The British ran over every high road of this country; penetrated every neighborhood, plundered every city and town to the Gulf—but lost the game. Their successors in tyranny will lose like them, unless the descendants of those who lived "in the times that tried men's souls" have infamously degenerated.

JULY 31, 1863.

THOSE blessed persons who expected nothing from England are filled to-day. Periodically there is a fuss in the British Parliament over the Southern Confederacy. It is time that this farce should tire the audience. We have no worse enemies in the world than the British Government and the majority of the British nation. Not that they are friends of the North. They hate the whole American people and gloat on their ruin. All their diplomacy has been, and will ever be, employed to prolong the war, by preventing the interference of any other nation.

The South never had, and never will have, reason to expect aught but evil from Great Britain. But in no event need any one expect Great Britain to do any thing more than intrigue in this or any other imbroglio. She will not only never go to war, but will not take any step that may possibly involve a future appeal to arms. In judging that country, one fact should never be lost sight of—that, in the present generation, it is the most peaceably inclined of all nations. The British people of our day have been educated into a horror of war as the most costly of all extravagances. Napoleon defined the English to be a nation of shopkeepers. The definition was then but partially true—and they convinced him of it before they were done with him. The British was once a combative as well as a mercantile race. But it is no longer so. Many wars have saddled it with an immense debt, and thus weighted all its movements with enormous taxation. The people who live in those islands have been taught that wars mean taxes. They pay the price of their ancestors' glory, and have fixed deep in their hearts the conviction that glory costs more than it is worth. A ministry that appears to keep the nation out of the ring where broken heads are plenty, and brickbats flying around, will always find itself on the strong side, and never have the least difficulty in settling the Roebucks and their like.

But France is a very different entity. The French, too, have had their wars. But they have not swallowed the opiate of a national debt. From time to time, France has coolly repudiated its debt, and neither this or any other generation of Frenchmen are deaf to the voice of active ambition. To be popular in France, the ruler for the time must bestir himself, must enlarge the sphere of French influence, and treat the people to a dish of carnage now and then. Napoleon is wise in his generation. He knows better than the *Rois Fainéants*. Even if he had not Mexico, it would be reasonable to look for his finger in the American pie. But the possession of Mexico appears to render his interference compulsory, whenever it shall become evident that this Confederacy will cease to exist without it.

A new throne is about to be erected, whose occupant shall be the puppet of France; that *Idée Napoleonienne* which has already been once embodied in a kingdom of Italy and Victor Emanuel, is to receive a new shape, habitation and name on the American continent. But it will soon turn to airy nothing again—that throne will prove an unsteady seat, that crown will be a fragile head-dress, that sceptre will break like a reed, on the day when the subjugation of the South shall be completed and the power of the United States be restored. To prevent this consummation is now a political necessity for the master of France.

AUGUST 5, 1863.

"OHE! JAM SATIS!"

THE present crisis of affairs in the Confederacy not only sanctions, but imperatively demands the closest, most searching inspection by the people, and the prompt institution of rigid reforms by their representatives. It is useless and childish to attempt to disguise the fact that gross official blunders and culpable negligence, long continued, have brought the country, within the last few months, under very great misfortune. Upon whose shoulders should the weight of a nation's just indignation be laid?

When the disastrous results of the battle of Corinth, glaringly published the incapacity of General Van Dorn to properly handle the Army of the Mississippi, which the doting fondness of Mr. Davis had intrusted to his management, the people insisted upon an immediate change of officers, and all eyes turned upon General Price for the command. Why was he not placed in it? Simply because the President entertained a personal disinclination to him. To the profound chagrin of the country, General Pemberton was created lieutenant-general, and ordered to the Department of the Mississippi. Ominous forebodings accompanied him as he travelled thither. Though discontented, we hoped for the best and awaited the result. Very soon it became painfully apparent, to even the most obtuse, that the general whom South Carolina distrusted, because of his course at Charleston, was rapidly wrecking the fortunes of the West. His incapacity and ill-luck could not be concealed by his fussiness; distrustful mutterings filled the land. What did these, together with accumulated warning, protestation, and pleading avail? Serene upon the frigid heights of an infallible egotism sat Mr. Davis, wrapped in sublime self-complacency, turning a deaf ear to all, and resolved to maintain his protégé, though the cause should sustain irremediable injury. The result proved the superior wisdom of the masses and the culpable obstinacy of the President. It has been said of him by one who knew him well: "He prides himself on never changing his mind; and popular clamor against those who possess his favor only knits him more stubbornly to them," of the truth of which assertion the retention of Mallory is a painful exemplification. There is an old Spanish adage which might with justice be quoted here: "A wise man sometimes changes his mind, but——,"&c.

Vicksburg fell, through an improvidence for which there exists not the shadow of palliation. Either General Pemberton is a traitor, or so completely incapable that he was unfit, not merely for the command of Vicksburg, but for any command requiring forethought. Upon one or the other horn of the dilemma he must inevitably be gored. Yet even now, in the midst of the disasters necessarily incident to his conduct, the country is disposed to credit the charge of incompetence rather than accuse him of treachery. Who is responsible for the loss of Vicksburg and Port Hudson, the sacking of Jackson, and the devastation of Mississippi? Mr. Davis, alone—for retaining in command a man who, the whole country foreknew, months ago, would ruin that State, which protested against him. The apologists of the President have attempted to cast the blame on General Johnston, and to blacken the hard-won reputation of the ablest strategist in the Confederacy. The people, clinging fondly and proudly to their old battle-scarred favorite, pointing to Richmond, angrily proclaim: "*Not General Johnston, but Mr. Davis is to blame.*" Unfortunately General Johnston is not ubiquitous; he was set to watch two men in different sections, neither of whom could be trusted in matters involving military acumen or strategy. If he left General Bragg to himself, blunders were immediately committed; if he left General Pemberton with orders to collect provision and ammunition, and sped to Tullahoma, to rectify errors, lo! Vicksburg is starved out. All that human skill could devise, and human energy accomplish, the people believe that General Johnston did; and they cannot be hoodwinked, deluded or persuaded to cast one iota of blame upon him. They know where the responsibility belongs, and there they are determined it shall rest. Despite the sneers of Absolutists and of those who incline to military dictatorship, VOX POPULI, VOX DEI.

The people are weary of the flagrant mismanagement of the Government. The spirit of resistance is as strong as ever, and the devotion to our cause as fervent and unshaken; but we are disgusted and disheartened at the course pursued by the Administration. But people have waited and hoped for a change, deeming in inexpedient to complain publicly, until the abuses and grievances have grown colossal and national patience is exhausted. Look beyond the Mississippi! What a humiliating spectacle meets the eye? Missouri utterly abandoned to her persecutors; while Missouri's troops, which never surrendered before, were made to stack their arms by order of General Pemberton. A large portion of Arkansas overrun, simply because Mr Davis's protégé No. 2—General Holmes—is kept in command, despite the prayers of the State and the irrepressible complaints of the army. If General Holmes be not in his dotage, the English language possesses no synonym to indicate his stupidity and inertia.

Will no one who has the Presidential ear render the Confederacy a service by reminding him of the celebrated anecdote of Louis XII., which he must have read when he studied Vattel? That monarch was urged to prosecute an old, personal feud, but he sternly and indignantly replied: "The King of France does not avenge the injuries of the Duke of Orleans." Had the people dreamed that Mr. Davis would carry all his chronic antipathies, his bitter prejudices, his puerile partialities, and his doting favoritisms into the Presidential chair, they would never have allowed him to fill it. Little did they imagine that some of our noblest, purest patriots, greatest statesmen and ablest generals would be immolated to the obscure hatreds of provincial politics, or the forgotten quarrels of the War Department at Washington. He seems to have mastered but one axiom of Machiavelli: "The dissensions of individuals contribute to the welfare of the State."

Mr. Davis has alienated the hearts of the people by his stubborn follies, and the injustice he has heaped upon some whom they regarded as their ablest generals and truest friends. The people do not share in his chronic hallucination that he is a great military genius, and can direct the campaigns in distant States with unerring skill. They would rather trust Generals Beauregard and Johnston, Ewell, Price, Kirby Smith, Breckinridge and G. W. Smith, and would be better pleased if he would employ himself in correcting evils near his own door: namely, the mismanagement of the Post-Office Department, the depreciation of the currency, and the gigantic mischief resulting from the present system of blockade-running.

The country is not discouraged by federal advances, but we know that, unless the errors of the past are promptly corrected, the future holds no promise. God forbid that our fair and beloved land should be ruined by our own mal-administration, or that our people should lack the proper energy and independence to teach their Executive that he is their servant, not their master—their instrument, not their dictator.

AUGUST 7, 1863.

THE army of the Confederacy contains the best and the worst of its population. The wisest heads, the noblest hearts, the strongest hands which this country affords, are in that organization. They are not always officers. Many of the purest and brightest spirits are in the ranks; men who have entered the army not from selfishness or vainglory, but truly to help their dear country; men who have sought no promotion, shirked no duty; who have borne fatigue, borne rough usage, endured every privation; who have not done this as "high private," but as "common soldier." When this war is over, these men will be rewarded by a degree of respect, an esteem, a love, from all who know them, which no officer under a commanding general who has won victories, can hope to have, or can possibly deserve.

But by the side of these, the truest heroes the sun ever saw, are many of the lowest scoundrels that disgrace humanity. A moment's reflection is enough to satisfy even those who do not know the army by experience, that the fact must be so. An army gathered as ours has been, is a great drag-net, that collects the dregs as well as the brightest ornaments of society. Mischief is done by indiscriminate, fulsome laudation of every thing that calls itself a soldier. On the real soldier the country should, and will, shower its blessings and rewards. But he must be the real soldier; he who remains at his post; he who asks few furloughs, and is never absent without leave; who never straggles on the march; who does not skulk from the fire; who is seen in the ranks of the army or in the hospital, but never at home; never in the wayside house; never in the cities, unless with a broken limb. To him be honor and reward; the respect of man and the love of woman; the first places of the nation will be his by right when his work shall be finished—not before, and not otherwise.

But what is the due of those wretches who straggle to rob and beg; who skulk or are sickly at every pinch; who are visible here, there, and everywhere, except in their companies when the roll is called? Are they entitled to any part of the consideration due to their comrades in the camp? Is it not a cruel robbery of the brave and true to call them soldiers? Their name is deserter, the vilest of malefactors! As such they should be treated by every man, and every woman, and every child, every civil and every military functionary. The house that gives such a one shelter is disgraced. Those who feed them, harbor them, or who, knowing of them, do not promptly inform the proper authority, partake of their crime, and stab their country.

The President and General Lee tell us that if all these shameful creatures were in their places, doing their duty, our armies would at this moment be numerically superior to the enemy. If the absent, the skulking, the straggling, were driven back to their duty, there would be no need for further tinkering with the conscription law or new drafts on the country. Those who are at home because of age, or occupation, or condition, can do much towards accomplishing that great object. But it is the proper administration of the military laws, it is the strong hand of the Government, that can alone deal effectually with this matter. A plaintive proclamation is not the measure which the case requires. An amnesty for the past will do more harm than good, unless accompanied by prompt, terrible, and invariable punishment for the least dereliction, or an hour's absence, in the future. Of what avail are eloquent appeals to men, the most of whom are destitute of the first rudiments of education, or devoid of a single spark of honesty, courage or patriotism ? The only cure for desertion is the death penalty; and if the Government and its generals would seize every opportunity to shoot and hang these men; if they would capture them as malefactors, try them at the drum's head, and put them to death without mercy, they would perform only the first duty of military authority, and they would soon cease to have reason to complain of skeleton regiments or nominal brigades.

AUGUST 12, 1863.

The legislature of Virginia will be convened in extra session, to take into consideration the measures necessary for the defence of the State. No one will object that such a session of the legislature is unnecessary. If a legislature is a useful branch of government at any time, certainly now is that time. If there is a fault in the meeting of the General Assembly, it lies in the need of calling it together. It never should have adjourned.

The same remarks may be made with double force upon the indolent Congress of the Confederate States. The members of that body should also be in their seats, or in the ranks of the army. They should work in one way or the other. Congress should not have adjourned while every day teems with new events, requiring the immediate consideration and action of the representatives of the nation; but, as they have dispersed and will not meet again for four long months, it is the duty of the Confederate Executive to convene them in special session without delay.

Are there not matters requiring the immediate interposition of the law-making power, and the prompt application of the remedial authority of the whole Government? What of the currency? Is it to wait four months for some effectual surgery? Will it wait?

If any thing is palpably true, it is that the Confederate Congress should at this moment be doing, or endeavoring to do, something to check the decline in Confederate paper, sinking under its own weight and the joint pressure of blockade-runners and the brokers, the dealers in gold who have the strongest of human motives to increase the disparity of the relative value of gold and Confederate notes. The present laws are manifestly insufficient for the magnitude of the evil and its causes. It was, indeed, easily foreseen that they would prove insufficient when they were made. Their intention was good; they were steps in the right direction; but they were half-measures, palliatives, which do not cut the root of mischief. If Congress were now in session, it is believed that it would no longer hesitate. It would see the worthlessness of the complex, involved, and timid financial system of laws which it invented, and laboriously brought forth last winter; and would resort now to those simple provisions which alone can render the Confederate currency adequate to the maintenance of the country. It would put a stop to the trade in gold; it would shut up that great drain on the country's vitals, the practice of smuggling luxuries into the land from the Northern States, which are paid for in cash or its equivalent. It would render compulsory the funding of the myriads of Confederate notes extant. It would boldly draw from the people all the money that it needed by an equal and rigorously collected taxation. It would retrench the sinecures and lop off the useless parts of that expensive machine called the Confederate Government: a machine with the like of which our forefathers did not encumber themselves in the successful struggle for independence of '76.

These, or similar measures equally decisive, Congress might adopt now, if it had remained in session to watch the march of events, or if it should meet at this moment. If not now, certainly in some brief period, the exigencies of this war will force Congress and the Executive on a more decisive and energetic course than they have hitherto pursued. But even if we are mistaken in thinking thus, we can scarcely suppose that any serious person will dispute the propriety of a continual session of the legislative branches of the State and Confederate Governments during this struggle for life. Composed mostly of the ex-members of the old Federal Congress, the politicians, to whom the people intrusted their business, have not yet gotten rid of the idea that their present position and duty is but a continuation of the life they led at Washington. But they will be forced to forget the habits and practices of that life by the dangers which now encircle them. The Confederate Congress has functions to perform very different from those of the body which held a short session and a long session in the house on Pennsylvania Avenue. Its true prototypes are the Senate of Rome when the Gauls besieged the city, the Long Parliament of England, the Perpetual Convention of France, and the Continental Congress of the revolted colonies. When did those bodies have their comfortable "recess?"

AUGUST 24, 1863.

FAST days and Thanksgiving days strike the Southern ear with a puritanical sound, always disagreeable, and, now, pre-eminently hateful. They smack of Latter Day sanctity; savor of the nasal twang and recall disagreeable reminiscences of Praise-God-Barebones, the Pilgrim Fathers, and their Yankee descendants.

National respect for religion and acknowledgment of the overruling hand of the Deity are consecrated by immemorial usage and natural instinct. Supplication in the hour of adversity, and Te Deums in the exultation of victory, are quite the correct thing, whether judged by the promptings of natural religion or the example of earthly potentates. The Roman legion marched confidently to victory, after the victims had promised the favor of the immortal gods; the Spanish infantry of the Middle Ages serried their iron ranks with the cry of Santiago, nor did the Protestant English meet them with a less assured trust in the protection of Heaven.

Some mode of invoking higher than human aid is common to all ages and nations. The Turk rushes to the breach, with the shout of "Allah Akbar," not less fervently than the Crusader with the cry of "Holy Cross." The late Czar Nicholas ordered many manifestations of piety during the Crimean war; while Sebastopol was besieged, he always rode out with a large cross suspended on his breast, and would frequently stop his horse in the streets to ejaculate passages from the penitential psalms. And Pelissier, while regarding the assault of the Malakoff, was heard to utter various remarks of a theological character, especially when any of his troops evinced "a foolish hankering after existence." Nothing could exceed the religion of the Austrian Government during the Italian war. The Emperor and all his court happened to be walking at the head of a huge procession through the streets of Vienna on the very day when the battle of Magenta was unexpectedly fought. Napoleon and Victor Emanuel, it is true, restrained their devotional ardor till some months later.

It is well that the Confederacy should display a trust in Divine aid, ingrained, as it undoubtedly is, in the hopes, the thoughts, and the progress of the people, as well as approved by the universal practice of the world. Still, it is to be regretted that the phraseology we use should be unfortunately associated with all that is repugnant to our taste and our feelings. It is one of the many consequences of our long intercourse with the Puritan members of the late Union. They, by the way, do not seem now to rely on fasts and humiliation. They have recently indulged in thanksgiving for victory, but their panacea for defeat seems to be fresh levies of men, more ironclads and additional fifteen-inch guns. Otherwise, Lincoln & Co. steadfastly ignore defeats.

It may be that the sanctimonious terminology derived from the Yankees should not be allowed to militate against a custom laudable in itself, but there are other accessories more deserving of protest and reprehension. One of the most serious political, moral, and social curses which afflicted the Union and precipitated its downfall was the prevalence of political preachers. It was a much easier and more inviting road to wealth and fame to mingle in political strife, and to agitate the questions of the hour, than to inculcate the precepts of charity, or to expound the doctrines of the Gospel. A man of good presence, easy elocution, and redundant vocabulary, could readily fill his church and his pockets by stimulating the vagaries of fanaticism and hunting novelties for the popular taste. It was both easier and more lucrative than to plod through the subtleties of ecclesiastical lore, or to seek to guide the wayward public in the narrow path of reason and virtue.

"The pulpit, that safe and sacred organ of sedition," has often been used for political purposes, but never so habitually, nor to such an extent, as among the Northern States during the lifetime of the now defunct Union. It descended into the arena of faction and courted the lowest breath of popular applause. Homilies on slavery and sanctimonious arrogation of superior virtue, both tickled the vanity and pleased the taste of Yankee hearers.

There are indications that the South is not free from this dangerous malady. That in times of high excitement the clergy should share the feelings of the community is natural; and it may be difficult to prevent all confusion of earthly and heavenly considerations in pious discourses; yet the nature of our government, wisely adverse to the union of the secular and the religious arm, forbids it, and our respect for the priestly character tells us that it is rather their duty to soften the passions aroused in the contests of the world, and withdraw our thoughts from their fevered excitement, than to stimulate them by passionate discourses.

This revolution should secure us social as well as political independence. We should get rid of Yankee manners as well as of Puritan laws; and one of the most obnoxious is the vice of political preaching. Let the Southern clergy, then, be assured that they will win more lasting respect, and exert more legitimate influence, in abstaining from a custom discordant to our manners. Let them inculcate virtue, stimulate patriotism, and expound Christianity, but let them argue from universals and trust the good sense of their hearers to make the application to particulars. Let them, in their clerical capacity, confine themselves to the holy province whose separation from temporal interests is alike conducive to sound religion and good government. Let the purity of the priestly robe not be sullied by the mire of the furious struggles of daily life. Let our preachers, in imitation of the Divine Founder of Christianity, utter their meaning by typical language, conveying unchanging principles of ready application to the purposes of life. The persuasive influences of unobtrusive piety will be more beneficial than the vehemence of sensation sermons. Let us not have the Southern pulpit converted into a rostrum for political harangues, or a lecture-room for the dissemination of peculiar philosophical tenets. Let not our preachers discourse of Lincoln, or of Seward, of Davis, or of Lee. Let them fulminate against Pharoah and Holofernes, and exalt Gideon and David. We have broken asunder from Yankee statesmanship and government; let us eschew their morality and manners We have lowered the portcullis and manned the battlements against the assaults of Seward, Greeley and Lovejoy. Great will be our mortification and sorrow if Beecher and Cheever should slip in by the postern.

AUGUST 25, 1863.

RECONSTRUCTION of the Union has been, and still is, one of the cries and catch-words in the North. There are persons in the South, quite sincere in patriotism, who are nevertheless injudicious and credulous enough to believe that something might be done to heep the cause of their country by encouraging that cry in the North, and by entering into some species of conference with the party who use it, to ascertain what they mean by reconstruction. Such negotiations, they doubtless intend, shall be in the nature of pious frauds. They propose to distract and divide the enemy. In a word, they propose a game of cheating with Yankees. In such a game, played by such parties, who would be the loser? When have North and South ever dealt in this way that the North has not been the successful cheater, the South invariably cheated? Trust the experience of all your lives, men of the South, and say as few words as possible to the enemy. Especially, say nothing that you are not prepared to perform. Our own people will always believe their leaders quite in earnest. They will take them at their word; and the moment that negotiations are begun, they will believe the independence of the South to be an abandoned cause.

What terms any minority in the United States would be willing to give the South if its people would lay down their arms and submit, it is not worth while to inquire. What terms the Government of the United States would give us are authentically and certainly known. Those terms are declared in the *laws* of that country, and would be executed through its military and civil courts. What terms the people of the United States would grant us, have been shadowed forth by the treatment individual citizens of the South have invariably received when in their power.

No doubt can be felt by any creature not an idiot, that if the Government of the United States believed for a moment it could persuade by promises, proclamations, words of any kind, the armies of the South to disband, the Confederacy to disorganize, and its citizens to take oaths of allegiance, that it would spare those words. To conquer the South without fighting has been the great desideratum of that Government and people from the beginning of the war until this time. This prime object would be in a fair way of attainment if the Southern States, or any portion of their citizens, would enter into negotiation with the Northern States, or any portion of their citizens, on such a subject-matter as reconstruction of the Union. Cheating might then begin—gammon would have a chance—thousands of promises kept to the ear and broken to the hope could then be heard and have their fatal effect on the weary, the cowardly, the base. There is but one only means of preventing the United States, people, politicians, parties or Government, whatever their promises, from carrying out their cruel purposes; those means we are using, not with all the success we could desire; but with enough to prevent that utter destruction which would be the certain and immediate consequence of the abandonment of their usage. So long as the Southern Confederacy can keep an army in the field, it is a belligerent. The Southern people are still entitled to such protection as the laws of war can give; Southern soldiers still prisoners of war when taken captive. They have not to blush, to cringe, to tremble and to hide. But the moment this war shall end without securing the independence of the Confederacy, every Southern soldier is converted into a FELON; that must be the legal status of all who have borne arms against the Union. There is no escape or evasion of it, or any of the shame, the loss, the misery that accompanies that condition.

Even if subjugation were a moral certainty, every hour through which the fight could be continued, would be an hour of relief and life. But no people ever were subjugated, no people ever can be subjugated, who will not submit. The South will never submit; and, simple as the people are, they can never be bamboozled into a belief that "reconstruction" is aught else than submission. The very mention of negotiations about a reconstruction of the Union is an insult to the humblest understanding. The state of things which existed ten years ago can never be again on this continent. The most foolish, the most ignorant, can see that. But even were it possible, what man is base enough to be willing, for his own good, to restore the "Union as it was?" Even the meanest has some regard for friends and kindred. Two hundred thousand of our finest young men have lost life or limb in this war. They shed their blood, they risked and lost their lives under the impression that they were doing an honorable and rightful thing,—THAT THEY WERE FIGHTING FOR THEIR COUNTRY! Their fathers, their wives, their children, are proud to say, my son was killed at Gettysburg, my husband fell at Richmond, my father, my brother, my uncle was one of the brave men who bled for the land in the great war. But what were all those persons if the Union never has been dissolved—if the Confederacy is an illegal combination—if its "so-called" laws have no authority? There is no uncertainty—they were criminals, traitors. Their graves are dishonorable graves. They did not fight for their country. THEY FOUGHT AGAINST THEIR COUNTRY. They lifted up parricidal and sacrilegious hands against that thing which every good man was bound to protect. They did not kill enemies, but committed murder on their fellow-citizens. Their names must be disgraced, their memory a memory of shame to all their posterity, friends and relations. Is there any man so mean and poor of heart as to be willing to reward the friend, the son, the father, the cousin, who has fought for him and his, with that ignominy? Perish all things; perish all together, rather than so desert, so betray the generous and the unfortunate.

SEPTEMBER 7, 1863.

WHETHER ferocity, folly, or beastly vulgarity is the predominating characteristic of the monstrous utterance with which Lincoln, the Yahoo President, to-day insults the human kind is a question not easily decided. That such a creature should be the chief figure in such a period; that this compound of brute and buffoon should be master of the situation in one of the most awful convulsions remembered by history; is a fact not indeed unparalleled, but of rare occurrence. Cromwell was a joker, and Cæsar a filthy man; but they kept their jests and their lusts in chambers, and displayed their stupendous abilities and terrible power to the world. But the Representative Man of the model republic and its revolution delights to display the proportions of his mind and the qualities of his heart undisguised, in official papers, as in bar-room talks.

"Nor must Uncle Sam's noble fleet be forgotten," says the grog-shop President. "At all the water's margins they have been present. Not only on the deep sea, the broad bay, the rapid river, but also up the narrow, muddy bayou, *and wherever the ground was a little damp, they have been and made their tracks.*"

Shade of Washington! is this thy successor? Can this be the man in whose hand rest the resources of the United States, and who controls a million of soldiers? Nero, Claudius, Marat, even if they were what Tacitus and Thiers describe, would have blushed for this. Sancho, when ruler of the island Barataria, would scarcely have written a letter parallel in style to that from which this passage is quoted.

Yet the reader will not smile, and disgust will vanish before stronger sentiments, when he has reflected on the intent and prospect revealed in this degraded language. Lincoln propounds as fact, which none of his race deny, or doubt, that he is invested with what he calls the "law of war." This law of war is explained by him to mean the right and power of inflicting unlimited injury on the Southern people. "A few things," it is true, are considered "barbarous," and he will refrain from doing them. What is it he will refrain from? "*The massacre of non-combatants male and female.*" This is the point at which he will stop. He will not order the extermination of Southern women, or the slaughter of little children. All short of that the ruler of the North intends to do. Every particle of property, real and personal, is the prize of the victors, and, what they cannot take, he will "destroy." Such is the future of the war. Such is the man of destiny.

SEPTEMBER 15, 1863.

WHILE it is perfectly obvious that the whole Yankee nation look upon the operations of the French in Mexico with a rage all the more bitter on account of its impotence, it is equally clear that their own condition imperatively forbids any course of action likely to embroil them with so formidable a power as France. The "great rebellion" demands all their attention and overtasks all their resources. The bluster of their journals and the rhodomontade of their demagogues are insufficient to conceal this fact from the world, or even to disguise it to themselves when suddenly brought face to face with imminent danger, and forced to grapple with a question of practical importance. In such a case they will at once perceive the prudence of abstaining from measures likely to produce hostilities, although they lack the dignity to suppress the ebullition of spite.

Napoleon has well chosen his time. The last three years have afforded the United States many opportunities for the cultivation of the Christian virtues, forbearance and humility. Their vanity has met with bitter disappointment at the hands of the Confederacy, and their pride has been forced to stomach grievous mortification in their intercourse with European powers. It may fairly be presumed that they have profited by their experience, and, that on an occasion demanding an unusual degree of self-control, they will rise, (or sink) with the emergency. To direct a foreign policy exacting such sacrifices of pride, no one could be found endowed with more suitable qualities than their Secretary of State. An impassibility of temperament and a callousness to insult, rarely to be paralleled, fit him admirably for a diplomacy where swaggering menace is to be followed by prompt abasement, and where a shallow cunning and disingenuous deception, in which he has had the practice of a lifetime, are considered an adequate substitute for grasp and comprehensiveness of intellect. During his long service in the United States Senate, and in the imperturbability shown by him amid the most exciting scenes of angry debate and sectional discord, he was learning a lesson, useful for the conduct of foreign affairs in a crisis which demands the sacrifice of all the most cherished feelings, the most susceptible jealousies, and the most vital interests of the Yankee nation.

The intense humiliation of our enemies is gratifying to the Southern people. Their own immediate interests, however, as well as the boundless prospects of the future, afford scope for serious reflection. Every age has its different forms of cant. In the present, popular rights and sovereignty of race are the fashionable themes, even for absolute potentates. Napoleon III. proclaimed to the world, when he was at Milan after the victory of Magenta, "that if there were men who did not comprehend the spirit of the age, he was not of the number." He readily comprehends that the tendency of the world at present is to accomplish by indirection and contrivance what simpler ages performed with undisguised force.

The establishment of a sovereignty, dependent upon France, upon our southern frontier, is replete with questions of the gravest interest for this Confederacy. They would demand the most patient investigation and the most jealous care in ordinary times, but, in this crisis of our fate, when we are struggling for mere existence, questions for future policy must necessarily be subordinated to the momentous issue of the hour. The attainment of independence will be the mighty labor of this generation, and we are naturally disposed to postpone all considerations of the future for the care of our successors, and say with Louis XV., "after us the deluge."

SEPTEMBER 17, 1863.

The Yankee Secretary of State has gratified the public with another of those little interchanges of sentiment with the English abolitionists, in which he and they have, from time to time, indulged since the beginning of the war. A committee of these gentry, not only extend their good wishes to Seward, but promulgate a little philosophy on the character and tendency of the war. While expressing deep sympathy in the success of the Yankees, they assert that, if the South is successful, it will be the first instance of the establishment of a government based upon African slavery. Seward accepts this idea as if it were a new revelation, and assures his correspondents that, to the numerous weighty reasons which influence himself and his party against the acceptance of the revolution, they have added another of decisive weight.

This great argument with which these people have enlightened Seward is simply nonsense. Unless African slavery be, in their opinion, a more heinous sin than white slavery, the same objection might be made to the most formidable empires and the most enlightened States of antiquity, and even to their own institutions arising from mediæval serfdom. The truth is, however, that the Confederacy is based no more upon African slavery, than upon cotton, tobacco, rice or Indian corn. It uses and maintains the system of labor established in the colonial state, expanded by time and favorable development, and it cultivates the products congenial to its soil. In both cases it perseveres simply in the plain path of reason and experience, content to receive and, if possible, improve the circumstances with which nature and the operations of mankind have surrounded it. The Southern war for independence is based upon the right of a people to alter their government, and to withdraw from an association in which vested rights were assailed by blind fanaticism, and plunder perpetrated under the guise of canting humanity. The domestic institutions of the Southern people are not obtruded by them upon the world. They simply defend themselves, and maintain the battle of order and steady progress against the wild schemes of rapacity stimulated by a self-sufficient and spurious philanthropy.

SEPTEMBER 23, 1863.

THE deep-seated antagonism of two antipathetic peoples, linked together by temporary requirements of political necessity or geographical position, under the American Union, was intensified by the collision unavoidably springing from their enforced juxtaposition, and manifested itself in every mode of expression, from angry invective to bitter ridicule. For seventy years, repugnance in the mode of thought, diversity of social customs, and contrariety of manners, displayed their natural effects, until they finally chafed asunder the fetters which bound them in discordant alliance.

We may now look upon the political actions, the literary taste, and the manners of our enemies, with as calm a spirit as the excitement of war will allow. If we read their newspapers, we will find the same insolent menace and the same clownish ridicule directed to foreign observers who presume to doubt the success of their arms, or to criticise the policy of their Government, that were formerly familiar to ourselves as favorite weapons in the attack upon our society and upon our rights. Nor are we forgotten amid the host of antagonists that the widely-spread ramifications of the war have caused to feel the force of their vituperation.

Southern chivalry was always a favorite theme of ridicule with these people. While their heavy artillery of argument and slander was directed against our more serious and permanent objects of solicitude, the missiles of ridicule were directed against our social peculiarities and domestic affections. The attempt to establish a more exalted code of manners and a more delicate morality, was laughed to scorn as the insolent assumption of affected aristocrats. Strict equality was, in their opinion, to be secured by the libelling process. Those who rose above the dreary uniformity were to be reduced to the common standard, instead of attempting to exalt those who were below. The lowest propensities of human nature were gratified by the systematic depreciation of all aspirations after a more elevated ideal, and by the constant derision of the Quixotism which refused to regard the market value as the sole standard by which to measure the worth of refinement and honor.

Even now, amid the terrible convulsion which shakes the Continent, and in presence of the fearful agony of desolate homesteads and crushed affections, we are shocked to catch the sound of idiotic laughter and apish gibes rising above the wail of broken-hearted despair. It is impossible for a man of ordinary feeling, or even of correct taste, to read the journals which may be presumed to be correct types of the Yankee mind, without profound disgust, and a feeling of misanthropic contempt. Is it possible that such beings are not only of our own race, but that, until within a recent period, they were united with us under the same Government?

Ridicule is a formidable weapon. In the hands of a Lucian, a Swift, or a Voltaire, it may change a religion or overturn a government. Its keen edge may be made to strike inveterate abuses or to defend the cause of innocence. When it is turned against the cherished principles or the lofty aspirations of an entire nation, it ceases to be respectable, even if it is tempered by the refinement of wit. It is doubly contemptible when the brutality of the ruffian is expressed in the language of the clown. The sneers with which the Yankee journals deride the struggles of a brave people would have been equally applicable to the reverses of the men of '76. They evince meanness of nature as well as poverty of invention, and their vulgar boasts have, if we may trust the news from the West, received a fitting reply from the gallant men whom they were intended to ridicule.

SEPTEMBER 26, 1863.

The New York *Tribune* complains that "Appleton's Encyclopædia," in some articles of current history, speaking of "the rebellion," "uses the language of the London *Times* and the Richmond *Examiner*." The main charges against the Yankee encyclopædists are, that they have styled the people of the South "the Confederates," and used the terms "United States" and "Confederate States," in speaking of the belligerents, instead of Mr. Greeley's pleasant antithesis of "the Republic and the Rebellion."

The criticism appears at first puerile; but it has really an important and curious significance. There can be no real objection to our recognition as belligerents. The authorities at Washington have long ago conceded this recognition, and the penny-a-liners of the Appletons can do no less. But it is remarkable that recently, on all possible occasions, in their literature and in their public intercourse, the abolitionists have deprecated the use of terms which imply the distinct character of the people of the South, and have been busy in claiming community of race and blood with us. In Mr. Seward's recent address to foreign courts, he is at especial pains to declare to Europe that the manifestations of courage and tenacity in this war are to be ascribed to the fact that the belligerents are of the same blood and the same mould of American manhood.

This affectionate claim of community of race and manners with us, and the constant protest against the use of terms which imply any natural difference between the Yankee and the Southerner, is something new in the war. At the commencement of hostilities, "the rebel" was a despised creature, and the Southern slaveholder was "hell-born." Now, the prime minister at Washington, and the scornful knight of the *Tribune*, are anxious to claim kin with the infernal progeny. They fiercely resent the assumption that the types of manhood or the traits of character in the South are in the least different from what they are in New England, and they denounce the barest suggestion, even by the use of distinct terms, of any dissimilarity between North and South.

The fact is, that the Yankee has a certain pride in the splendid reputation which the South has won in this war, even though it may have been at his sole expense, and hopes to claim some partnership in it through the association of the name of "American," or some other common title of nationality. We all recollect the Yankee encomiums of "Stonewall" Jackson, and the busy advertisement of Mr. Junkins, that he was father-in-law of the distinguished "rebel." These incidents give the clue to the Yankee disposition. They are now proud to claim kin with the countrymen of Lee and Jackson, and to assert a partnership in the glory and applause which the South has obtained in this war.

It is scarcely necessary for us to protest against this insolent assumption by the Yankee of a common national name and a common temper with us. We have had enough in times past of stuff about fraternity, and the ties of "Uncle Sam's" progeny. We assert that the people of this Confederacy are distinct from the Yankee in blood, in institutions, in ideas, and in all the elements of a separate nationality. The war of our independence illustrates this fact. Whatever may be its fate, impartial history will, at least, separate us from the old titles of the Union, and give us the credit of a name and national character distinct from that of the Yankee.

OCTOBER 5, 1863.

In the opinions of those shrewd observers who are always expectant of great events, and who scent in every breath of wind indications of change and convulsion, the presence of a few Russian men-of-war in New York harbor is ominous of an alliance between the Czar and the American Dictator. There is no rational ground of apprehension that any such combination is about to be formed. The sympathies and the interests of the two parties, it is true, run very much in the same channel. The two despots of the West and the East sit grimly regarding each other across the intervening world, and say God speed to the glorious work of "order" in which both are engaged. "*Idem velle atque idem nolle, ea demum firma amicitia est*," says Sallust; sympathy in love and hate begets a sort of friendship; and certainly between the Empire of Russia and the so-called Republic of the United States there is the greatest identity of likes and dislikes. Both have an unlimited desire for territorial expansion; both have an utter antipathy for freedom of speech and of the press; both delight in enormous armaments; have the barbarian love for vastness and display, and despise the restraints of law or humanity when opposed to the gratification of their wishes. At present, too, they have an additional bond of union. Both are annoyed by rebellions. One is striving to crush the embryo national independence of a free-born race, while the other struggles to repress the efforts of a gallant people who shake the yoke to which long years of injustice and oppression have failed to render them submissive.

There are other points of resemblance between these two nations, so recently supposed to be the opposite poles, as it were, of humanity. In both there is a barbaric love of magnificence; in both, a gloss of civilization covers the intrinsic savagery of nature This, in the Russian boyard, takes the form of diplomatic refinement and courtesy; in the Yankee, it appears as a sham intellectual culture and pseudo-philanthropy. Each looks with nervous sensitiveness to the opinion of Europe. The Russ, recently emerging from Scythian rudeness, desires the applause of that civilization into which he is a new comer, while the Yankee looks back with servile admiration and craving for praise to the society in which he knows his progenitors held but an humble place. The points of contact arising from social peculiarities and similar potitical position have, of late, been increased by similarity of government. Both are now military despotisms, and have a common interest in the suppression of every struggle for liberty, and the suffocation of every lofty aspiration.

The Russian despotism, enjoying the advantages of age and long habit, is naturally superior, in many points of detail, to the recent growth of America. The rapidity, however, with which the latter advances, gives ground for the assurance that in no distant future, Washington will have but little cause for envy of St. Petersburg, while, in the essentials of arbitrary government, its proficiency shows already that nature has to a great extent supplied the want of practice.

The Czar, descended from a long line of rulers, and brought up in the elegance of a court, may look with some disdain upon his brother despot, so recently caught in his native wilds and exalted to his present perch of power. Yet' a not very remote period in the life of nations will show the House of Romanhoff almost as obscure as that of Lincoln. The master-hand of Gibbon has portrayed the early state of the Russian empire, and has shown us, with lifelike vividness, the rude traffic of a barbarous tribe. He has described the descent of the Don,—in boats not very dissimilar to those in which the American Czar formerly plied his vocation on the Mississippi,—and narrated that fierce attack of Constantinople, which Nicholas was anxious to repeat, and to which the capture of New Orleans by the hordes of the Upper Mississippi bears considerable analogy.

These considerations, however, although they abundantly explain the reciprocal sympathy between the two Governments, and the cordial good will with which they respectively desire the suppression of the Polish revolt and the subjugation of the South, are insufficient to warrant the formation of an alliance. No benefit could well result to either party from it. The Yankee Czar has his hands full, and could, of course, furnish no assistance to the Muscovite. The latter might send him ships, but of these Abraham has a sufficiency, and an addition to the number would not increase his power. Immense as is the Russian army, the ordinary necessities of the empire, the complications of European politics, and the Polish war, render it improbable that men could be spared to act against the Confederacy. Such an event might, however, be within the bounds of possibility, and the Yankees might carry into practice the scheme which George III. vainly attempted against the men of the American Revolution.

The report of a Russian alliance with the United States comes as a sort of counterpoise to that of French alliance with the Confederacy. But we may dismiss the idea of such an actual alliance as a chimera. Alexander may wish his parvenu brother success, but his wishes are not ripe for action. The Russian fleet in Manhattan bay is perhaps intended as a public sign, a demonstration, a hint to the world of what may be under contingencies, but nothing more at the present moment.

OCTOBER 12, 1863.

"So fought the Greeks at Thermopylæ," is the simple comment of Herodotus at the close of his animated description of that heroic achievement. For more than two thousand years the deeds of Leonidas and his Three Hundred have been regarded with admiration, and extolled as without a parallel. Yet, after all, he was defeated. The glorious death of the Spartans delayed the march of Xerxes, cost him many of his best troops, and secured valuable time to Greece. In a moral point of view, it rises to the highest pitch of sublimity. Regarded as a simple military operation, it can only be classed as an affair of outposts, of no decisive influence upon the fate of the war. It has been reserved for America totally to eclipse this vaunted exploit of antiquity. This continent has the longest rivers, the biggest lakes, and the fattest oysters. It has produced the greatest "rebellion" the world has ever seen, and it is but proper that the most extraordinary feat of arms should be performed upon its soil.

Forty-two men, we are informed, repulsed twelve thousand Yankees at Sabine Pass. Leonidas had three hundred Spartans, not to speak of the auxiliaries, at Thermopylæ. The commander at Sabine Pass—fame has not yet recorded his name—could number only forty-two men, "principally Irish." These Forty-Two, like the knights of old, took their position and defended the Pass against all comers.

But it is not only that the present victory has been gained, but that an advantage which should be rendered decisive of the war presents itself to us. Admitting that these Forty-Two are the sole specimens of their class, granting the violent supposition that in our armies there are none to match them, what an important use may be made of this number! Victory for the South is reduced, in the future, to a simple equation. A re-enforcement, equal in value to a moderate-sized army, can be transported promptly in a single railroad car. They may fight at Chattanooga to-day, and three days hence on the Rappahannock.

Uneasy doubts may suggest themselves to the minds of some as to the truth of this marvellous exploit. It is certainly wonderful, but not more so, perhaps, than some of the adventures of Ariosto's hero or of the gallant knights whose adventures excited the chivalric soul of Don Quixote to deeds of valor and knight-errantry. Granting that there is much exaggeration in the story, enough will remain, after making all reasonable deductions, to warrant the highest expectations from the services of this wonderful band.

It is the common complaint of poets and romancers that the progress of science is inimical to the graceful fancies and pleasing imagery of their art. The advance of enlightenment has destroyed the power of the fairies and extinguished the belief in ghosts. The researches of philosophy and discoveries of chemistry have dried up the source of many beautiful conceptions, and given a prosaic solution to many phenomena around which poetical imagination was wont to weave its texture of fable and mystery. This objection, like most of those urged against every fresh development of progress, has been shown in many instances to be causeless. There is a compensating action in the increase of knowledge for any partial or temporary damage it might inflict upon the system of labor of the operations of the intellect. The history of inventions abounds in instances of the one. The progress of poetry can show examples of the other. If some of his favorite themes are taken from the bard, his domain is expanded, on the other hand, by new realms of thought and more elevated grandeur of conception. The telegraph is a striking example of the close alliance between the advance of science and the expansion of the imagination. It was at first regarded as the simple messenger of news, the slave of commerce, the chronicler of variations in stocks, or the details of daily traffic. To view it thus was to circumscribe its sphere and to clip its tireless wings. It is worthy of a higher destiny. It can bear the amplification of the poet as well as the dull ciphers of the merchant. Even now it may be engaged in this loftier office. The Trans-Mississippi country, in its present state of isolation, is peculiarly adapted to stories of the marvellous. The wonderful details of the victory of Sabine Pass may be creations of the imagination. If so, we must console ourselves for the loss of the solid advantages that might be drawn from it by visions of future fame. We shall have legends and ballads worthy of immortality, and our Forty-Two will go down the tide of time with Jack the Giant-Killer; the Palladins of Charlemagne; and that Irish Brigade, of whose exploit at Fontenoy Marshal Saxe never heard, and which no French historian relates, but which is too well known by the rest of mankind to require further illustration here.

OCTOBER 12, 1863.

THE depravity of mankind is in nothing so manifest as in the detraction which attends excellence of whatever description. It would seem, indeed, that the inevitable consequence of human grandeur is human meanness and littleness. By so much as the balance is elevated on the one side, just by so much is it depressed on the other; so that great and good men may almost be said to be the cause of their opposites—the bad and contemptible. The illustration which the poet has drawn from natural phenomena hardly meets the case, for while the traveller ascending the mountain side reaches at length an elevation destitute of animal or vegetable life, his upward progress cannot be said to occasion, much less to multiply, the venomous reptiles which crawl at the mountain's foot. But this appears to be the surprising peculiarity of the moral world, where virtue, wisdom, purity and nobility of character seem actually to provoke into being vices which otherwise would never have had an existence.

Let the metaphysician explain it as best he can, the fact is incontrovertible, that mankind are so constituted that they cannot witness the superiority of their fellow-men without becoming a prey to prejudices the most unreasonable and to passions the most fiendish. The confession is, in the last degree, mournful, and all the more so because human progress, so-called, and the fancied beneficence of civilization, in nowise diminish this lamentable perversity of man's fallen nature. The teachings of experience and the lessons of history are of no avail, for the sorrowful truth is that frail man is to-day precisely what he was when Moses, the meekest of men, was overwhelmed by the upbraidings of the people he had delivered from Egyptian bondage, and when Socrates, that "most Christian heathen," was forced to the fatal cup of hemlock because his virtues were intolerable to the age in which he lived. Follow the course of the centuries, from the advent of the Christian era to the present hour, and the same sad story is told in every generation, in every class of society, every condition of life, with a uniformity so constant that the theme of envy has long since ceased to attract even the passing notice of the philosophic historian, and has passed into the hands of the moralists who conduct the trite exercises of the infant schools.

In letters, the arts, the sciences, the religious world, and, above all, in political affairs, malignity and defamation are the inseparable attendants of excellence. As far back as the days of the Jewish kings, the penalty of literary skill was so severe and so inevitable, that Solomon, with all his wisdom, could only describe it by the famous exclamation, "Oh! that mine enemy would write a book." The career of the artist, replete with every misery, is admirably exemplified in the brief and touching story of Pallissey the Potter. If we turn to the sciences, the single line of Broussais, "Harvey passed for a fool when he announced the discovery of the circulation," discloses at a breath the torrent of abuse with which every inventor or discoverer is invariably saluted. In the religious world it is well known that the fate of the "man of sorrows and acquainted with grief" is that of all who dare even to attempt to imitate their Lord in pureness of heart and holiness of life.

But it is in the arena of politics that we find the most illustrious victims of detraction. How often, during the untoward moments of this cruel war, have we had occasion to revert to the history of our own immortal Washington; and when calumny and reproaches assailed our living leaders, what sweet consolation have we not found in remembering that the mighty dead were wronged in like manner. It was hoped that this great conflict might terminate without the display of those base passions which assaulted the Father of His Country not only during the stormy periods of the Revolution, but after peace was established and every just cause of discontent had disappeared. Yet how accurately, alas! history has repeated itself. Envy, jealousy, malice, spite, venom, and all that the petty vengeance of disappointed ambition could suggest, have been hurled upon one who in due season will be hailed as the Father of His Country. As Washington was calumniated, so will be all the great, the good, the wise, the pure and lofty of the present generation. And oh! how refreshing to think the base arts of the adders that hiss at the feet of the present greatness will fall harmless as they did in the days that are gone. The bitter blows and blasts of the evil-minded do but assimilate and identify the heroes of to-day with the immortal patriots of the past; and they who suffered what Washington suffered will surely shine in the future even as Washington now shines, and will continue to shine until the last syllable of recorded time.

OCTOBER 16, 1863.

WE have been pained by the misconstruction of a late article in this newspaper upon the glorious victory gained over twelve thousand Yankees and a fleet of gun-boats by the unaided valor of forty-two Irish, or principally Irish, fellow-citizens. How any Hibernian reader could suppose that the writer was disgusted by the happy circumstance it is difficult to imagine. We have published our delight at it, and we are charmed to learn, on equally good authority, that the Confederate army contains no less than fifty thousand Irish of like quality. An *easy* calculation will prove that if forty-two can whip twelve thousand, fifty thousand can as easily dispose of fourteen millions of the enemy.

Which of the Confederate armies in the field contains this large body of invincible troops? We are unable to answer the question, but hope they are just now under the command of O'BRAGG. Another question which often troubles the mind is whether there are any native Confederate troops at all. Last winter some remarks about the Jews were misconstrued, and this newspaper was severely reprimanded therefor, because the Confederate army contained fifty thousand Jews, principally under Lee, whose real name was Levy. In the beginning of the war some other remarks about Yankees were misconstrued and this journal was rebuked by a member of Congress who declared that the Confederate army contained fifty thousand fellow-citizens of Northern birth. Supposing the Germans, the French, and others to claim only an equal number, what part of the Confederate force consists of the wretched natives? Are there any natives? Do people ever get born here? This writer has often met enlightened foreigners who maintained the contrary. One official gentleman who had passed eighteen years here assured his countrymen that two-thirds—two full thirds—of the American people were of European birth. It was vain to argue with him that the original English population was prolific, that they ate much meat, married early, and begot sons and daughters during two hundred years He trusted to his senses, he said, and two out of every three people he saw here spoke no English.

As to the battle of Fontenoy, it is rather stale news; but as an allusion to it has been equally "misconstrued," and as we are assured that our fifty thousand Irish soldiers will not fight unless justice to their personal conduct in that battle is done, we publish the true history of that immortal day, won by the Irish brigade, under Lally, an Irishman, born in Dauphiné, France, who was an officer in the French artillery. In this faith was the present writer reared, and often has he been disgusted and astonished by the mendacious accounts of that battle in French histories and encyclopædias. While perusing them, the well-informed reader often asks himself, where, then, is the Irish brigade? When is Lord Clare about to begin? When will O'Brien rush on? But they never rush on in the French accounts. The Irish brigade fills only half sentences, and is always second; while the authentic accounts universally represent the whole French army broken and running away, with King Louis foremost, and the Irish coming forward and winning the victory by themselves. *Such* is the "exploit of this Irish brigade," at Fontenoy, to which allusion was made in this paper. It is hoped that no further unkind misconstructions will be made. The Irish are the bravest soldiers of all the armies of the world; they have won all the victories in all countries, except in one,—and that exception is, doubtless, due to the fact that the mercenary auxiliaries they have with them elsewhere, are not in their places there, as they should be.

OCTOBER 27, 1863.

"THE very interesting colored barber, direct from Richmond," whose arrival in Washington and whose revelations of life in Richmond were thought of sufficient importance to be telegraphed to the New York *Times*, has turned up in that city with "a handkerchief full of locks of hair, shorn from the heads of rebel notables, obtained in the course of business," and has been doing a good stroke of trade by selling them to the fanatical dupes. A special meeting, to receive him and hear his stories, was held in the basement of Cheever's church; reporters were in attendance, and the particulars are given in a copy of the *Tribune* of the 32d futuro, which was forwarded to us by an obliging friend in the signal corps, and received at a late hour last night. We have room only for a few of the most remarkable passages:—

"Quite a collection of prominent ladies and gentlemen were assembled last evening in the basement of the Rev. Dr. Cheever's church, to pay their respects to the very interesting colored barber from Richmond, whose arrival in this city has been anticipated with so much anxiety. Among the celebrities present, we noticed Mr. Greeley, of the *Tribune*; Mr. Raymond, of the *Times*; Mr. Stephen Pearl Andrews; Miss Dix; Professor Fowler; Mrs. Kemble; Dr. Hodge, of Princeton Seminary; Dr. Guernsey, of *Harper's Monthly*; Rev. Dr. Pyne; Dr. Cheever; Mrs. Swisshelm, and others. The meeting was opened with prayer, by the Rev. Dr. Cheever, who then introduced the distinguished guest, Mr. Jupiter McFarland, a tall, salmon-colored gentleman, about thirty years of age, quite handsome, with intelligent black eyes, hair almost straight, and a decidedly pleasing address. After shaking hands with the principal personages, Mr. McFarland, who 'has in his veins the best blood of Virginia,' stood up in the middle of the centre aisle, and answered in an audible tone, the questions put to him by Dr. Cheever and others. His education being imperfect, Mr. McFarland's English was not altogether elegant; but his melodious tones and his frank directness of manner made him easily understood."

We pass over the incidents of his escape, which are minutely, and no doubt falsely narrated, and come at once to the important questions and answers, as given by the reporter, who makes a feeble attempt to imitate the mulatto lingo.

" Q. Are you acquainted with the rebel leaders ?"

" A. Yes, sir; intimately. They come regular to my shop to get shaved."

" Q. All of them ?"

" A. All 'cept Mr. Benjamin and the 'Torney Gen'ral; they is too busy."

" Q. Does Jeff. Davis come?"

" A. Yes, he is de fust one, every mornin,' sure as de sun shines."

" Q. What sort of a man is he?"

" A. Well, he don't cuss none sence he jined the Church, but he is potty rambunktious when he can't git no good segars from Cuby to smoke."

" Q. Do the people like him?"

" A. Some un'em does and some un'em doesn't. Them that lives in the Departments swars by him, but the rest says he apint mean gen'rals, just to spite the people."

" Q. His cabinet fear him very much, do they not?"

" A. Well, as for cabinet-makers, thar hain't but mighty few left; most un'em havin' took to makin' coffins." [Suppressed laughter.]

" Q. There are a great many deaths in the city, then?"

" A. Yes, sir; we has berried nigh on'to four millions of 'Fedrit soldiers since the war begun." [Sensation.]

" Q. Does Jeff. Davis get shaved every day?"

" Q. No, he gits shampood; and then he sits in a cheer and smokes, and spits about, and talks politics to his friends."

" Q. What other persons come to your shop?"

" A. Mr. Letchers comes to git his hair curled, and so does Mr. Seddons. Mr. Memminger and the Press Gen'ral, Mr. Northup, they comes to git their mustaches confumed, and bathes together."

" Q. You don't mean to say they bathe in the same tub, at the same time?"

" A. Yes, I do; they washes one another with castile soap. They is great friends, and plays into each other's hands."

" Q. How do they do that?"

" A. Why, Mr. Memminger, he makes money accordin' to the claims of the Press Gen'ral; and the Press Gen'ral, he is a fierce old man; he says, he bedam if he aint going to press every thing the people raise to eat, so as to make expenses light."

"*Q.* There is great scarcity of food in Richmond, then?"

"*A.* Yes; people dies every day of starvation."

"*Q.* That's the reason there are so many mobs of women?"

"*A.* Not adzackly; for Govermint is afeard of their risin, like they did last winter, and so they gives 'em plenty of money; but it's mostly the rich planters that's been drove away from home and lost every thing, that perishes for the want of something to eat, and is 'shamed to say any thing about it." [Loud and prolonged applause.]

"*Question by* Mr. GREELEY.—How about the rebel rams?"

"*A.* I declar', sir, I don't know. I aint taste sheep meat for two year. I don't love it."

[The merriment of the audience at this unexpected reply, says the *Tribune* reporter, could not be repressed, the lecture room shook with laughter, in which Mr. McFarland joined when his mistake was explained to him. He then stated that the rebels had three or four rams completed, and about two dozen more, of the largest size, well under way, at the little town of Fluvanna, about five miles above Richmond.]

"*Question by* Miss DIX.—There are a great many low women in the city, are there not?"

"*A.* I don't know, old Mistiss—"

"MISS DIX, *interrupting.*—I am your sister, not your mistress; recollect you are free now."

"*A.* So I is. I forgot dat. Well, sister, the women is mostly about your height, some a leetle higher, may be."

"*By* Mr. PEARL ANDREWS.—Society is in a very disorganized state, I imagine?"

"*A.* A good deal that way. Since the war broke out the furriners has quit comin' with their organs and monkeys."

"*By* Mr. RAYMOND.—How long do the rebels think the war will last?"

"*A.* About five-and-twenty year, unless the flour and meal gives out."

"*Q.* I suppose they hate us very heartily?"

"*A.* They don't do nothin' else; and the little boys is worse than the grown folks. If they catches any of your men in the street, trying to git back home, they chokes 'em down and takes 'em in the back yard of the cullerd folks jails, and turns bull-dogs and bloodhounds onto 'em tell they tears 'em to pieces. Cap'n Alexander, at the Libby, has got a big hound that has eat at least two hundred prisoners alive. But they never lets this be known." [Intense indignation and excitement, especially among the ladies.]

"*Q.* Money is very scarce in Richmond, isn't it?"

"*A.* Thar's plenty on it, but it don't buy nothin' because the Govermint ain't got the sense to manage its business. When I was in Washington, Mr. Chaste larfed at his brother Secretary, as he called him, and said he could wind him around his little finger. He had been patterning hard after him, but that had just brought him into trouble, for the two countries warnt in the same fix at all."

[This financial revelation of the Richmond darkey was hailed as a positive proof of the great intellectual capacity of the African, and elicited many compliments from Raymond. At least, this is what the Yankee reporter says.]

" *Question by* General McClellan, *who had just come in.*—How many troops are there in and around Richmond ?"

"*A.* A good many. Thar is the Armory Band and the City Battalion, and Gen'ral Brown's horse company, and the militia, and about a thousand hundred niggers."

" *Q.* Are the negroes armed ?"

" *A.* Yes, sir. They makes out like they was working on the fortifications, but they has as many and good arms as anybody. I seen 'em."

" *Q.* Who commands the whole force ?"

" *A.* I haint sartin for sure, but I expect Cap'n Freeman and Gen'ral Brown, the President's fust cuzzin."

[Here says the *Tribune* reporter, the important part of the conversation ended, and Mr. McFarland opened his handkerchief and disposed of a lot of hair trinkets, made out of the capillary excrescence of the noted rebels, male and female, whom he had, at various times, attended in his capacity of barber. Most of the articles brought high figures. A lock of Jeff. Davis' hair sold for $10 ; a curl of Governor Letcher's for $5, and a neat watch-guard, made of the plaited tresses of two kinds of beautiful hair, one straight and the other curly, but sweetly harmonizing, was knocked down to Mr. Greeley at $40. Bracelets made of the hair of other secesh belles sold at less remarkable rates, but Mr. McFarland must have netted between $300 and $400 by the night's operation, " with a few more left of the same sort," which may be had on application to him at his lodgings, with Miss Dix, on East Thirty-fourth Street. The doxology was sung, the benediction pronounced by a clergyman from Boston, whose name we did not catch, and the meeting broke up harmoniously.]

NOVEMBER 3, 1863.

The war, with all its long train of evils, has furnished nothing comparable in depth of tragic interest and intensity of pathos to the grief of Meade when he found that Lee had retired without fighting. Rather than that Lee should have escaped without a battle, *ipse dixit*, he would have lost an eye-tooth. Here is "the touch of nature that makes the whole world kin." We cannot all be generals or statesmen : but we can all appreciate the pain of drawing a tooth. All can appreciate, then, the magnitude of the sacrifice that Meade was prepared to make. History records no greater act of self-abnegation than this. Agamemnon yielding up Iphigenia, Richard III. immolating his nephews, or the Virginia Legislature abolishing the faro-banks, are not more heroic.

It is strange what apparently contradictory appearances sometimes conceal the real wishes of men. With all this anxiety on the part of Meade, it had really seemed that he avoided the battle that Lee pressed upon him instead of courting it. Could Lee not be forced to fight? O! Marius, if thou art a great general, come down and fight. O! Sylla, if thou art a great general, make me come down and fight.

In this fearful calamity which has overtaken Meade, he has the satisfaction, at least, of being sustained by his countrymen. That singular people display one amiable trait of character, which is refreshing to note as a change amidst the stream of vituperation that has poured upon them for the last two years. They are always in the best possible humor with themselves. If they are disgracefully routed at Bull Run, they actually seem to glory in the completeness of their defeat and the exaggeration of their panic. If they gain an advantage by dint of overwhelming numbers or a combination of land and sea forces, it is straightway magnified into the greatest victory since Marathon. If defeated, they congratulate themselves on escaping complete annihilation. If they are foiled in advancing and forced to fly, all disappointment at the failure of their plan is lost in admiration of the skillful retreat. Under all circumstances they are faithful to this optimist philosophy.

The Yankees excel in the art of description, as in all other matters. No feat of arms has passed uncelebrated. In fact the warriors have been more deficient than the poets. In default of those brilliant victories which it was expected would be furnished so abundantly by their generals, these men of the pen have been forced to invent, and to atone for deficiency of skill or prowess by fertility of imagination. They surveyed the field and talked in sounding phrase of "the Grand Army with its right resting upon the Mississippi and its left upon the Atlantic."

Great commanders have been, more or less, celebrated for skill in particular departments of the science of war. Hannibal was famed for ambushes and stratagems; Frederic, for handling cavalry; Napoleon, especially, for his celerity of movement and relentless pursuit. The Yankees seized the vacant post of priority in conducting retreats. Xenophon, it is true, gained immortal honor by the retreat of the Ten Thousand. Moreau, in modern times, distinguished himself by the retreat through the Black Forest. Yet these generals did not rest their fame exclusively on these feats. It was reserved for Meade and some other Yankee generals to attain the highest summit of renown by the skillful performance of retrograde movements alone.

Brilliant as is the reputation he has won for himself in this war, Meade evidently aspires to something more. Hence the affecting declaration respecting the eye-tooth. Let him beware lest he be toppled from his present pinnacle. The nation he serves is somewhat fickle. They praise a general one day and revile him the next. They wheedle and pet the victim while they are actually whetting the knife to decapitate him. Was there ever a nation in which a question could arise like that between Burnside and Hooker, where the latter's fate trembled in the balance and he hardly escaped being ignominiously broken in order to rise to be commander-in-chief. With such masters the most skilful retreats will fail to avert one's ruin.

NOVEMBER 4, 1863.

WITH that fondness for analogies which is so characteristic of all theorists, writers on both sides of the great controversy between the North and the South, have endeavored to set forth the relations between the members of the old Union under almost every conceivable form of partnership. But, oddly enough as it might seem, if we looked merely at the surface, the Southerners, in spite of their traditional, hot-blooded, impulsive temperament, have always taken the quiet, business-like view of the connection between the two divisions of the late model republic, and have invariably represented it under the figure of a mercantile firm; while the Yankees, who had palmed themselves off on their own tribe, and on the rest of the world as cool, unpoetical calculators, have as uniformly developed an astonishing amount of maudlin sentimentality whenever this subject has been broached. Notorious as they are for the matter-of-course way in which they are wont to put off the ties of nature, they could yet grow eloquent when descanting on the brotherhood of all American citizens, or the sisterhood of the States. When first secession "reared its awful form," they called us "erring brethren," and "wayward sisters," "rebellious brethren," and "estranged sisters," "a little more than kin and less than kind," and so they ran on through all the gamut of appropriate epithets to their unfraternal relatives of the South. Then they became still more affectionate as we grew less fond, and next assumed the paternal type; Uncle Sam found out that his nieces were his own children; and imported citizens in Wisconsin and Minnesota mourned in High Dutch, and wept in lager beer over the unfilial conduct of South Carolina and Georgia. But the climax of sentimentality for the North, and of insult to the South, was attained when the Yankee worked himself up to the amatory pitch, and represented the Union of the States under the symbol of wedlock—the Northern States the bridegroom, and the Southern, the bride. We all remember how the fit idol of these modern Egyptians, their god Anubis, their chosen chief, Abraham Lincoln, aired this comparison on his way to Washington, and how he enlivened the parallel by ribald allusions to free love and elective affinities.

We said that the difference between the modes of representation might have seemed strange in view of the popular conception of Northern and Southern character; but the fact is, that the true standard-bearers of the South—her statesmen and her thinkers—were never so much given to bursts of sympathy as the declamatory champions of the North; and now that the fiery trial of actual warfare has brought out the stamp of each nationality in clear outlines, no one should wonder that the Yankees have the monopoly of the sentimental department; for sentiment is always idle, always selfish; real feeling alone is active and self-sacrificing. Still we have too high an estimate of Yankee shrewdness to suppose that these displays of rhetoric are meant for any other ears than those of the groundlings; and the initiated have, no doubt, a far different idea of the real nature of the Union. They are not imposed upon by brotherhoods and sisterhoods, by the bonds of a "common descent, a common language, and a common history." They, too, take a business view of the connection, and look upon the Union as a great life insurance bubble. And how well they understand the working of such institutions our Southern policy-holders know to their cost. The peculiar form of insurance company after which the Union, as they have it, was framed, is technically called a Tontine, and the brief exposition of the system is conveyed in the familiar regulation, "The longest liver takes all." The Southern States, according to them, had so many inherent elements of weakness, that they were to die out, and the North was to succeed, by virtue of survivorship, to the rents of their less vigorous neighbors, and, meanwhile, by dexterous management in the board of directors, to cheat them out of any annuities which might be due. But the process of dying out was very slow. Some of the incorrigible Southern shareholders actually had the impudence to increase and multiply at a time of life when such behavior was a breach of good taste, if not of good breeding; and Virginia, the oldest representative of the Southern branch, though declared *effete* a thousand times; though shown by skilful Northern diagnosis to be suffering from dropsy of the brain, tubercles in the lungs, cancer of the stomach, phthisis, enteritis, borborygmus, and a general complication of disorders, suddenly took a new lease of life to the great discomfiture of the Northern shareholders, and bade fair to prolong her span by a couple of centuries. In short, it soon became evident that the "course of ultimate extinction" was very tardy, and it was deemed expedient to aid nature a little. As the Tontine was an Italian device, Italy, the mother of poisons, slow and quick, and the home of the stiletto, was appealed to for help, and not in vain. But the slow poisons were too slow; the quick poisons only acted as emetics, and the stiletto glanced from the ribs of the Southrons. Then they tried to smother us in our sleep between feather-beds of compromise measures, and to strangle us by a cordon of "free States." Wholesale murder—the last resort of Yankees as of kings—is their present experiment, and it promises to succeed no better—nay, to be a more lamentable failure for them than their previous efforts.

If we drop the parable and ask ourselves, with becoming seriousness, which of the two contending social systems has better stood the test of this "storm and pressure" period, we may well look for a cheering response to the question. Here the devil's livery of Red and Black—Black Republicanism faced with Red Republicanism— finds no wearer. Our hodden-gray is sadly threadbare, but it is an honest dress, and we need not be ashamed of it. Here no conflicting interests array section against section. Here no foreign element threatens to absorb and assimilate our native culture. Here we do not feel the weight of a leaden tyrant in every breath we draw; we are men and walk erect.

They said that we were tyrants dancing on a slumbering volcano, and as soon as the Yankee stokers stirred up the sluggish mass, we would be consumed. The Yankee stokers have stirred up the sluggish mass, and there has been no explosion. The South can never be a St. Domingo, in spite of all that the ingenuity of Yankee hate can do; for our negroes are better Christians and truer gentlemen than their would-be liberators. Nor are we much disturbed at the opprobrious title of oligarchs. Oligarchies are bad enough for those who do not like them, but they have the advantage of a tough vitality; and, oligarchy or not, our form of government and our social organization give promise of a longer life than the mob-rule of the North, with attendant man-worships and monkey-worships. Not that we think ours is the best of possible republics, and the present the most agreeable epoch in the world's history. There are endless abuses rife in the Confederacy, and many a man since the beginning of the war, has wished to change places with his grandfather or his grandson; but the fabric of our social life remains, as a whole, unshaken, and in lieu of pleasure we must console ourselves with the philosophical reflection, that, after all, happiness is not the highest good, and that our descendants will wish that they had lived in the stirring times of the Great Revolution.

NOVEMBER 7, 1863.

An obvious and striking peculiarity of the war is the complete ignorance manifested on both sides as to the resources, views and sentiments of their adversaries. This, in itself a noteworthy phenomenon, is likewise a key to the solution of many problems connected with the origin and duration of the struggle. It was this blindness—the arrogant confidence arising from it—that urged the aggressors to persevere in the destructive policy which caused the war. The same cause produced the gradual expansion of the struggle. To it are to be attributed the apparent failure to appreciate the true importance of the crisis—common to both sides—the make-shift policy, and the continual expectation of a speedy termination of hostilities which have filled the general mind with such a series of illusions. Both countries may be said—as Lord Aberdeen said of England in the rupture with Russia—to have "drifted into war."

It is now apparent even to the Yankees themselves that they had grossly miscalculated the power and the temper of the Southern people. The South fell into an error similar in character, though not equal in degree. Her statesmen clearly saw that the marvellous wealth and prosperity of the North was based upon that of the South. They then jumped to the conclusion that the damming up of this abundant source would at once cripple Yankee power and preclude the possibility of a great war. They knew, too, that the character of the hostile people was averse to enterprises of doubtful gain, and they confidently argued that sober reflection would deter the Yankees from the gigantic effort to conquer a whole and united people. In this reasoning they underestimated the power of that accumulated wealth which seven decades of prosperity had collected in the populous centres of the North, and overlooked the pecuniary resources that could be brought into play by the dexterous working of financial machinery. Nor did they foresee, to its full extent, the power which the dominant faction would obtain of controlling so entirely the full resources of their people and of stimulating them by the combined operation of appeals to interest and patriotism and by the pressure of terrorism. From these mutual mistakes each nation has seen its task swell into giant proportions.

Inscrutable as the future now appears, there are some cheering indications of the final crash which is destined to overtake the invader, unless he can gain more decisive advantages than any he has obtained since the tide was first turned against him after the fall of New Orleans.

Our surgeons say that the Confederate wounded display much greater fortitude in the endurance of suffering than the Yankees. They attribute it to the high spirit of the men. In the same way, a tithe of the distress, borne unmurmuringly by a large part of the Southern people, would drive the masses of the North to despair.

NOVEMBER 12, 1863.

The various shifts adopted to supply the want of some general organic provision for the withdrawal of the surplus circulation of Confederate notes, and their reduction into funded debt, have all failed of their object. Men no longer impose implicit confidence in Confederate bonds. Now and then we hear the old patriotic phrases: "If these bonds are not good, nothing is good; for if we are subjugated we can call nothing our own." But men are beginning to see the want of logical sequence in this popular syllogism; and it is now conceivable that the Government might be bankrupt, and yet the country not subjugated. The old view is the better for the honor of our cause; but the new mode of looking at the matter is certainly in accordance with experience. As Machiavelli saw, long ago, gold and silver are not the sinews of war; and we can thrash the Yankees with empty pockets, as we have thrashed them with ragged trousers, and jackets out at elbows.

All patriotic considerations have lost their weight in the general demoralization attendant on a prolonged war. The people are disgusted with the confusion and uncertainty which the waxing plethora of paper money has introduced into every department of business and every branch of domestic economy. No one knows what to charge for his wares, except that he cannot charge too much. An advance of thirty or forty per cent. a week on articles of prime necessity, is a phenomenon that has ceased to excite the slightest astonishment; and in the general despair of a fixed standard, some are reverting to the clumsy method of barter; some are making contracts, to be adjusted at a distant future, in which, it is hoped, the relations of value will be more settled than they are at present.

This disgust extends itself to the externals of Confederate money, —as well it may. The people are disgusted with every shade of Confederate notes; with every line of the coarse engravings; with the lopsided capitol at Richmond; with the portraits of distinguished cabinet officers and statesmen, who frown or smirk from their pillory in the vignettes. Any change would be welcomed which should put Mr. Memminger's assignats out of sight—"anywhere, anywhere out of the world."

We count largely, then, on the general loathing, on this surfeit of paper and printers' ink; and, under the pressure of the popular opinion, Congress will doubtless attempt to devise some comprehensive and vigorous measures for reducing the inflated currency and preventing the return of this paper deluge. To be effective, these measures must be simple, and the personal agency required be reduced to a minimum. Expedition is all-important under the circumstances. The operation of the stringent measures of a comprehensive and expeditious system may seem harsh in individual cases, but cannot be harsher than the conscription system, which has blighted the prospects of tens of thousands, and marred some of their noblest and dearest plans of life. Like the conscription, it will teach men that they belong to their country and not to themselves, —a lesson which is not always best learned by voluntary sacrifices. Of course the system must be carried out thoroughly, and to this end it must be self-working, so far as human wit can devise. Trust to personal agency and we shall have but another illustration of the old saw, " a good beginning makes a bad ending." It was of a financial reform that Tacitus wrote, *Acribus ut ferme talia initiis, incurioso fine.*

NOVEMBER 14, 1863.

IF the reputation of the Yankee Secretary of State as a statesman depended upon what is generally regarded as the highest attribute of that character, and were to be measured by the degree of foresight exhibited in his various predictions, he would be deemed totally unfitted to hold the helm in times of tempest. During that period of plethoric peace which carried material prosperity to such a height in the United States, and stimulated so greatly the passion of gain, Seward was qualified to be one of the rulers of men. Subtle chicanery and dexterity in party tactics, supplied the place of those broad principles of generalization which are necessary to secure the highest and most permanent welfare of a nation. In such times, the adroit leader of a faction seems to be endowed with all the qualities that confer success. The triumph of a party is considered synonymous with the prosperity of the State.

It is no matter of surprise that the remarkable skill displayed by Seward in forming and directing the energies of a party, should have won him the reputation of a consummate statesman among his colaborers. He himself did not, evidently, appreciate the magnitude of the new circumstances by which he was surrounded, when, on his advent to power, he found himself face to face with a great revolution, to which his own efforts had, contrary to his expectation, so powerfully contributed. With that incapacity to appreciate the true value of great events, so characteristic of narrow minds, he looked upon the agitation of a nation's heart as the ebullition of a disappointed faction. Hence those ridiculous prophecies of a restoration of concord and re-establishment of the Union repeated with such perseverance, long after they provoked the derision of the world.

He is now chary of making predictions, to be accomplished in a limited time, though this veteran intriguer still extends his view to those whom he is pleased to term "his Southern brethren." To serve the purposes of metaphor, we have been forced to fill nearly all the modes of relationship with our would-be Yankee brethren. We have been barbarous ingrates to the tenderest of mothers; then we have sought to dissever the bonds of conjugal union; we have been erring sisters; Cain-like brothers; and now Seward felicitously depicts us under the type of the Prodigal Son.

He assures us that the fatted calf will be slain upon our repentant return. Neither men nor angels can prevent that, he says. As to the men of his own region, his knowledge may entitle him to speak; but his means of ascertaining the opinions of the angels is not so clear. Neither is it evident why the angels should be desirous of forbidding the feast, even had they the power, which he positively denies them. Ever since he compared himself to the Saviour, upon the taking of Vicksburg, his knowledge of heavenly matters must be taken for granted, and we are bound to suppose that he possesses equal sources of information upon two subjects so essentially distinct as the power of the angels and the movements of New York politicians.

The prodigal son was abandoned to his evil courses until, having wasted his substance in riotous living, he sought the shelter of the paternal roof. Thus, too, Mr. Seward declines to extend us any invitation, although he is ready to give us so cordial a welcome back. May we not suggest to him the propriety of following his exemplar with more exactness? The father of that dissolute young man did not attempt to reclaim him by force. He awaited the natural consequence of his conduct, and when his own misfortunes caused him to return, he was joyfully received. Let Mr. Seward advise Lincoln, who must be taken as the impersonation of the venerable and sorrowful father, to withdraw his armies and endure a little while, until the repentance, which will soon take possession of his undutiful son, drives him to seek admission into the paternal mansion. The longer he persists in his evil courses, the more thorough will be his repentance, according to Seward. Let no obstacle, then, be opposed to the consummation of the good work, but let him rather be encouraged to persist until the harvest is ripe. In the mean time we can assure Mr. Seward that the South has already much reformed, especially in the article of riotous living. True, we pay very high prices, as he has no doubt heard, but our estate is not seriously diminished by them, since the great magician who converts leaves into money by a stroke of the wand, defrays all our expenses.

Then, again, the Northern statesman changes the metaphor, and regards us as a property, of which Abraham Lincoln has been unjustly defrauded, and appeals to those natural principles of justice which warrant the possession of his goods to every owner. We are compared to horses, boats, or houses, and Lincoln is said to be merely defending himself against robbery. Here it might possibly have suggested itself to him that the argument was susceptible of another turn, and might have done duty on the Southern side. Without the faintest appearance of consciousness, or the least blush of shame, he goes further, and insists upon the natural right of defending one's country. Not the glimmer of a doubt appears that the South may be engaged at this moment in that laudable work, and the inference is irresistible, that, in taking possession of our country, the Yankees are only reclaiming what is their own, and that the sectional vote which gave Lincoln proprietary rights over the country, carries, as a corollary, the ownership of the soil and its produce. His subjects are well disposed to acquiesce in this view of the case. The good old rule sufficeth them, the simple plan, " that they should take who have the power, and they should keep who can."

Mr. Seward seems to ignore human feeling altogether in his calculations as to " his final success in the great work of restoring the Union." In the blandness of his own nature he can see no obstacle in the three years of war to prevent a re-union of North and South. The thousands of victims, the laceration of war, and the catalogue of sufferings that follow in its train, are not valid reasons why their memory should not be obliterated, and Southern men give the hand of friendship and political association to those who have inflicted upon them all the woes that invasion and conquest accumulate upon the heads of a devoted people. Let him read human nature, not as developed in the pulseless frigidity of his own heart, but as mirrored in the stream of history.

NOVEMBER 20, 1863.

IT is a wise provision of nature for the happiness of the human species, though it may not be so conducive to its solid improvement that renders us blind to our own weaknesses and ridiculous traits. In vain does the disinterested good-nature of our friends seek, by open remonstrance or subtle innuendo, to enlighten us and lead us in the path of reform. We obstinately refuse to be convinced, and assure our well-wishers, with as much confidence as the Archbishop of Grenada did Gil Blas in the affair of his sermons, that they are entirely mistaken: faults we have, of course, but the particular foible they have selected for animadversion is the very one from which we are entirely free. Thus, too, a dandy of the Tittlebat Titmouse stamp often struts along with the air of most perfect satisfaction, entirely unconscious that he is a subject of ridicule to the critical public, and attributing the smiles provoked by his bad taste to the admiration he excites. All of us are reluctant to acknowledge our imperfections. Even the pious Christian, who, in the fervor of his humility, lifts up his voice on the Sabbath, accuses himself of all the sins in the decalogue, and grovels in the dust with the worm, has a dim and consoling consciousness in the background that he is, by no means, the abject creature he professes himself to be. Out of this prostrate and hebdomadal state of abasement he knows that he is to rise to a glorified week of existence, and that, for six consecutive days, he will have the proud satisfaction of being lauded by the community as a most excellent member of society, and a bright ornament to the church. All his protestations of his worthlessness are to be taken in a Pickwickian sense. He does not intend that God shall believe him too implicitly.

Even if this disposition to see every thing relating to ourselves in a roseate hue impedes our progress in some respects, yet it makes ample amends in the happiness it gives. Setting aside the prosaic realities of life, such as eating and drinking, which no force of imagination can entirely dispense with, illusion is a much greater constituent of human happiness than reality. Surely it is better to live in that fairy world where the glittering veil of self-conceit hides every deformity, and softens every line of beauty, than to have the chilling touch of displeasing reality continually pressed upon us. Better continue hugging our frailties, in the belief that they are virtues, than to aim at a distant ideal, whose difficulty of access depresses our spirits and unbraces our energy. "Know thyself" was very bad advice to the mass of mankind.

Never was this principle of philosophy so beautifully illustrated as in the case of that most interesting and advanced nation, whose chief business for some time past has been to cut our throats and steal our property, all in the name of civilization and humanity. For the last three years they have been the objects of the almost unmixed derision and abhorrence of the whole world. Their attempts at the magnificent and the heroic have been hailed with shouts of "inextinguishable laughter," while their cold-blooded barbarity has excited the opposite emotion of horror. Scarcely a dissentient voice has been heard, save from those whose fanatic enthusiasm would lead them to approve any enormities in the holy cause, as they deem it, or from those, the identity of whose situation and principles renders them sympathetic with every form of tyranny. It is useless to cite the opinion of the Southern people, as their testimony would be naturally subject to suspicion, it being evidently difficult for men who have been chased from their homes, despoiled of their property, or wounded in their affections, to judge the perpetrators of these acts with impartiality. The testimony of the neutral world is sufficiently clear.

How wretched would we suppose that nation to be under this load of obloquy! We know them to be very thin-skinned. We know how miserable they were made by the satire of Trollope and Dickens; how it cut them to the soul to be ridiculed for eating with their knives, talking through their noses, or indulging in the cross-examination of travellers. Even now they are reviling Dickens for his ingratitude in abusing them after the kind reception and the magnificent ball they gave him. They taunt the British nation with its base requital of the honor done the Prince of Wales in lending a semi-recognition to the Confederacy and building it a few ships. With true commercial instinct they looked upon their balls and parades as judicious ventures, which were to bring them in good returns. The pen of the novelist and the alliance of a nation were to be bought at the cheap rate of a plentiful supper and the precious boon of an association with a select company of New York aldermen, with women to match. On this principle Thackeray's vocation were gone. Every snob would catch him up and invite him to dinner, and gratitude would seal the mouth of the caustic satirist.

Strange to say, the Yankees who winced under the sting of irony and satire, seem now to be as impervious to these lighter missiles, and to the heavy artillery of invective, as their own iron-clads. The abuse they return with interest. They stand up with matchless effrontery against the condemnation of the whole world, and impudently claim to be the model people of the globe.

The monarchs of Europe rejoice in the discredit the Yankees brought upon the cause of republicanism, and feel that their example of democratic misgovernment has strengthened the cause of despotism more than mighty armies could have done. That brilliant light of the model republic which once threatened to be a firebrand to the monarchical system of the world has now become a beacon to warn the nations of the perils of democracy. Such is the work the Yankees have accomplished in the last three years.

Yet in the midst of their confusion and disgrace, with organized anarchy enthroned over them, shamefully beaten in the field by a nation of a third of their numbers, they have the impudence to assert that Europe is amazed and awe-struck at the stability of their institutions. They obstinately refuse to see themselves and their deeds from the stand-point that they are viewed by the rest of the world. Certainly, for their present happiness, they may be thankful that they are blind; let them rejoice that nature, when she affixes the brand of vice and meanness upon her creatures, kindly deprives them of the power of appreciating their misfortunes.

NOVEMBER 25, 1863.

There is but a single ground upon which the privilege of [supplying their prisoners in the Confederacy with rations and other necessaries can be accorded to the Yankee Government. Of the two horns of the dilemma so tauntingly offered us, we can accept only that which exposes our poverty in defending our humanity. We cannot acknowledge that we are, in the malignant language of our enemies, "desperately barbarous," and therefore neglectful of the usages of civilized war. We must, then, gratify their hate by avowing that we are "desperately poor," and, being unable to supply these suffering patriots with the numerous comforts their grateful country desires for them, we are forced to devolve upon their compatriots, native or adopted, the pleasing task of furnishing those luxuries which the ravages of war or the strictness of the blockade preclude the Confederacy from giving them.

The Yankee policy with respect to the exchange of prisoners has been clearly exposed. It is based upon the simple principle that our men are intrinsically worth more than theirs, and that if they continue to hold our prisoners and to allow their own to remain in our hands they will be the gainers. Such, in fact, is the whole scheme of the war. If, by dint of superior numbers and a lavish expenditure of blood, they can inflict such losses upon the South as to render it incapable of further resistance, their point, they think, is gained. It is useless to say that this reasoning is as stupid in a military, as it is shocking, in a moral point of view. But it carries conviction to the minds of a set of men whose conduct has proceeded upon the assumption that superiority of numbers rendered success a mathematical certainty.

While this savage and cold-blooded idea is at the bottom of their reasoning, they are aware that it is necessary to cloak their purposes under as decent a veil as they can find. It will not do to tell their soldiers, or the classes from which they expect to recruit their armies, that they regard them merely as fighting animals, to be used sparingly, or sacrificed wantonly, according to the varying necessities of the case. It would be ruinous frankly to avow that they are delighted to retain a certain number of Confederates in prison at the expense of an equal or even greater number of their own men. An excuse must be found which will throw the odium of refusing exchange, upon the Confederacy. Yankee ingenuity, unhampered by the restraints of an adherence to truth, can easily accomplish this. Is the Confederate Government prepared to aid them in this notable scheme? Are we to submit to the inauguration of a system which dooms our prisoners to hopeless captivity? Shall we allow these invaders of our soil to be supplied with all the luxuries which the abundance of the means at the disposal of their Government can furnish them, while our brave men are to suffer the rigors of a Northern climate, to be exposed to the brutal tyranny of Yankee officials, or to the no less repugnant exhibition of an insidious appearance of kindness which aims, in conjunction with the depressing influence of time and captivity, at sapping their allegiance to their country? It is earnestly to be hoped that no such concession will be made to our faithless foe. We have sought to carry out the cartel of exchange in good faith. Let us not allow the Yankees to take advantage of their own wrong, and, while they avoid the odium attaching to the desertion of their prisoners, retain the advantage of neutralizing thousands of our soldiers.

That such is their object there can be no doubt. The unwilling tribute of an enemy's praise belongs, in the fullest measure, to our gallant soldiers. Gladly would the Yankee Government, in order to deprive us of their services, agree to lodge them at the Fifth Avenue or the Metropolitan, and to feed them upon turtle soup and champagne. It would be a vastly cheaper way of disposing of them than maintaining armies of hirelings to oppose them in the field.

Let our enemies be distinctly informed that their prisoners are as well treated as the condition of the country permits; that they are not exposed to as great privations as our own brave troops; and, that if they are forced to drink the muddy water of the James, it is a hardship shared with them by the citizens of Richmond, who have learned to bear it with fortitude. Let them be told, moreover, that if real scarcity is to try our people, it is neither proper nor prudent that they should witness the spectacle of thousands of well-fed men who have been the direct agents of their own sufferings, while they are pinched with hunger. Common sense will show that grave consequences might ensue from such a state of things. Let them be told that if they wish to relieve these men, it can be done at once by the legitimate operation of the cartel.

NOVEMBER 26, 1863.

THE result of General Bragg's useless and unsuccessful attempt to hold a worthless position in front of Chattanooga, will not disappoint any over-sanguine anticipations of the public mind. The Confederate army did very little harm from Lookout Mountain to the Federal forces in Chattanooga. Under these circumstances, a retreat to the old field of Chickamauga appeared reasonable and was expected by the country. But General Bragg held his position until forced from it.

How has it happened that, with his splendid army and with unquestioned superiority of position, he has sustained an acknowledged reverse? The answer will be made with considerable unanimity, that General Bragg is incompetent to command—that he is maintained in his important position by Mr. Davis against the judgment and protest of both country and army; that neither troops nor officers have confidence in him; that he has lost battle after battle by a faulty arrangement of his troops and want of military talent; and that it is right and reasonable to suppose that he has lost another in the same way.

The result is, that we have lost on Lookout Mountain the advantages gained in the great and bloody battle of Chickamauga. That battle must be fought again, either in the next fortnight or in the spring of 1864. Now, will Mr. Jefferson Davis any longer persist in maintaining General Bragg in the command of the army on which depends the fate of the Gulf States? This is an inquiry which will be anxiously made by every citizen who reads the news this morning, and who really desires the success of this Confederacy. If that general is kept in place in despite of all the proofs that he is the wrong man for such a business, it is possible that the Confederate army may incur a disaster on the banks of the Chickamauga commensurate with its former victory. But we refuse to believe that the consequences, even of a defeat in a general battle there, will be any thing like those which hasty minds assume. They would not be the loss of a State or penetration to the Gulf. The Federal army could not advance five miles farther, even if victorious, without risking annihilation, nor will the Gulf States be subjugated by the loss of one battle or twenty battles, unless they are inhabited by a very different breed from that which peoples Virginia.

NOVEMBER 27, 1863.

The shameful and lamentable ignorance which Europeans generally exhibit in regard to all matters pertaining to America, has long been a fruitful theme for all book-making tourists from the United States. Without stopping to inquire whether the complainants are justified in their indignation by their own superior knowledge of foreign parts—without stopping to examine them on the character of the Germanic Confederation, and the number, names, and geography of the States which compose that union, or to exact a minute description of the territorial domains of Austria,—we are willing to concede the ignorance alleged, although we doubt whether it is as shameful to the one party, or as lamentable to the other, as it has been commonly represented. Aside from the relations of trade, the interest of educated Europeans in America is about as lively as our interest in Australia or New Zealand. That we have attracted more attention in the last twenty years—that some American books have been read and republished on the other side of the water, is due, partly to the spread of a cosmopolitan spirit, which welcomes to its catholic embrace the last effusions of the Timbuctoo muse and the last novel of CHIN LING and MIEN FUN, as well as the latest publications of Harper and Appleton—partly to the Mutual Admiration Trans-Atlantic Telegraph Company, the working of which has profited the shareholders and amused the initiated for many a day. Of course, Yankee vanity would not admit that even benighted Europeans could be ignorant of the vast superiority of Americans in the sciences; but we admit it freely. Sad to tell, Morse is not so well known as Faraday, nor Benjamin Peirce as much revered as

Newton or Euler. The very name "American," which the citizens of the United States persistently appropriate to themselves, often seems to convey no definite idea of nationality to people unaccustomed to contrast themselves with the denizens of other quarters of the globe; for no inhabitant of Europe ever says, with becoming pride, " I am an European." The Germans, for instance, who are wont to mark sharply the lines of their " narrower fatherland," and to distinguish accurately between Hohenzollern-Sigmaringen and Hohenzollern-Hechingen—between Reuss-Greiz and Reuss-Schleiz— are sorely puzzled when their minds are allowed to expatiate over a whole boundless continent; and we cannot wonder that, at German tables, gentlemen from Terra del Fuego and Patagonia have been solemnly introduced to their "countrymen" of New York and Baltimore. As to the interior of Europe, some crude notions about primeval forests and oceanic rivers, George Washington and the War of Independence; some vague doubts as to the complexion of the inhabitants; some general conception of a country half Eldorado and half Botany Bay; some dim recollection of grisly bears, opossums and cockatoos, constitute the American idea of many people, who certainly are well-bred, and who are at least as well informed as their neighbors. Carolina rice, Virginia tobacco, and New Orleans cotton, are current terms; but Presidents were made and unmade without exciting the curiosity of the great European Sleepy Hollow; and the war of 1812;—the war with the Seminole Indians; and the war with Mexico, are not as well remembered as the exploits of the vikings and the border feuds of barons who died half a millennium ago.

But American travellers have long been known to Europe. Time was, when none but gentlemen crossed the water, first to visit their English kindred, and then to make the grand tour; but that time passed away soon after the Revolution; and for years and years it has been advisable for every American of breeding to preserve, as far as possible, a strict incognito while on his travels abroad. Americans are but too well known; too well known to the innkeeper, who speculates on their extravagance, and even then hardly repays himself for the trouble which they give; too well known in every haunt of low dissipation in the great capitals of Europe; too well known for the comfort of some of their own number, as many a man can testify, who abhorred the spread-eagle passport which he was doomed to carry in his pocket, even before that remarkable bird assumed the character of a carrion crow. Extremely annoying to the Southerners, in days gone by, was the fraternity thrust upon them by every stray Yankee; and among the various little comforts of secession, not the smallest was the full release from any Yankee claims to brotherhood on the score of a common nationality.

But although as one nation we may have been slighted heretofore, as two nations we are attracting attention enough now that all Europe has found out that there is a great struggle going on here. The conservatives of European society are generally with the South; the radicals with the North. But all this partisanship is sheer dilettantism. It means nothing. If we are defeated, Freedom's shrieks will be drowned in the bustle of other revolutions, or faintly re-echoed in the groans of a degraded and unpitied nation. If we are successful, the new Confederacy will be a nine days' wonder, and we shall at last have the honor of entering into the "system of civilized powers."

As this latter issue is, for the present, nothing but "a melancholy *utinam*"—as a quaint writer has it—it may be as well for us to look more narrowly into the way in which the Confederacy is unofficially represented in Europe. We had our suspicions, even before "diplomatic dispatches" had been intercepted by the enemy, that the Confederates now in Europe were hardly a shade better than the Federals of former days. It is a pity, if it is so, that we have but the dregs and the froth of our society to represent us abroad; and yet it must be. High-spirited men would not seek Europe in such times as these except under a solemn conviction of public duty. Great souls scorn to save themselves apart from their country. But we might hope that the Southerners who are abroad, conscious of the attention which they must attract, would at least be studious to avoid the offensive characteristics of the Yankees. They should remember that they are defendants in a suit which is not decided—a suit which involves honor as well as property, and that a decent sobriety of demeanor would be advisable during the progress of the case. How much better would it have been if, at the outbreak of the war, our Government could have ordered back by a stern ukase all Confederate sojourners in Europe (except those who could give proof of some rational occupation), under penalty of disfranchisement and confiscation of their property. Yes! better appear a magnificent nationality because unknown, than unjustly condemned because imperfectly known by our would-be representatives. We are not afraid that our merits will be exaggerated by the European public. The heroism of our true men is worthy of any age. And this is the only reputation we desire. As for diplomacy, culture, refinement and all the minor morals of social life, we will waive our claims to them until we ascertain who our representatives are. Some of our agents seem to be foreigners; and, while we may make use of their accomplishments, we can claim no national credit for them. We may be wrong. They may be native Southrons; but in all the nomenclature of Southern families, we find no such names as those they bear.

DECEMBER 1, 1863.

IT appears that Grant is doing his best to fulfil the arrogant orders of his masters, and that Bragg has been getting himself whipped again near Ringgold. Never, perhaps, in history, has the consequence of incompetent generalship, and want of confidence between commander and troops, been more manifest than at present in northern Georgia. We have no doubt that General Bragg has done the best that he could, and for all the ill that has befallen him and us, Mr. Davis alone is responsible. It is clear, that if he persists longer in the pitiful perversity which has retained Bragg in the command, in spite of remonstrance, in spite of facts, in spite of common sense and duty, that the army of Georgia will be disorganized and lost. Similar policy in the Southwest has already cost the Confederacy a great army,—one of 42,000 men, originally good soldiers; but they were disorganized by repeated defeats, in which the President's incompetent *protégé* was generally surprised, and always routed, with the loss of artillery, and finally shut up by him in a town invested on land and water, where surrender was only a question of time. Is the Confederacy about to lose a second army?

If General Bragg is longer intrusted with its destiny, the danger of such a catastrophe is really great. Let us hope that Mr. Davis is not weak enough to trifle longer with the interests of his country, and that he will immediately appoint some other man to the command. Who should that man be? Any man is better than Bragg, whatever his abilities; for towards no other man will the same distrust be felt by the troops; and, of all lackings in a general, want of confidence, faith, and affection, on the part of his officers and men, is the worst. It would be difficult to find another, save, perhaps, Pemberton and Holmes, who would not inspire more confidence than General Bragg, and almost any change would be, in this most essential particular, a benefit to the Confederate army in Georgia.

But if it is asked, who, among the officers of high rank, would most properly replace General Bragg, scarcely any man of candor could fail to answer with the name of Joseph Johnston. He is, indeed, the only man available who can at once rally, reorganize, and restore that unfortunate army. He has, it is true, been much abused by the sycophants of power, but all know that he is a general of first-class ability and knowledge. It is often said by impartial persons that he has done little in the war; that Manassas, Williamsburg, and Seven Pines are all his battles. But this much more may be said of him—that he has never incurred a single defeat, and never lost an army, not even a brigade, not a regiment.

It is, however, certain that the achievements of General Johnston in this war have not been commensurate with the public opinion of his ability; he has never had a chance, nor is there reason to hope that the President will so far forget his individuality as to give him the command of that army. If after Manassas, Johnston and Beauregard had written briefly thus: Glory to God and Davis, Bull Run's ours—they would have been wise, and might have rendered their country many services since, which they have not had the means of doing. Unfortunately, and unwisely, they wrote long dispatches, said little about the President, and gave to him no glory at all. From that day to this they have had no chance that the President could keep from them. For some cases already beyond hope, they have been summoned, to serve as scape-goats. One of these patients, however, Beauregard has redeemed and restored, and if the matter grows worse in Georgia, perhaps the Executive will remember that a Joseph Johnston still exists. Things are not at that pass now, though it is too evident that they soon will be, if the command is not instantly changed. There are many good officers,—and any of them is better than a general who has always been favored by his Government and always frowned by fortune.

DECEMBER 2, 1863.

IN calculating the chances of their ultimate success, our enemies have always counted largely, or pretended to count largely, on the weakness entailed upon us by the aristocratic character of our social organism. Certainly they have long spoken and written, and still speak and write, as if they believed that the Southern people are under the sway of a small slave-owning oligarchy, and that it is only necessary to get these factious noblemen out of the way in order to revive the Union feeling. If they are not in earnest, we cannot conceive what they mean by repeating the falsehood, unless they wish to swell their collection of "Useless Lies, which nobody can believe" as a companion volume to their compilations of "Useful Facts, which everybody ought to know;" or unless they hope to verify the remark of Henry IV. of France, "They will lie so long that they will wind up by telling the truth." However, from time to time, we have seen signs of weariness in these jabbering theorists, and the more advanced disciples of the abolitionist school are bent on extending the area of extermination beyond "the oligarchs," until it embraces the whole white population of the South. The first step in this task they have assumed is, to be the dispersion of the "rebel armies,"—a costly step. The next will be the annihilation of the guerrilla bands that will infest the country. Then, the gibbet and the axe; then, an army of executioners, imported Chinese, the most expert headsmen in the world, and native Yankees, who will soon throw the famous invention of Dr. Guillotin into the shade, and make the ghost of Sanson blush at his awkwardness.

Among the valuable auxiliaries to this depletive course, they count deportation and voluntary exile. Where the future Cayenne of the Yankee Government is to be, we do not know. We may be huddled together in the everglades of Florida; in Okeefinokee swamp; on the keys of the Gulf; or, by a treaty with the Czar, be transferred to the regions about Tobolsk and Irkutsk. The voluntary exiles will be scattered over the face of the globe.

From the very first, exile was put down deliberately among the chances of the war; but we fear that the time is passed when this heroic determination of the best people of the South would have appalled the Yankees. We suspect, rather, that they desire nothing better than a general exodus of the rebels, and so far from refusing to let us go, they would help us on our way into the wilderness, and lend us any number of gun-boats and transports if the Red Sea should not repeat its miraculous division. Indeed, the Northern press has given us numerous hints to the effect that it is time for us to collect our shattered hosts and be off to Mexico, with such bag and baggage as they have left us. Here again the old fallacy of an oligarchy peeps out. "If," they say to themselves, "if the priests, and the nobles, and the warriors of the Southern people were to 'emigrate' in a body, we could easily reduce the rest to bondage." But the priests, and the nobles, and the warriors, with their wives and children, would simply be the whole Southern people; and Brother Jonathan and Uncle Tom would alone be left to discuss the terms of surrender.

The truth is, matters will have to come to a far worse pass before it will be true patriotism in any Southerner to think seriously of abandoning his native land. Every now and then we hear of persons who have slipped out through the blockade, and who, evidently, have no intention of slipping in again. The temptation is strong, and we have no quarrel with human nature because it prefers luxury to privation, any kind of peace to any kind of war. Most of these blockade-runners are wealthy, and some of them have become wealthy by the war, or, in other words, at the expense of those who continued to bear the grievous burden from which this gentry have withdrawn their shoulders. Let them go. All cannot get into the life-boat when the ship is sinking, and then they will do as much good by sending back brandy and overcoats to the shivering passengers on the wreck, and they will describe so well the heart-rending scenes on board the foundering vessel to enthusiastic audiences around the breakfast-table and the tea-urn. But the ship is not sinking, and the enthusiastic audiences will soon lose their respect for men who took fright at the snapping of a mast or the springing of a leak; and the fellow-passengers of those who deserted the vessel with such convenient despair will hardly wish to see them on board again. As for those who venture abroad without any capital except their heads and hands, they will find that the change is not unconditionally to their advantage. It is one thing to ramble through Europe with a circular-letter of credit, another to elbow one's way to a livelihood through a crowd of eager and better qualified competitors. Our Confederate bread may lack savor, but the European bread of dependence would be too bitter salt; and while our road to glory may be a Via Dolorosa, it is not as hard a path as Dante found the mounting and descending of a patron's stairs. All employment vouchsafed to a Confederate would be regarded as charity, and sympathy would often look marvellously like insult. Although we do not give full credence to the exaggerations of the Northern press, we must believe that there is a considerable number of Confederates in Canada, and we fear that the Yankee accounts of their condition have some foundation in truth. Let their fate be a warning. Better endure the discomforts of our present state than accept the patronage of "cheap Englishmen," as Canadians have been well styled.

It may be said that the class to which these remarks apply is small. True. Our hope and stay of the army cannot emigrate.

But there was some foundation for the indignation which the French people manifested toward the *émigrés* in the Revolution; and the example of our *émigrés*, though it cannot spread very far, is pernicious. While it may not be necessary as yet to adopt any legal measures in this matter, still the moral sense of the community ought not to fall asleep over this case of conscience as it has done over so many others.

DECEMBER 3, 1863.

A THOUGHTFUL biographer of Ignatius Loyola, while vindicating the claims of his subject to true greatness, has tersely expressed the true secret of the eminence attained by the founder of the Society of Jesus in the brief sentence: "The discerning of spirits is the foundation of power."

We need not ransack history for illustrations. They come unbidden. Every man, who has succeeded in establishing an empire, or in creating a nation, has owed his success to his insight into character. The knowledge of the human heart is the basis of the science of government. Two things the true ruler must understand—the character of the people whom he governs—the capacity of the agents whom he employs. Official position will not give a man this insight. The best intentions in the world will not give it. Men of the best intentions have often been the worst governors. The most resolute will cannot give it. The will has no power over an organ that does not exist.

How little this people has been understood by the men whom an inscrutable Providence has made our official representatives every step of this revolution has shown. The great body has always been far in advance of its supposed leaders. The generals—as often happens in war—have brought up the rear, but, as ought not to happen in war, they always keep in the rear. Had those in authority sounded the depth of national feeling, our army would have been as large in 1861 as it was in the summer of 1862; our finances in 1863 would have been in no worse plight than in 1861; the navy would now have a tangible existence and the State Department be something more than a Confederate reading-room. But, as it is, our whole history, thus far, has served merely as a commentary on Machiavelli's famous thesis, that a nation is wiser and more constant than its leading men. Had a little discretion been shown, the Government might now have the enthusiastic support of the millions of the South. Our honor was interested in upholding what seemed to be our choice, and no one wished, by unnecessary opposition, to lend a handle to our enemies. But when the people found that their voice was utterly disregarded; that every suggestion, which did not proceed from an official quarter, was looked upon as an impertinence; that dire necessity alone compelled the Government to measures which had been advocated months before by every reflecting man; that wrong courses were persisted in long after the evil effects, which were predicted, had set in—it is not to be wondered that the people began to dissociate themselves from the Government—to support its existence without upholding its authority—to acquiesce, instead of applauding. It is some comfort, we grant, to have a President who does not disgrace us by Hoosier-English, but it is a comfort which is dearly bought at the price of a Memminger and a Bragg.

For this is, after all, the great grievance; the utter want of judgment in the selection of our officials—high and low—civil and military; and, what is still worse, the unreasoning, selfish obstinacy which retains the incompetent in their posts. The choice once made, if it does not justify itself, every thing is done to justify it; and good money is thrown after bad with a prodigality which would be ridiculous if that good money were not the life-blood of our nation. Personal considerations may not *consciously* lie at the bottom of these obnoxious appointments, but there is no bias which so easily eludes self-inspection—none which is so patent to the world at large, as favoritism; and the current expression, "The President's Pets," shows what is the popular view of the matter. In military command, the confidence of his soldiers is an essential element in the success of a general. No matter what the cause of distrust, the distrust itself is sufficient to disqualify the commander for his position; but if that distrust is confirmed by repeated disasters, it is not worth while to argue the point on any grounds of which a court of inquiry could take cognizance. "Murad, the Unlucky," may owe his ill-luck to himself, or he may owe it to circumstances; but soldiers are superstitious, and do not want any heroes of a hundred defeats. On the other hand, popular favor may be misplaced. But how often has it been misplaced since the beginning of the war? Was the public wrong in its estimate of Jackson before his threatened removal? How do we know that the public is wrong in its estimate of Price?

It has been suggested long ago that the President was guided in the selection of his cabinet officers by the example of Napoleon III.—that he wanted only clerks, not statesmen, so that the real power might be his, and all the credit redound to him. But if he has made his appointments in good faith, it must be admitted that "the discerning of spirits" is no part of Mr. Davis's encyclopedia of the sciences. This is the point in which he fails to reach the romantic standard which he has doubtless set up for himself. Agamemnon does not at first present a very imposing figure in the wise old Epos, but the careful student learns to respect him more when he sees how the "king of men" strengthens himself in the affections of his adherents, and wins back the revolted spirit of Achilles.

Under this severe trial of patience and devotion, the attitude of the Southern people is sublime. We hear complaints, we hear expostulations; but we have no "factious opposition," such as administration organs would scent out in every honest criticism of governmental measures. The country has borne every provocation from the President, fixed on them by the early fates, in heroic silence. He has taught us, not only in his proclamations, but also by his policy, "to cease from man," and in lofty faith, to look to God for our help. It is very pious. But is it very wise? Will resignation sweeten ruin? Had not the nation better think of altering the course of the ship? When Hercules saw the condition of the Augean stable, he did not roll up his eyes to Jupiter, but turned a river into it.

DECEMBER 10, 1863.

MUCH eagerness prevails to catch the first words from Congress indicative of the temper and intentions with which it has assembled in this most important session; and for that reason we surrender our space to-day to the reports. Although, therefore, the able message of the President possesses an interest and importance which arrests attention and provokes much comment, we cannot do more than recapitulate the chief points.

We cannot but admire the ease with which Mr. Davis glides over "grave military reverses," and the delicacy with which he omits every allusion to their causes. In half a sentence he recounts the surrender of an entire army at Vicksburg; but does not tell Congress whose orders shut up the army in that trap, and set aside the orders of General Johnston for its evacuation when the field had been lost. He refers to the invasion of Arkansas and "the control of the enemy" which has followed, but forgets the favorite general whose command had been the source of stagnation, mismanagement, distrust, and disaster. He stigmatizes with bitterness the demoralization and misconduct, in other words, the cowardice of the troops which lately broke and ran on Lookout Mountain, but does not state the cause of that demoralization, confusion, and cowardice to have been the fact that they were utterly destitute of confidence in a leader, who had been first put into a position to mortify a hero, and maintained there long after results had proven him incompetent to the army he commanded, and to the country he had lost. In telling of Longstreet's bootless errand to Knoxville, he might have informed us what military genius conceived the idea of dividing a small army into two detachments, and separating them by rivers, mountains, and hundreds of miles, in the presence of a much larger army, at the moment when the latter was re-ceiving heavy re-enforcements. Although the message is long, a candid statement of the whole truth upon those points would be a useful addition to the two concise pages devoted to the important events, which have rendered the history of the last five months a sombre chapter in the annals of the war.

That portion of the message which relates to what the President is kind enough to call our Foreign Relations, is an admirable compendium of all the insults we have received from the British Ministry, and of all the failures of our own Government to aid the country by diplomacy. The conclusion, which is presented with crystalline clearness, is one which this journal often expressed at the outset of the matter, that we have neither help nor sympathy to expect from Europe,—that there will be no intervention, except such as may come from the selfish interests of France, or to prevent a reconstruction—and that the Confederacy has nothing further to do in the way of Foreign Relations, but to "wait for a returning sense of justice." Mr. Davis might have added that it is possible for us to do that much without supporting a State Department, and without paying twelve thousand dollars in gold to each of a numerous and distinguished diplomatic corps, which holds no communication with any Minister of Foreign Affairs, other than his excellency, Mr. Judah P. Benjamin, at Richmond.

The section of the message devoted to the absorbing subject of the currency, is a long and copious narrative of facts proving incontestably that the Government has been destitute of foresight and good management in all its financial affairs. The story, however, is so told as to make it appear that the chief faults were those of Congress in not making wiser laws, and of the Yankees in continuing the war for a time so much exceeding the expectations of Mr. Davis and Mr. Memminger. The latter sage, as we learn from the message, has presented in his report "the outlines of a system," for reforming his currency; but his report has not yet been printed.

On the present force and organization of the army he gives little information. On the interesting and tender question of substitution he is brief and undefined. But so much can scarcely be said of the recommendation to abolish all exemptions, and put every man in the country, old and young, on the pay-roll of the army, and allowing the President, his Secretary, and other officials, his creatures, to give the privileges of exemption to whom they please, under the name of "detail." Such a project would not increase the army by one man. It would, however, double the expense of the military force; it would also open the widest door that ever gaped to receive the ruin of society, by bribery, corruption, fraud, favoritism infinitely ramified, private malice infinitely gratified. Perpetual martial law all over the land would be but a trifle to a law which would place every man, old or young, sick or well, whatever his occupation or its necessity to the material and political existence of the nation, under the thumb of the present office-holders at Richmond, with full power to order them to Arkansas if they did not kiss their feet, or to stay at home if they paid them well.

The rest of the message is devoted to the Trans-Mississippi Department; the navy of Mallory, and the cruisers which are happily beyond his reach; to the Post-Office, which appears at least to pay its expenses. The story of the Yankee cartel is clearly told; but no reasonable excuse is made for the unprecedented indulgence which permits the enemy to send luxuries to Belle Isle, while our soldiers starve in captivity on Johnson's Island. An eloquent recapitulation of the barbarities of the enemy concludes the message, which contains no account of the motives which induced Mr. Davis to threaten retaliation and not to fulfil his threats. The entire document is written in excellent style, and the sprucest English. Indeed, the same may be said of all the President's messages. If we kept a

President for that purpose alone, we could not make a better selection; for the merit of Mr. Davis is, that he possesses a degree of literary talent which is adequate to the composition of an official document. If he would confine his public communications to these things, and avoid juggling telegrams and popular harangues, he might descend to posterity as a worthy rival of another ruler who never said the foolish thing, and never did the wise one.

DECEMBER 12, 1863.

A RESOLUTION has been introduced in the Senate which may prove the source of a great reform in the Confederate Administration. A law is proposed to limit the term of office for the cabinet ministers to two years.

There are certainly two classes among those who speak, and pretend, at least, to think about public affairs. One would shut every mouth that is not filled with idle, wicked praise of those who have frittered away the might of the South. They would even deny that there are any disasters. The currency is admirable. Chickamauga was a glorious Confederate victory. Bragg, Pemberton, and Lovell, are beloved servants of the South, and deserve medals of honor. The Confederate navy is all right. Our European prospect has been brightening every day since the war began. Or, if it is found necessary, at times, to acknowledge something to the contrary of this, we are imperiously informed that the welfare of the country requires the country to hold its tongue, shut its eyes, and especially not to utter a word of censure, or to search after the causes and the authors of misfortune. There is a large number of weak, low-minded persons who like this advice, and call it patriotic. With neither fortitude, nor honesty, nor courage to look the truth in the face, they want to be told every morning that nothing is wrong, and that we are getting along swimmingly. But can no one, for the love of his own skin, be prevailed upon to think for one moment, where we are swimming, where we are going on this fine road, where this system leads?

Many things are wrong! We have suffered vast misfortunes. Nothing happens in this world without a cause, and like causes will produce like effects to the end of time. If we, the sovereign people of this country, refuse to inquire into the causes of the military, financial, diplomatic, administrative misfortunes which have befallen this country, and to remedy, or, at least, to change or interrupt their operation, those causes will continue to operate, will continue to produce disaster after disaster, progressively worse, until they arrive at their natural conclusion—the subjugation, the catastrophe and death of the nation. What man in his senses can, with candor, question these truths? What levity, what wickedness, to refuse them consideration because they are painful, or because it is pleasant and popular to tell the old women that all is well!

If many of our affairs have been mismanaged, the persons who constitute the Government have mismanaged them. They are the causes and the sources of misfortune, and they are the things to change, if we are not careless of our fates. It is impossible to believe that they have not done as well as they could, but that has not been well. They have lacked foresight and ability. That much is proven; proven by the results; proven by their fruits; proven by the spectacle before the eye that looks on the map of the Confederacy. They have not been competent to manage the business which they undertook; and, instead of amusing ourselves with lies about open facts which deceive nobody, common sense and the instinct of self-preservation should make us strive to expel them, if their own consciences will not cause them to withdraw. Where will you find any better? says subserviency. Frankly, anybody who has not proven—proven himself by his acts to be bad.

Here is a law proposed which will enable the country to reach the sources of incompetency. It will produce something like accountability and responsibility in the executive departments. Fix things as one may, the heads of those departments do control, have controlled, and must always control many of the chief movements, as well as the infinite details of government. A narrow-minded, short-sighted, inefficient man in one of those posts communicates his character through every ramification of the business over which he presides. It is difficult to imagine an objection against the expediency of instituting that check on the course of folly or corruption. Such a limit can do no harm, and may do infinite good in a Government like this. He who has proven his wisdom, energy, and integrity, by his acts in office, will always be approved; and it is right that he who is a load of stupidity, listlessness, or corruption, should not be borne on the back of a groaning people during six long years, in which they must struggle for their lives with a remorseless enemy.

DECEMBER 31, 1863.

To-day closes the gloomiest year of our struggle. No sanguine hope of foreign intervention buoys up the spirits of the Confederate public, as at the end of 1861. No brilliant victory like that of Fredericksburg encourages us to look forward to a speedy and successful termination of the war, as in the last weeks of 1862. The advantages gained at Chancellorsville and Chickamauga have had heavy counterpoises. The one victory led to the fall of Jackson and the deposition of Hooker; the other led first to nothing, and then to the indelible disgrace of Lookout Mountain. The Confederacy has been cut in twain along the line of the Mississippi, and our enemies are steadily pushing forward their plans for bisecting the eastern moiety. No wonder, then, that the annual advent of the reign of mud·is hailed by all classes with a sense of relief—by those who think and feel aright, as a precious season to prepare for trying another fall with our potent adversary.

Meanwhile, the financial chaos is becoming wilder and wilder.

Hoarders keep a more resolute grasp than ever on the necessaries of life. Non-producers, who are at the same time non-speculators, are suffering more and more. What was once competence has become poverty, poverty has become penury, penury is lapsing into pauperism. Any mechanical occupation is more profitable than the most intellectual profession; the most accomplished scholars in the Confederacy would be glad to barter their services for food and raiment; and, in the complete upturning of our social relations, the only happy people are those who have black hearts or black skins. The cry of scarcity resounds through the land, raised by the producers in their greed for gain, re-echoed by the consumers in their premature dread of starvation and nakedness. We are all in the dark, and men are more or less cowards in the dark. We do not know what our resources are, and no one can tell us whether we shall have a pound of beef to eat at the close of 1864, or a square inch of leather to patch the last shoe in the Confederacy. Unreasoning confidence has been succeeded by depression as unreasoning, and the Yankees are congratulating themselves on the result, which they hawk about as the " beginning of the end."

Theologians will tell us that the disasters of the closing year are the punishment of our sins. This is true enough; but a cheap penitence will not save us from the evil consequences. There is no forgiveness for political sins, and the results will as certainly follow as if there had been no repentance. As all sins are, in a higher sense, intellectual blunders, we must strain every fibre of the brain, and every sinew of the will, if we wish to repair the mischief which our folly and our corruption have wrought. The universal recognition of this imperative duty is a more certain earnest of our success than the high spirits of our men in the field, or the indomitable patriotism of our women at home, from which newspaper correspondents derive so much comfort. The incompetence and unfaithfulness of Government officials have had much to do with the present sad state of affairs, but the responsibility does not end there; the guilt does not rest there alone. Every man who has suffered himself to be tainted with the scab of speculation, has done something to injure the credit of Confederate securities; every man who has withheld any necessary of life, has done his worst to ruin the country; every one, man or woman, who has yielded to the solicitations of vanity or appetite, and refused to submit to any privation, however slight, which any expenditure, however great, could prevent, has contributed to the general demoralization. It may be said that, with the present plethora of paper money, such virtue as we demand is not to be expected of any people made up of merely human beings. But some such virtue is necessary for any people whose duty it has become to wage such a contest as ours. And if the virtue is not spontaneous, it must be engrafted by the painful process through which we are now passing. We cannot go through this fiery furnace without the smell of fire on our garments. We can no more avoid the loss of property than we can the shedding of blood. There is no family in the Confederacy that has not to mourn the fall of some member or some connection, and there is no family in the Confederacy which *ought* to expect to escape scathless in estate. The attempt is as useless, in most cases, as it is ignoble in all. A few, and but few, in comparison with the whole number, may come out of the war richer than when they went in; but even they must make up their minds to sacrifice a part, and a large part, of their riches, in order to preserve the whole. The saying of the stoic philosopher, "You can't have something for nothing," though it sounds like a truism, in fact conveys a moral lesson of great significance. Men must pay for privileges. If they do not pay voluntarily, their neighbors will make them pay, and that heavily.

We all have a heavy score to pay off, and we know it. This may depress us, but our enemies need not be jubilant over our depression; for we are determined to meet our liabilities. Whatever number of men, or whatever amount of money shall be really wanting, will be forthcoming. Whatever economy the straitening of our resources may require, we shall learn to exercise. We could only wish that Congress was not in such a feverish mood, and that the Government would do something towards the establishment of a statistical bureau, or some other agency, by which we could approximately ascertain what we have to contribute, and to what extent we must husband our resources. Wise, cool, decided, prompt action would put us in good condition for the spring campaign of 1864, and the close of next year would furnish a more agreeable retrospect than the *annus mirabilis* of blunders which we now consign to the dead past.

JANUARY 1, 1864.

STANDING upon that narrow isthmus of time which connects the two segments of the calendar, the old and the new year, it is natural that we should pause to reflect; should cast a keen retrospective glance upon the troubled tide over which we have passed, and peer intently into the Cimmerian darkness which envelops our future path. In the most tranquil periods of existence, these artificial divisions, the "relay houses," where the "Fates change horses," are suggestive of solemn thoughts; regret for the past and fitful resolutions for the future. The present epoch of troubled and anxious portents, when all the usual cares and plans of life are dwarfed into insignificance before the one all-important concern of maintaining national life, naturally stirs the deepest recesses of the heart, and awakens the greatest solicitude for our future course and prospects.

What does the impenetrable face of 1864 conceal of good or of evil for us? Will the year, like its immediate predecessors, be distinguished by glorious and hardly won victories of the Confederate arms, checkered occasionally by unavoidable mishap, and stained at times by unaccountable imbecility or imprudencies, yet presenting, in final result, military glory, tarnished by loss of extensive territories and accumulation of embarrassment?

A momentous question, and the answer to it is not, by any means, dependent exclusively upon the nod of Jove. Once before, in the progress of the war, did gloomy clouds contract the horizon. The eventful spring of 1862 may be considered as the first great crisis and turning point of the struggle. A parallel state of things exists at present.

The cool and statesmanlike glance which takes in at once the whole field, which appreciates the danger without exaggerated alarm, which preserves its calm in the midst of danger, and applies methodically the proper remedies, is what we now need. Excitement and rashness are always detrimental in affairs which cannot be transacted without a considerable lapse of time. Our armies must be maintained on a proper footing, and they and the population in general must be fed. The necessary productions of mechanical skill must be furnished, both for the well-being of the army and the daily business of the country. Above all, and before all, the political liberties and institutions of this country must be preserved *intact*. These are the things that we fight for. Once let the nation grasp the idea that these things are lost, and it will refuse to go on with this war. Let all who are concerned be warned of this in time.

What we want is that sane legislation in Congress, and that patriotic spirit among the people, which will give the requisite military strength and the supporting influence which backs military power by the energy of an industrious and provident people. It is idle to indulge in the crude speculations and projects which captivate hasty and superficial thinkers only; of converting a whole nation into a camp; of collecting a single army from the strength of the nation, and staking all upon the issue of one campaign. As well resort to the chivalric method of the middle ages, and propose to decide a war by a single combat or a pitched battle in a *champ clos*. We require a policy which embraces the whole field, which provides for all our necessities, and faces all our dangers; not the contracted view which takes in fragmentary ideas, and thinks that when it has secured a point of the game, it has done everything. A temperate boldness and sagacious deliberation will bring into play all that is necessary to be done by a people who still really abound in resources, and upon whom the impression that has been made by the enemy's arms, however pregnant with distress to portions of the country, is absurdly disproportioned to its conquest. Let but a wisdom commensurate at all with its valor distinguish the Confederacy, and the new year will make evident the folly of the design which the enemy propose, and which is only beneficial or necessary to the execrable junto which now rules at Washington.

JANUARY 2, 1864.

VIRGINIA has a new Governor. Tuesday evening last John Letcher made his adieu to the gubernatorial mansion in Richmond with a bowl of "apple-brandy toddy," and a festive speech. There was something about the speech more remarkable than the free toddy and the mutual admiration society which celebrated the occasion. After nearly three years since the commencement of the war, Mr. Letcher comes before the public with an after-dinner explanation of his course on the secession question, and proves, with the logic of liquor, that he was the original evangelist of secession in Virginia. He says that he opposed the Convention that took the State out of the Union because he preferred Lincoln to force it out; and then there would have been no division of parties, and all would have unanimously resolved to rescue their liberties.

After three years of taciturn virtue, mistaken calumny and undeserved censure, the out-going Governor finds this occasion for the triumphant vindication of himself. But, unfortunately, the argument is not original. It is precisely the same with which HICKS debauched Maryland, and which, at the beginning of hostilities, was in the mouth of every wretch who designed, under an affected indignation and postponed threats, to secure the ruin and subjugation of the South. Wait to be kicked out of the Union, they said, and the affront will be mortal, and, therefore, sure of resentment. But that is every coward's argument and artifice—waiting for the paramount insult, without taking notice of inferior assaults; and it invariably ends in his taking the slap in the face quite as submissively as the preliminary affronts.

With the bluster of what he would have done, and what he did not do, Letcher makes his exit and retires with the God-speed of every individual who wishes the country well. The occasion is one of too much thankfulness to be disturbed by criticisms of the past. Let him go to his "mountain home" quietly, with no more toddies, speeches or shows, and especially without tarrying for that sword which the wise men of the city have voted for his services on Joseph Mayo. We have only to pray that Virginia may never look upon his like again.

The inaugural address of his distinguished successor, the General and Governor William Smith, occupies our columns to-day. While it is the sincere wish of all that his administration of the old laws of Virginia may be wise, just and patriotic, we are compelled to enter this early protest against many of the theories and projects for legislation which it contains. But intellectual speculations and daily acts are different things. We hope that some of the Governor's views, when developed and explained, will be found less wild than they look; and, in any event, we feel confident that he will administer the business of the State according to its ancient constitutions, established laws, and known usages. These are good; the people are good; and the only means of bringing forth the strength of Virginia is by an adherence, both in letter and spirit, to her old customs and policy.

JANUARY 13, 1864.

UNITY of will is absolutely essential to the successful command of an army. By an easy, though delusive, process of ratiocination the same principle is extended to the operations of government and the uncontrolled will of a single individual supposed to be the fittest instrument for administering the business of a State. Many, who demur to the unlimited acknowledgment of the principle, give it their adherence in so far as it relates to a state of war. Whatever may be the theoretical beauties, or the happy operation of constitutional checks and balances, or of free discussion in peaceful periods, they deem them out of place in the trying times of a great and pitiless war. The fashion of late years, more especially among military men, has been to dilate upon this supposed inferiority of free governments in the vigorous conduct of hostilities; and many zealous defenders of liberty have conceded the point, only claiming for their cherished system a preponderance of benefits, when the whole field of national life is taken into view.

It is a superficial analogy which confounds the arbitrary will necessary to the direction of military operations in the field with the enlightened supervision requisite for evolving the resources of a nation with the greatest practical efficiency and the least detriment to the public welfare. In the one case, plans are formed which demand secrecy and energy, but which are based solely upon considerations of a military nature, requiring, no doubt, genius and ability, but which are infinitely less complex in their character, and demand very much less consideration of extraneous agencies and disturbing causes, than the other. Nor is it true, as historical sciolists are so fond of asserting, that despotic governments are alone capable of the vigorous conduct of war. Leaving out of view the facility with which the absolute rulers of Asia have always succumbed to the free genius of Europe, it will be found that an enlightened system of representative government, however obstructed by the want of celerity incident to free debate, and the greater publicity which attends its measures, has, in general, proved superior to the more concentrated but less vigorous efforts of absolutism. Above all, is this the case when the whole life and energy of a people have been signalized by the prevalence of free principles. To change its whole course of action in such a case, under the pressure of impending danger, is like a change of front and order of battle in presence of the enemy.

It can hardly be deemed necessary, in the course of a war waged for the establishment of sound constitutional principles, to inflict so severe a blow upon them as to deliberately throw them aside in the heat of conflicts as cumbrous impediments. Such a proceeding would bring deserved discredit upon them, not only throughout the world, but among ourselves. The inference would be just and reasonable that whatever success they may have met in the past was due to favoring circumstances, and that the more difficult state of things which will exist in future on this continent demands a reformation of antiquated ideas.

The fortunate results which so often attended the choice of a dictator at Rome are much prized by the advocates of unlimited authority. Rome, with her aristocratic Senate, her divisions among the orders of the State, and her irregular and crude method of legislation in her early days, can hardly be cited as a complete exemplar for a people whose traditions and habits have so thoroughly educated them in the maintenance and exercise of well-regulated representative government. Yet, if we could find a Camillus or a Cincinnatus, it might not be improper to invest him with the authority which they possessed. If we cannot, let not our legislators and statesmen abolish those guaranties of liberty which are sufficiently imperilled by the mere existence of war; let them not introduce an element into the State which will certainly replace civil by military leaders; and let not the chosen guardians of liberty commit a deliberate act of political suicide.

JANUARY 20, 1864.

MARTIAL virtue is quite distinct from military efficiency. The Romans were essentially the military people of the ancient world, though, in bravery upon the field of battle, it was impossible to excel the warriors of Germany and Gaul. Yet, in the thorough and systematic organization which pervaded the legions of Rome was found a principle which overcame all the efforts of desultory bravery, and finally made her mistress of the world. The feudal lords of of mediæval Europe displayed conspicuous prowess on every field, yet were they subject to such complete routs as are unknown to modern discipline, and their mode of fighting became obsolete with the introduction of improved infantry tactics.

France is undoubtedly the first military power of the present day. Yet, though at Albuera, at Badajos, and at Waterloo, the steadiness of the British infantry maintained the ground, in the Crimea it was clearly shown how insufficient for a great and continued struggle is the valor which is only prepared for the brunt of a single battle. Complete order, all-pervading system, looking to the comfort of the soldier, and consequently insuring his efficiency in actual combat, were the great military requisites, which were conspicuously displayed in every department of the French army, and which can never fail to secure its excellence in protracted campaigning.

It is impossible to deny the Southern soldier that bravery which he has proved on many well-fought fields, but it is equally certain that the thorough organization of armies is not the praise properly attributable to the Confederacy. Much, no doubt, is to be attributed to the manifold difficulties with which we have had to contend, the want of so many indispensable requisites which go to make up the complex machine of an army. Much, however, must be ascribed to official incompetency or negligence. The character of the soldier himself, too, renders it difficult to secure that complete efficiency which marks the perfection of a disciplined army. The very reckless bravery which gives him his victorious *élan* is difficult to reconcile with the strict discipline, the sleepless vigilance, which are indispensable to success in war. Free-handed and improvident, the Southern volunteer is disposed to be thoughtless of the future, and to purchase present convenience at the price of future hunger and discomfort. Experience and long campaigning have a tendency to correct these faults, but it is more in the watchful supervision of officers that we should look for amelioration.

The French soldier, careless and thoughtless by nature, seems to assume a new character with his uniform. He becomes alert and cautious. He is provident and contriving in alleviating the hardships of camp, and increasing his stock of comfort. To his superiority in this respect, as well as to the excellence of the French commissariat, many of the advantages enjoyed by the French over the English in the Crimea are attributable. His shrewd care of the *cuisine*, his dexterity in foraging, and the skill with which he dressed his food and prepared his soup, contrasted advantageously with the improvidence of the British, and secured him great advantages in the exposure of the bivouac, the fatigue of the march, and the ordeal of the battle.

Three years of war should have rendered us a thoroughly military people. That they have not produced this effect is evident. Our troops out-fight the Yankees, as they have done from the beginning; yet the latter have made greater strides towards the constitution of a thoroughly organized army. The material they have had to work with, naturally less endowed with military aptitude, is yet more pliant to the moulding operation of discipline, and thus, with them, art has to some extent supplied the deficiencies of nature.

It is important that a similar improvement should be made in the military efficiency of the Confederacy, in view both of the possibility of the indefinite prolongation of the present war, and the armed attitude of watchfulness which will have to be maintained in consequence of the future changed condition of affairs on this continent. Enthusiasm and the ardor of high-spirited courage must be supported and invigorated by the bracing hand of a discipline and a system which will give concentration of energy without impairing individual enterprise and daring.

Without resorting to the Yankee plan of immolating every officer who is unfortunate, we may, at least infer, from the improvement which seems to have attended their generalship, that a stricter accountability and more exacting supervision of our own officers would not fail to produce a decided amelioration in the Confederate army, a military engine, the admirable parts of which only require to be properly combined and harmonized in order to produce unparalleled results.

JANUARY 21, 1864.

THE vain and unreflecting North are deceiving themselves with the delusion that the South is already conquered. From the begin ning they have regarded the task as constantly on the eve of accomplishment; they now think the work already done. There are a few plain considerations which ought to teach them that they are laboring under an error. The South not only is not conquered; but, *if she chooses*, she never can be.

In a population of five millions, there is one in five capable of making resistance; capable of exerting effective effort, in some form, in opposing an aggressive power. If true to herself, the South is capable of successfully resisting a million of men. Can a people thus possessing an army of at least four hundred thousand brave men be conquered by any foreign power unless they choose to be?

The North boasts twenty millions of people. One in twenty of this number is more than it has yet succeeded in placing upon its muster rolls.

The plain deduction from this statement of the case is, that if the South has suffered reverses in the contest to the extent of bringing her cause into any sort of peril, it has been either from want of valor in the People or of capacity in the Government. It is for the public to determine where the blame lies; our own opinion is well known. The whole male population, between the ages of eighteen and forty-five, with a few necessary exceptions, have been placed at the disposal of Government; and our impressment laws have exposed to it the whole available substance of the country, which they have seized with a strong and used with a lavish hand. If our cause has been brought into peril, it need not remain so for one moment, if those who are charged with responsibility but perform their duty with wisdom, with honesty, and with ability.

JANUARY 21, 1864.

"RECONSTRUCTION" is an absorbing topic with the enemy at present. The fighting being so nearly concluded, Lee's army exterminated, Johnston's starved to death, Beauregard's buried under the ruins of Sumter, it becomes a serious question what is to be done with the rebels. A variety of opinions exist upon the subject. Lincoln's decimal system is, of course, favored by official influence, but there are others to which their partisans are not less devoted. There is the territorial system, under which the Yankees are to control absolutely the destinies of a population which has forfeited all the rights appertaining to the States by their wicked rebellion. There is the free-farm system, by which everybody is to be endowed with rich lands, fruitful in cotton, rice, or tobacco, and new blood infused into the languid South; and there is also a feeble remnant of antediluvian politicians, who call themselves democrats, and are much laughed at for their innocent pertinacity in demanding the restoration of the States to all their rights, and the maintenance of that obsolete instrument called "the Constitution."

One sage philosopher, discoursing upon the subject, with all the gravity and wisdom of Minerva's bird, wisely comes to the conclusion that the manner in which the Southern people will be treated depends very much upon themselves. They may, says he, remain sullen and indifferent, stupidly obstinate and insensible to the blessings of the restored Union, which comes in such a charming guise —heralded by the roar of artillery and the groans of the wounded and dying. They may be unartistically and unpoetically callous to the beauties of the "old flag." In that case, evidently, they will have to be treated with severity. On the other hand, he thinks there may be a violent revulsion of sentiment. Conquered and crushed, they will, in an instant, turn their rage upon those who have deceived them. Unwilling to take any fault to themselves for their misfortune, they will denounce those whom they have heretofore trusted as the authors of their calamities. They will pass, then, at once from antipathy to the Yankees into an excessive love for them. A paroxysm of loyalty and devotion to the Union will seize them. Such sudden changes of popular feeling are recorded in history. The restoration of Charles II. is a case in point. The exiled monarch was received with every demonstration of rejoicing, and the whole nation testified its loyalty by the most extravagant exhibitions. Why may not this be the case at the South? Why should Lincoln not be received with salvos of artillery at Richmond? Why should Butler not be welcomed at New Orleans with joyous strains of music, and garlanded with flowers by the admiring fair, whose favor he has won by the courteous consideration he has always displayed for them? In the full tide of returning loyalty, such things may well be.

There is, however, one little defect in this sage philosopher's historical parallel. The outburst of loyalty which welcomed Charles back to the throne of his ancestors was the spontaneous feeling of a people who were all desirous of his return. Forcibly had he been expelled, and peacefully was he recalled. The case is precisely opposite with the restoration of the Union. It comes supported by bayonets and reeking with blood. Such a restoration is not likely to be hailed with any boisterous manifestation of delight.

The restoration of the royal line in England, too, was an uprising of the people against the dreary fanaticism and hypocrisy under which they had groaned for years. They had tried the Puritans of the genuine Pilgrim Father stamp, and were disgusted. We, at the South, have had experience enough of their antitypes, the modern Yankees. We have already had our rejoicing at being quit of them, and are no more likely to welcome them back than the English were disposed to reinstate the Rump Parliament and its reign of pestilent cant.

JANUARY 22, 1864.

CERTAIN of our contemporaries seem never to weary of ringing the changes on the necessity of harmony. Æsop's bundle of sticks is lugged in every now and then to break the stiff neck and the unbending back of the "opposition." The bad Latin motto of Austria, *viribus unitis*, is daily expounded for the benefit of those who do not appreciate the measures of the best of all possible administrations. What proportion of these homilies is due to patriotic motives, what to truckling subserviency, we will not stop to examine. But as there is danger lest some well-meaning people may be dinned into the belief that the time has come for the suspension of all individual judgment, and as we have a sincere regard for all well-meaning people, it may be worth our while to offer a brief vindication of the course which so many representatives of the press have found it their duty to pursue.

We need no Œdipus to tell us that criticism is easier than performance. *That* is the burden of countless proverbs and parables without number. Still criticism has its uses, and fault-finding is, after all, often the cause of fault-mending. Sometimes the result is direct; the exposure of the error leads to its reparation. More frequently yet, the lecture is applied in a different way; and in spite of an obstinate adherence to a mistaken policy, new plans are shaped under the influence—more or less consciously felt—of a vigilant censorship. The administration has been slow to heed the advice of those who stand without its magic circle; but it has been forced to yield point after point, and these concessions, though tardy and ungracious, show that it is not entirely beyond the reach of such cogent arguments as the consentient voice of the country. For months and months the administration was let alone, and with what result we all know. Henceforth it can expect no renewal of the hazardous experiment, and must content itself with being but one of the powers of the State. Harmony, indeed! If the harmony of our first love had continued unbroken, it would have been the only thing unbroken in the Confederacy. *Sufflaminandum est.* The brake must be put on although the wheels may creak under the cruel treatment.

Nothing is to be feared from the independent utterances of the press. There is no "opposition" in the invidious sense of the word. There is no dispute about the end, which is the same in every true patriot; that there should be much debate about the means is not only natural and legitimate, but eminently useful. Nobody inveighs against the war as unnecessary; against our separation from the Yankees as a heart-rending divorce of brother from brother. No respectable journal hints at reconstruction. Blunders in the conduct of affairs are freely criticised, and the fulfilment of repeated prophecies is often employed to give a keener edge to the criticism; but we have seen no trace of the malignant exultation which prefers to be in the right, like Cassandra, rather than in the wrong, like Jonah. The opposition, as called, may be hard to please, but the administration is harder to please. The Government assumes a bold position—somewhat late in the day, it is true—in the matter of our foreign relations, we reaffirm our approval of that position; we strengthen it by illustration and argument; we maintain the wisdom of the policy. Our approval, our arguments, our advocacy are regarded as so many covert sneers. It is well for the peace of mind of all journalists who undertake to review, impartially, the state of public affairs, that the pleasure of the administration is a matter of no importance whatever.

But, we are told, the Yankees derive great encouragement from our wrangling, and expect the dissolution of our league to follow close in the wake of our dissensions. If these dissensions had any reference to submission; if we were debating the expediency of accepting Lincoln's amnesty, the Yankees would do well to be jubilant; but as our disputes relate simply to the best method of repelling the invader, as we are all agreed on the policy of dispatching Cerberus, and not appeasing him, we can see no reason why our enemies should be exultant. Far better reasons would they have for rejoicing, if our Congress should pass any of the desperate measures which that body has suffered itself to entertain; and whether the Yankees are exultant or not, we must learn, once for all, to walk in the good old paths of hereditary constitutional right, without regarding the frames and feelings of that mighty emotioned people. The true danger is lest our own people should be alienated from the cause by the misconduct of those who are at the head of affairs, and, by pointing out errors and urging reform, an independent press can do more to promote a higher harmony, than by a mute resignation to accomplished facts, or loud appeals for such a unity as can be brought about only by an abnegation of thought, or a renunciation of liberty.

JANUARY 26, 1864.

GAMING, if not entirely suppressed by the recent law framed for that purpose, has, at least, had its wings clipped. It no longer holds high carnival in spacious halls and tempts with luxurious banquets, but is confined in barricaded recesses, and contracts its bill of fare to dimensions more appropriate to the present times in which "Starvation Parties" abound. With this diminution of its splendor, there is a corresponding decline in the number of those who frequent the "hells."

Law can do much to correct the vice of gaming, but not all. The suppression of the gaming-houses in France greatly diminished the vice. It fled to the clubs, where, of course, the mass of the population are unable to indulge in it. Apart from these privileged localities, it is principally in the apartments of faded "lorettes" that indiscreet young men are fleeced in Paris.

In that part of America lately called the United States, the vice was fostered by some peculiarities of life, as well as by the natural propensity to try one's luck at games of chance. It is intimately connected with the same spirit which has caused the erection of mammoth hotels, and collects a gregarious and omnivorous mass at enormous *table d'hôtes*. In other countries, people prefer to eat in select parties; and it is considered more pleasant to be one of five than one of five hundred. The Yankee, however, whose indefatigable and aggressive spirit has controlled these affairs on this side of the water, is fond of the vast and tawdry magnificent. Hence his hotels, his steamboats, and hence, too, his faro-banks. People flock to these establishments under the combined influence of the taste for living in public, and the mania for gambling. The one assists and develops the other.

Now this love of crowds is a Yankee propensity, which they have succeeded in engrafting upon the South. We should rid ourselves of it, along with other "notions" of theirs. Our hotels, instead of being immense caravansaries, where a man, unless in the good graces of the clerk, is forced to clamber up innumerable steps, like a wolf seeking his lair, should be framed more upon the European model. Instead of the palatial fronts, the vast corridors, and the endless tables, the hotel should aim at giving the traveller the repose and quietude of home. Comfort should be desired rather than show. The *table d'hôte* should be a place where people come to satisfy their hunger with well-cooked food in an unpretentious way; not an immense exhibition, where ladies are to appear, at four in the afternoon, in "*décolleté*" dresses, and resplendent with diamonds and lace.

Such establishments would really contribute more to the comfort of respectable travellers, than the vast style instituted by the Yankees. They would be also of a much more elevated tone, and would not be liable to the objections and disorders which make our present system so ill-adapted for the residence of families. The tastes and habits of Southern ladies and gentlemen would naturally lead them to seek for greater privacy than that afforded by the hotels established upon the model of the noisy and bustling Yankee. This change will be an addition, too, to that stock of radical differences which already separate us from that people, and in the cultivation of which national character will be best developed.

An entire change in the hotel system would greatly contribute to the diminution of the vice of gambling. Accustomed to a quieter mode of life, men would not rush to the gaming-house, under the impulse of a desire for gregarious feeding. The fashion of such things would change; and, when deprived of the allurements of the table, and of that secret sympathetic feeling which takes possession of crowds, and spurs them on to greater excesses than any individual of them would commit, men will play solely from the naked love of gain, and the desire of giving an active motion to the sluggish sensibilities.

Then life will pass in a mode more congenial to the character and structure of Southern people. We shall have the tranquil progress of the family coach, instead of the express-train, high-pressure rate of the Yankees, which has intensified and made manifest the want of harmony between the two peoples. Then the Southern gentleman, when he travels, will surround himself with an air of solid substantiality, instead of a mass of *rococo* frippery. Then, if he has not altogether conquered the old Adam, and thinks there is no great harm in investing a small sum upon the investigation of a problem of chances, he will intrust it to the keeping of a favorite thoroughbred, not rush madly into the vortex of desperate play, with the apparent object of dissipating his means in the shortest possible time.

FEBRUARY 15, 1864.

In a column of extracts from exchanged papers, containing the public news, the following paragraph from the Columbus (Ga.) *Sun*, was printed in the last edition of the *Examiner*:—

"A FAT CONTRACT.—In a valley back of the little town of Hamburg, South Carolina, opposite Augusta, Georgia, an immense distillery is going up, the proprietor of which is said to have a Government contract for five hundred thousand gallons of whiskey. He has the damaged corn and some molasses ready, also pens for fattening hogs on the swill. What is odd, the owner of this distillery is Collector of the Port of New Orleans, and draws salary as such. At least his name was sent in as successor of his father, who was the father-in-law of Jefferson Davis, and no one has ever heard of its rejection."—*Richmond Correspondent Columbus (Ga.) Sun.*

The present writer was made aware of the foregoing by the two notes which he had the surprise and delight to receive from the President's own secretary, under the official envelope of the Executive Department. One of them is addressed :—

RICHMOND, VA., February 13, 1864.

TO THE EDITOR OF THE RICHMOND EXAMINER:—

SIR—In the *Examiner* of this date is published an article headed "*A Fat Contract*," and purporting to be an extract from the Richmond correspondence of the Columbus (Ga.) *Sun*, each sentence of which contains one distinct falsehood.

Mr. William F. Howell, the gentleman evidently referred to, is not "Collector of the Port of New Orleans," nor has he "drawn salary as such," nor has "his name been sent in" as such. He is not "the owner of an immense distillery," nor has he "a Government contract for 500,000 gallons of whiskey."

The facts are, that Mr. Howell is a Navy Agent, and that under orders from the Navy Department, he has erected near Augusta, Georgia, a distillery for the manufacture of whiskey, to be used by the Medical Purveyor and as rations. Mr. Howell "has no contract," and acts in the matter simply as a Government officer under orders.

By publishing this you will oblige your obedient servant,

BURTON N. HARRISON.

The publication of the foregoing is ordered by the President's secretary in the following judicious, polite, and amiable language:—

[Private.]   RICHMOND, February 13, 1864.

MR. DANIEL:

SIR—Enclosed with this you will find a communication which you will oblige me by publishing in the *Examiner* of the 15th.

It is brief, and is a statement of facts relative to a slanderous article which some one in your office has inserted in the *Examiner* of this date as an extract from the columns of the Columbus (Ga.) *Sun*. Its publication by you is due Mr. Howell's friends as an act of justice for a wrong which has been done him, I trust, without your knowledge or consent.

Some time since a statement appeared in the *Examiner* relative to the burning of the President's cotton. Colonel John T. Wood at once addressed to the paper a communication correcting the errors it contained, and requested publication for it. So far as I am informed, the correction never appeared in the *Examiner*. Allow me to say that I am unwilling to believe that you, personally, had any thing to do with withholding it from publication, and that I am inclined to hope that this communication of mine will not share its fate. Otherwise, I shall be forced to the conviction that the *responsible Editor* of a public journal himself indulges the petty personal malignity which inspires the articles which assail the private character and personal concerns of the President and the members of his family.

Your obedient servant,
BURTON N. HARRISON.

As Mr. Harrison has no title to make us the confidant of his correspondence, nor the President's secretary to write us private letters on subjects in any manner concerning public business, we do not feel at liberty to suppress either of these interesting and necessary documents. We trust that the President and his secretary will be pleased at the present prompt compliance witht heir wishes. Perhaps they would like to hear why we did not publish the communication formerly sent us by Colonel Wood. In an article on the danger that the cotton crop should fall into the enemy's hands, it was remarked that very few planters burnt their cotton—even the President did not burn his own. This was all. Whereupon a long and confused missive was sent to us from the Executive Department, over the signature of J. Taylor Wood, enclosing a well-known telegram by the President about his cotton, an editorial of a Mississippi journal on the same subject, and other morsels of hard language, written on different pieces of paper, the whole forming an abusive but unsatisfactory contradiction to a charge that the President had preserved his cotton, when that of his neighbors was burnt by military authority. Knowing nothing of that matter, and not having referred to it, we thought proper to "withhold" Colonel Wood's lengthy communication. It did not "correct the errors" of the *Examiner;* this paper contained no errors or error on the subject. The remark that even the President had not taken the trouble to destroy his own cotton rested on the President's own published telegram, that he did not know what had been done with it. There, it appeared that he had neither burned nor ordered others to burn it. The remark was exact; the inference legitimate, that if the President himself neglected to destroy his cotton, few others would burn theirs. The papers sent by Colonel Wood had no application, raised a new issue, might possibly mislead, and his communication was rejected for that reason. There was another reason; we did not think such exhibitions of temper and manners by the President could be pleasing or beneficial to the country; these discussions and certificates are unseemly; nor did it look well that he should manifest such uncommon uneasiness about that other story, of which we had said nothing at all. Hearing such angry denials of what was not said, people might begin to think that there really was something in it. This, a patriotic, decorous, and public motive was what chiefly consigned Colonel Wood's documents to the waste basket. They appeared better fitted to damage than to do good. But the President's secretary explains our conduct by "personal malignity." After a misinterpretation so ungracious, we have no longer the privilege of consulting our own judgment, or indulging the feeling of compassion, which would prompt us to return his letters to their writer's address. Therefore we publish all the President's secretary has written in the President's office about the President's relative or connection, his place and his present occupation in the Confederate Government; and if he is wise enough to write us again, or if any of the President's aids, or the President himself, will undertake the task of giving more information on these topics, we will print every letter they will vouchsafe to send, without the delay of one day. Since they want publicity they shall have enough of it, or at least all that we can give.

There are many interesting points which might be thus elucidated, and no one has such opportunities for procuring the information as the President's secretary, who sits in his office and writes under his eye. We did not know that the Confederacy paid him for this kind of work, but since he has undertaken it, we are glad to see him usefully employed. He may explain how, and by whose authority he has connected himself with the matter; why he thinks a paragraph from a Georgia paper relative to a public functionary and public business can be due only to the inspiration and "personal malignity" of an editor in Richmond, or can be the just ground of "private letters" from the President's secretary; he may tell us what may be the exact personal relationship between the navy agent at the port of New Orleans and the President; and how the Confederate naval agency for the port of New Orleans and a Government whiskey distillery in Georgia, can be strictly considered "personal concerns of the President and the members of his family." Could he say what other offices are *tabooed* against public animadversion for the same cause? A wide field opens to the President's secretary, but we will suggest only one fruit which he might pluck there for the public. If he will only take the trouble to inform us which one of the President's family, and of the late General Taylor's, *is not* holding any office anywhere, we shall not only print it with pleasure, but the public will receive his information with a gratification heightened by surprise.

Descending from general to particular observations, it is clear that the President's secretary convicts the correspondent of the Georgia *Sun* of several errors.

It appears from the documents now public, that Mr. Howell is not "Collector for the Port of New Orleans," nor has he drawn salary as such, nor has his "name been sent in as such," nor has he "a contract for five hundred thousand gallons of whiskey."

On the other hand, Mr. Howell is "navy agent" for the port of New Orleans, he has "drawn salary as such," his "name was sent in as such," and he has erected an extensive distillery, not near Hamburg, in South Carolina, but near Augusta, in Georgia, on Government account, over which the navy agent for the port of New Orleans will preside, and make whiskey, five hundred thousand gallons, more or less.

The public will appreciate the differences. One point only of the slanderous *Sun* is not pronounced a distinct falsehood, and we may, therefore, be permitted to believe that Mr. Howell is not "the father-in-law of Jefferson Davis," but only his brother-in-law. Another Mr. Howell was navy agent at New Orleans before secession; was continued in office by the Confederate Government; died navy agent some time after the capture of New Orleans and the expulsion of the Confederates; and it was the name of his son that was then sent in for the place of navy agent at New Orleans, the same, we presume, who now, in the course of his naval duty, is called to the distilling of whiskey, five hundred thousand gallons, more or less, for the Confederate Government.

FEBRUARY 16, 1864.

"What becomes of the pins"? is an interrogatory of trifling interest compared with "What shall be done with our Treasury notes"? We mean, of course, the material fabric, the paper that has been wasted in the preparation of the promises to pay, the residuary rags which will soon begin, in a dirty snow, to come down upon and overwhelm Miserrimus Memminger. At this moment they are scattered over ever so many hundreds of thousands of square miles, the representatives of a most uncertain value; six months hence they will be massed together in this city, a vast bulk of utterly worthless matter; we say worthless, unless, indeed, there shall occur to the fertile mind of the political economist some happy method of utilization. We have heard of eccentric people who papered the walls of their rooms with cancelled postage-stamps, and the cancelled Treasury notes might possibly be useful in this kind of upholstery, but for the fear that madness would supervene upon the wretched occupants of apartments so ornamented, and thus the country be filled with Bedlamites. To see the faces which adorn these bills looking down on one forever, with that unchanging expression of ineffable melancholy which the engraver has given to all of them (for on the best specimens of the Confederate currency Davis is doleful, and Stephens saturnine, Hunter is heavy, and Clay clouded with care, Memminger is mournful, and even Benjamin the buoyant is *bien triste*), and to have constantly in sight the evidences of the country's travail and impecuniosity, were enough to drive even a well-regulated mind to lunacy. To make a burnt sacrifice of them after cancellation would, perhaps, be thought the proper thing, if men enough could be spared from the army to superintend the combustion. But this work would have to be done with great care, and would require many months to complete it. To set fire to the immense mass at once would imperil the safety of the city. Nor does such flimsy fuel answer well for the furnace and the forge, however convenient it might prove for heating the baths of a modern Omar. We have to suggest a disposition of these notes which commends itself to the attention of both the Confederate and State Governments; a twofold disposition, looking to ornament and defence, which will give a stimulus at once to manufactures and the fine arts in the Confederacy.

The impenetrable nature of paper, when closely packed together in layers or leaves, is well known. It is not easy to send a pistol-ball through a book of five hundred pages. A testament in the breast-pocket of a pious soldier has often saved a life upon the battle-field. Still less easy is it to pierce a succession of laminar pasteboards. The reader catches at our proposition now before it is announced. We are hopelessly anticipated. Let two-thirds of the waste-paper of the Confederate circulation be converted into pasteboard, and this substance substituted for iron in the sheathing of our ships-of-war. The superior lightness of the armor would dispel all fears of sinking the vessel. We congratulate Mr. Mallory upon having the means at his command for the speedy completion of his gun-boats, now building in Confederate waters. If it be said that the power of resistance in pasteboard to bombardment is an untried experiment, we can only reply that as all our gun-boats are designed for destruction by their own commanders, it is really of very little importance whether the *carton* would resist a cannon-ball or not.

So much for two-thirds of the paper money. As for the other third, let it be reduced to pulp, or *papier mâché,* and let this be moulded into statues for the completion of the Washington monument. The heroic figure of the Secretary of the Treasury might be placed upon one of the vacant pedestals, that which was designed for the FINANCE of the Revolution in the person of Thomas Nelson, Jr. There would be a beautiful fitness in this apotheosis.

FEBRUARY 20, 1864.

"MEASURES, not men," was some years ago a favorite cry with all parties. "Men, not measures," is the catch-word of Carlyle's hero-worshipping school. The true motto is the combination of both. The true philosophy of history — if there is any such thing — must keep steadily in view the mutual interaction of popular movements and of individual leaders. Those who are bent on seeing in Islamism nothing but Mahomet, in the English Commonwealth nothing but Cromwell, in the French empire nothing but Napoleon, must be sorely puzzled by our present revolution and be fain to exclaim, with Byron, "We want a hero." One name there is, which we all love and venerate, a name which has received the consecration of the grave, but the whole significance of this grand upheaval cannot be conveniently merged even in the illustrious person of Jackson. Valiant men we have had and still have in great numbers. The genius which understands how to evoke all the energies of a people; how to apply them aright when evoked, has not yet appeared on our stage, or has haply been hustled off in the crowd of supernumeraries. In this great revolution of little men we miss even the average intelligence, the average forecast, the average of enlightened patriotism, which the representative form of government is supposed to secure; and the citizens generally look with more dismay at the bearing of their delegates than at the gathering difficulties of the situation. The dissatisfaction of the people is re-echoed by the consciousness of their representatives themselves—some of whom were lately so frightened at the responsibility of their position, so thoroughly self-convicted of their incompetence to deal with the momentous questions before them, that they made, with all the boldness of despair, or entertained with all the calmness of resignation, the wildest propositions to divest themselves, and through themselves the people, of rights which have been regarded heretofore as almost indefeasible. In spite of this unwelcome phenomenon, we are not ready to pronounce the modern experiment of representative government a total failure. We are not ready to proclaim a dictatorship. The people are able and willing to instruct their delegates, and if these delegates will only listen to the voice of their constituents, all will yet be well. Meanwhile it may be useful, in view of future elections, to pass in review the causes which have put so many incompetents in the late House of Representatives.

Some of the members of the late Congress were elected on the rather unsatisfactory ground that they had served in the Congress of the old Union—in other words, that they had been party hacks. As West Point was the plant-bed of our generals, so Washington was the seminary of our statesmen. We acknowledge that routine has its value in its place; but the routine of caucus-holding, log-rolling, wire-pulling politicians, is worse than useless in a revolution. It is almost impossible for such men to rise to the height of the great argument which we are discussing; they have naturally kept up the old congressional jargon and played the old stage tricks, not knowing, or affecting not to know, that the time for all these corrupt traditions is either past or not yet come.

Then we had the usual proportion, or rather disproportion of lawyers—another unfortunate heir-loom of American politics. Lawyers have a weakness for politics, as mathematicians for metaphysics; and all experience shows how hopeless that weakness is. Wise and liberal legislation is not to be expected from counsel learned in the law; and some of the most astounding resolutions offered during the late session emanated from men who have a certain local reputation as practitioners at the bar.

Another cause of the deficiencies which we deplore is to be sought in the actual scarcity of good material. Most of the real ability of the country has been absorbed by the military service, and not, as some of our contemporaries would have us believe, by the department clerkships. When the war broke out, many of the foremost men of the land, and many of prominent promise, engaged eagerly in the duty of repelling the invader. Of these, some have risen to high positions, which they can not conscientiously leave; some have become wedded to a life which, in spite of its repulsive features, possesses a strange fascination; while others are shattered wrecks of their former selves, and a large proportion have sealed their devotion with their life's blood. We do not subscribe to the vile French proverb, *Vieux soldat, vieille bête*—but certainly the recent recommendations of so many distinguished officers in the matter of recruiting our forces in the field, are calculated to stagger our faith in the intellectual abilities of our chieftains, whatever we may think of their subordinates.

But the main reason, we take it, why the members of Congress seem to fall so far short of the just standard, is the intense thoughtfulness of the people. In ordinary times there were too many men of intelligence, of culture, of true, though somewhat indolent, patriotism, who disdained to notice the squabbles of politicians, who feared to defile their hands by touching party pitch. They were grievously in the wrong, as they now know; for these petty skirmishes indicated a general engagement, and all reform, from the cleansing of the Augean stables down to the purification of the Confederate commissary department, is dirty work. But there is no danger of any such error now. Indifferentism is impossible. The air we breathe is full of the questions of the day. The food we eat (or go without) suggests a variety of economic problems. The notes we handle are financial tracts. Not a detail of daily life but forces on our minds the thought of our ceaseless conflict with a powerful and malignant foe. This steady, eager, painful thinking has educated the best part of the people, and, so far from looking to Congress for advice and encouragement, they are themselves the true counsellors, and the true preachers. The people of the Confederacy can dispense with the address with which their representatives have favored them. Nay, Congress would do well to heed the various addresses which the citizens of the Confederate States are putting forth from time to time, through the public press, in order to rebuke the TRIBULATION TREPIDS of both Houses.

FEBRUARY 26, 1864.

THERE is buoyancy, after all, in the Confederate atmosphere. The air grows lighter and clearer around us; and men begin to feel with a full assurance that our Confederacy is going right through. This improved tone in public feeling is partly due to the resolute action of Congress in the bills for maintaining an efficient army, and recovering financial health. We are warranted in believing, on the strength of these measures, that the country means to use, and to exhaust, all its powers and resources of mind, body and estate, but it will win and wear the dear prize of independence. None so irrational now as to speak of any possible "compromise;" we can all see and appreciate what is to be our dreary fate in one event, our noble recompense in the other; and that between these two there is Nothing. This intimate conviction, and the open public pledge given by Congress that all of us shall submit to equal sacrifices in sustainment of the common cause, makes any nation of white men, of the right breed and blood, truly invincible. State is now surer of State, and each man surer of every other man, than they were three months ago.

Therefore, in spite of maladministration, or perverseness, or imbecility, there is a healthier confidence that the people will bring all right in the end. We are to have a splendid army in the field this coming spring; and one way or another it will be fed. That is enough; with that nothing can fatally hurt us. We can bear even General Bragg—for he is not to command any army in action; and he will surely scarce order Lee to fall back, or Johnston's troops to hunt the duck in the Mississippi, or Beauregard to evacuate Charleston, or Polk and Maury to raise the white flag on the forts of Mobile. One can even concede that even in his present dignity he may be rather useful than otherwise; and, at any rate, this Confederate people is going to carry our cause through, and the whole Government along with it. On the march for independence and victory, inspired by such a fiery passion and strong hope, we have force to make light of every weight: no incubus or old man of the sea, will weigh a feather. By heaven's blessing we will carry them all on our shoulders; will pull through the very quartermasters, and even, if that be possible, the commissaries themselves—there will be a heavy drag, indeed!

Sometimes there is comfort in calling to mind that tiresome saying of the Swedish Chancellor—that it is wonderful how little wisdom goes to the government of men—comfort, we mean, to the governed: for, as to the governing (for the time being) they rather disrelish that maxim while in office. They are in the trade, and must look wise—it is impossible to *be* so wise as they look,—and, at any rate, even if the maxim were true, and they most potently believed the same, yet they hold it not courtesy to have it thus set down; and for a great Chancellor, a Minister of State, and brother of the craft, to decry his own wares, and to spoil the trade in that kind of way, is a piece of weakness they cannot pardon in the too candid Oxenstiern. But to those who are, for the time being, not governing, but governed, it may be consolatory, while they see the incompetence and perversity of rulers, to remember that this is the way such things are done—that we may not be much worse off than others, as men usually go—that most great things are accomplished in the main, not by governments, but by the resistless will of a roused national heart—that, through all, and in spite of all, the unwisdom of rulers, a nation's destiny accomplishes itself, more or less, according to that nation's deserts—and that the world, on the whole, wags.

Here is the moral: that if we are resolved to be free, and worthy to be free, we shall be, in spite of the very devil.

Now, it is a great thing to stand upon a basis of simple fact and truth. In this struggle, whichsoever of the two parties first gets himself upon that firm ground must win the day; and we do not think that the Confederates are upon it now. They at least know that they must conquer or perish; that compromise there can be none; that the Federal power or the Confederate people must be ruined; that we must dictate a peace, or else our enemies will; we on our terms, or they on theirs; we on their ground, or they on ours; that they must be bankrupt and divided asunder, or we beggared and outlawed. Be it so; and better so. We protest that this position of affairs is altogether to our mind; if any Confederate shrink from abiding this issue, and in this exact form, it is time that such Confederate should gather up and clutch all he can lay his hands upon, turn it into gold and jewels, and sneak away across the lines, provided he can escape the robbers that infest those parts.

MARCH 5, 1864.

IF the Confederate capital has been in the closest danger of massacre and conflagration; if the President and cabinet have run a serious risk of being hanged at their own doors, do we not owe it chiefly to the milk-and-water spirit in which this war has hitherto been conducted?

It is time to ask, in what light are the people of the Confederate States regarded by their own Government? As belligerents, resisting by war an invasion from a foreign people, or as a gang of malefactors, evading and postponing the penalty of their crimes? It may appear a strange question, yet the answer is not so distinct as could be desired. The enemy's Government, we know, takes the second view of our position. To the Washington authorities we are simply criminals awaiting punishment, who may be hanged or who may be pardoned. In their eyes our country is not ours, but theirs. The hostilities which they carry on are not properly war, but military execution and coercion. There is, in their opinion, no equality of rights between us, no more than there is between the police and a gang of garroters which the police is hunting down. Even the one symptom of apparent recognition upon their part, of our status as a war-making people, namely, the exchange of prisoners (a measure to which policy compelled them for a little while), is at an end. We would not treat, forsooth, with Major-General Butler! The outlaws, indeed, pretend to tastes and preferences as to which of the efficient police-constables shall be sent to deal with them. The fastidious creatures demand to be brought back to their duty by gentlemen-like officers, and to be handled with kid gloves, do they!

This, we are all aware, is the manner in which our enemies view the subject; and, to do them justice, they act in accordance with their theory. But " we are to consider," it seems, "not what wicked enemies may deserve, but what it becomes us, as Christians and gentlemen, to inflict." Oh, hypocrisy; and thou forty-parson power which alone can sound its praise through thy forty noses! What cant is this! What comfort are these fine sentiments to the houseless families who have been driven from their homes, when they find that our armies, even on the enemy's soil, are withheld from giving the invaders a taste of real war in their own quenched hearths and blazing barns? For what have we set over us a Government at all, if it be not to protect us against our enemies; to avenge us when need is; to uphold our cause in all its fullness and grandeur, and to keep our banner flying high?—but *this* is lowering the cause, and dragging the banner through the dust: *this* is encouraging, inviting our invaders to ravage and pillage us at pleasure, sure that they will not be visited with the like in their turn;—the Christianity and chivalry of all this is for the enemy—to us and ours it is cruelty and contempt. It was not for this our fields have been soaked with the choicest blood of our children these three terrible years.

It is very painful to think it; still more to say it; but the simple truth is, that after all the hardships we have undergone, and the victories we have won, our enemy is gradually gaining over us the great moral advantage and prestige that officers of the law have over malefactors. So often and so long have we yielded to their pretensions of superiority, and suffered them to deny our equal right, that it must end in demoralizing and quelling our spirit. The Yankee now seems not to stand opposite to us with the sword, but to stand over us with the whip, which, from time to time, he *cracks*. And we are Virginians, Carolinians, the "chivalry" (God bless us!) of this Continent, and that policeman there, with his baton, is the vulgar and despised Yankee. Soon, at this rate, all the pluck will be taken out of us; we shall be rebels confessed; and it is not war that will finish the work, but criminal jurisprudence and prosecuting attorneys; not generals, but constables; not the sabre, but the handcuff. The sword is too bright, too high-tempered, too noble an instrument to be used upon such material; they will substitute the lash.

What, then, would we practically suggest? First, to put to death all "raiders" caught in the fact; secondly, to insist upon the most scrupulous carrying out of retaliation for murders, robberies, and other outrages, with the most punctual exactitude; we cannot afford *now*, if we would recover our rightful position, to bate them one jot or tittle; thirdly, on our next entry into Pennsylvania and the parts adjacent, to remember with jealous accuracy the proceedings of the enemy's generals on our own soil. We have no use for any Christian gentleman who will come short of these requirements. It is time that our kind and religious rulers should begin to show mercy to us; and as the first and most urgent work of necessity and mercy, it is right and expedient that the robbers and fire-raiders just apprehended on the peninsula meet with a quick trial and a dog's death.

MARCH 11, 1864.

The last homage which the Yankees have paid to the shade of John Brown in the late Dahlgren raid may yet cost the invaders dear. The Government is nerveless and vacillating as usual, but the temper of the people is at a white heat. Never in the course of the war have the devilish intentions of our enemies been so distinctly enunciated. This last lesson will not be lost; for luckily it is not too late to learn. At the outset of this campaign, in which the advantages are on our side, with our ranks filled and our financial troubles in the course of a happy adjustment, our foes have thrust a terrible weapon into Southern hands, a weapon, which, for various reasons, the South has hitherto forborne to use. It is, we admit, a sword that cuts both ways, a sword with a spiked hilt, which will gall the hand that wields it with an uncertain grasp, but it is an effective instrument, and it is better to employ it in any way than to bow our necks to the axe, or to bare our backs to the lash of those who set up to be executioners. If we were dealing with any other people than the Yankee nation, we should prefer to fight under the starry cross of our battle-flag; but we have no choice. The blackness of darkness has veiled the stars and hid the cross of our ensign. Chivalry and Christianity, as emblemed in our banner, as symbolized in our seal, and proclaimed in our motto, are not idle terms when we have to do with men. But mad dogs and mad Yankees are to be dispatched with the first implement of destruction that comes to hand. Let every Yankee robber die the "ignominious death" which their late leader expected for the stragglers of his pack of hell-hounds, and let us begin at once with the picked gang of marauders, whose fate should be decided, not by the amount of mischief which they actually accomplished, but by the outrages which they came to perpetrate.

We can stop these raids; we can paralyze these miscreants. That we have not done so more effectually heretofore is due to a pitiable imbecility in the administration, and, we regret to say, an equally lamentable supineness on the part of the resident population. What has been, hitherto, and elsewhere than in Richmond, the noble utterances of the farmers? "Bury the silver! Hide the bacon! Drive off the stock! Send the negroes 'southward!' Stay at home and beg the Yankees to have mercy on our women and children, and not consume all our corn and provender." In their vocabulary there were no such words as rifle, powder-horn and shot-pouch. Now, let it be distinctly understood, that when we handle such marauding expeditions as these, no quarter is to be given to them by the Government, and hence that the raiders will give none to those who submit to fall into their hands, and a very different spirit will animate the people, who are not cowards, but simply selfish. Let it be distinctly understood that though there may be exempts from regular service, there are no non-combatants in such a struggle as this, that every man who can raise a finger, MUST raise that finger in defence of his home; and efficient organizations will spring up in every rural neighborhood. And hang the robbers. That is a necessity. That thing must be done if the country is to escape pillage and the town conflagration. Hang them as soon as they are caught. Hang them and let them remain hanging, as a sign of the "Entertainment for Man and Beast" which we offer to the Yankee race.

MARCH 25, 1864.

A PERPETUAL wonder to the many who do not stop to think, is the cheerfulness of those who have lost every thing by the flood of invasion, and the patriotism of those who have been left by our receding armies within the enemy's lines. The leading optimists in the Confederacy are those who have had their mansions pillaged and then burnt; who have had their lands laid waste and their negroes carried off; who have lost all the elegant appliances of life, and have seen, with their own eyes, the treasured heir-looms of past generations carted off by a Yankee general or pocketed by a Yankee private. The leading pessimists are those who have thus far come off scot-free from the great reckoning between the two races, who have made money instead of losing it, who have been subjected to no sacrifices, who have kept up the old style of living, and have kept aloof from the new style of dying. When our armies are encamped on the debateable ground which has been raked time and again by the harrow of war; when our scouts penetrate into the regions which the enemy infest, they find a more cordial welcome and meet with more hospitable treatment than in those sections where the Yankee has never set his foot. The country is stripped, but from mysterious recesses something is brought forth for the hungry Confederate, who might ask in vain for food in counties which the Federals have not yet ransacked. The land is one vast common, but the little patches of ground which the impoverished owners still cultivate, seem to yield more than the broad acres of the wealthiest planters. The houses are in ruins, but the Confederate soldier is greeted more gladly under the shattered or charred roof-tree than in comfortable dwellings farther South. The homely, hearty appellation, " our boys," once so common, is now confined to the army itself and to the border country. Quarter a regiment of cavalry or a battalion of artillery in the interior, even if it be but a short distance back of our lines, and there is no end of lamentations, objurgations, and railing accusations. Alas! for the stuck pigs and the slaughtered sheep. The devil take the artillery! Alas! for the poultry-yard, "'henless,' and 'chickless' in its 'cockless' woe." The devil fetch the cavalry! Alas! for the hay-stack and the straw-rick! The devil seize the artillery, the cavalry, the soldiers generally!

But there is nothing surprising in all this; and it is not worth the while to quarrel with human nature because it is so mean or to deify it because it is so heroic. In this momentous struggle, it is a great gain for a man to bring home to his mind the reality of the issues before him; and the shortest road to that end is sacrifice—voluntary or involuntary. A few, and but few, in the whole Confederacy faced the great alternative calmly and deliberately at the very outset. The masses were right at heart, but they were not conscious of the full import of the phrases which they used so freely. Since then many—how many—have had practical illustrations in their persons and property as to the real meaning of the war and the real purposes of the Yankees. Of these, small is the proportion who have kissed the rod and bowed the knee. The vast majority are firmer than ever, and more buoyant than ever, because their doubts are all gone with their property. Their losses are investments which can be made good, if not in kind, yet in a higher sense made good by perseverance and the success which waits on perseverance. Their hearts are in their treasure. If defection comes at all, it will come not from those who have suffered most, but from those who have suffered least, and who hope that, at the worst, they can make a tolerable composition with the invader. If it is true that whoso loves much gives much, it is also true that he who gives much learns to love much; and what is true of individuals is true of States. Compare the late message of Georgia's Governor with the address of the exiled Chief Magistrate of Louisiana. We have no far inland Arcadia around which the tide of invasion has swept innocuous. All have suffered and all are true. But there is no sorrow like unto the sorrow of Virginia, and there is no faith more stanch than hers.

It is not without reason, therefore, that the grim wish is sometimes uttered that the Yankees would give certain lukewarm localities a taste of their quality, for a touch of Yankee, does, beyond a question, make all Confederates kin. But we hope that any further chastening of this kind is not seriously needed. There is reason to believe that the whole Southern community, with the ample sacrifices required, will henceforth serve the common cause with more perfect singleness of heart, and bear the common burden with a more patient spirit.

MARCH 26, 1864.

It is painful to be obliged to treat seriously so revolting an idea as that of receiving Butler as the Yankee agent of exchange; yet the matter is really a serious one: it gravely affects two most vital questions; first, the honor of the Confederate Government, and second, the whole policy and theory of this war. The first and main concern is, of course, the national honor of the Government; which, indeed, embraces and overrides the other consideration; because there can never be for any people either policy or expediency in self-abasement and degradation. No nation can afford dishonor: the expenses and sacrifices of years of war yet to come we can endure; but disgrace never. It would be the loss and ruin, in advance, of our whole cause. If there be any one thing good, heroic, invincible, in this Confederacy, it is the high, keen spirit of its best citizens: that heroic quality could not survive deliberate humiliation, deliberate admission by our Government that we cannot, or dare not, stand up to our word, and put our solemnly declared principles into action. The question at issue here may be represented as a trifling detail. Not so; it would be deeply, painfully felt by every man of principle in the country, to be a virtual surrender of our whole right and *status* as a belligerent power, a virtual admission that we are indeed nothing but rebels and criminals, evading justice and postponing punishment: and many a good old Virginian, who has sent his sons proudly and gladly to the field, to vindicate the sovereignty of a State, and the haughty independence of a National Government, would then bitterly grudge every drop of blood that his children have spilled. He would feel that the enemy has been allowed slowly, but surely, to surround himself with all the *prestige* inseparable from the party having law on its side, and therefore enabled to take a high tone, and deal with a high hand; while we Confederates take the airs and use the language of an equal and independent power, only by fits and starts, snatching here and there at a thin pretext of dignity, but ready to drop it hastily at the first summons of its real owners, and our real masters.

You cannot separate national honor from policy or expediency. Yet try to consider this latter part of the case by itself. Is it politic and expedient to teach our enemy that we are ready to yield up all our rights for fear of the consequences of exacting and enforcing them? That we are ready to say, if we retaliate any outrage the enemy will retaliate back again—let us not retaliate: if we keep our word in the matter of Butler, then they will hold our prisoners—let us not keep our word. Why not say, also, when they are marching into our country, if we fire upon them they will fire back at us; cease firing! Once entered upon this path there is no stopping; every day must give them more and greater advantage, until they have, indeed, the top-hold, the whip-hand: every communication between us then would not be a negotiation, but an order or edict *de haut en bas*. This cannot be policy in a struggle for national independence, which the present is supposed to be. On the contrary, it is we, it is the party assailed, invaded, and sought to be reduced to subjection, who cannot afford for one moment to bate one jot or tittle of our highest pretensions.

If we stand firm, Lincoln must yield and draw back from this insolent and outrageous demand. He has nothing to lose, personally, by appointing some less obnoxious agent: we, by accepting Butler, should lose all. We should lose our self-respect, our dignity, our honor. But if the Government be indeed so insane as to receive Butler, the evil effects will by no means be confined to this isolated humiliation, and the triumph of the enemy over our Southern " chivalry." Who cares for this Butler? And what are their vulgar boastings to us? But the case is this:—if the Government should, in this instance, belie its own proclamation, men would say, *which* of its proclamations, then, which of its declarations and solemn pledges, does it mean to observe, and which to violate? The President has, in other eloquent proclamations and declarations, enunciated certain principles and resolves—for example, that the Confederacy has determined to make itself independent at all hazards and sacrifices; that in no case, on no terms, will we ever live in political union with the Yankee nation again. The question would soon arise, Are these some of the things that the President meant when he said them, or that he did not mean? Seeing that one deliberate proclamation is trampled under foot, why not another? The whole question is open. Policy and expediency may any day dictate the quiet ignoring of some other declared resolve of the Government: considerations of humanity, wish to stop effusion of blood, a present from Mr. Lincoln of vaccine matter, chloroform, we know not what, may be urged as reasons to depart from the extreme rigor of these resolutions, and to make on one of them, or on all of them, some sort of *compromise*. As we write the word, we shiver.

The people (thank God!) are up to the mark, up to the work; they meant and mean to carry out all these proclamations and messages to their fullest extent. The soldiers have bidden adieu to their families and gone to the field, taking their lives in their hands, to rescue their native land from the pollution of a base invader, or else to die. They are either the soldiers of an independent Government, or else they are brigands and rebels, with no rights at all. They expect their Government to maintain their position, and its own: it is for that they have constituted a Government. It is sad when your leader has to be dragged and goaded, to make him so much as follow. A government ought to be the head and heart of a national movement, not the tail, not the posteriors.

MARCH 29, 1864.

THE result of the military council held at Washington in the early days of this month, was correctly stated in the columns of this paper, on better information than our generals sometimes get from their trading scouts. We endeavored to call attention to the decision of the United States Government—that the next campaign should be made against Richmond—that the whole veteran force of the United States should be consolidated in Virginia under Grant; and that nothing further should be attempted in the South and West until the chief object was accomplished. We understand that our warning created some merriment in official circles. Our military Solomons were too well satisfied that there would not be another great battle fought in Virginia during the war; and that the great campaign was to be looked after in Georgia. Official facts, now well-known to all, show who was right and who was wrong. Grant has even been made Commander-in-Chief. Not a commander-in-chief after the manner of Halleck; not a bureau officer at Washington; but Commander-in-Chief on the field. He takes the chief army in his hands, and does not ask Lincoln for more troops, but orders them up to his headquarters from any part of the country. His main object, like that of all other generals, is victory and success *where he in person shall command.* To secure success there, every general will, if he has the power, strip all other quarters of troops. To Grant that power has been given—a power hitherto unknown, except when sovereigns have been on the field as commanders—and Grant has assumed the personal command of the "Army of the Potomac." This fact removes all ground of doubt. The campaign of 1864 will be here, in Virginia, against Richmond. The war elsewhere will stand still. The best parts of the army of Chattanooga, and that of the Mississippi, will be seen here. Already they are assembling at Annapolis, in Maryland.

Grant is now the pet bubble of the Yankees, which that bubble-worshipping people are blowing as they never blew bubble before. Grant is the newly-discovered Hercules, who is to crush the eleven heads of the Southern hydra. Grant is the rebel-slayer and traitor-eater who is to make mince-meat of secession, exterminate the slave oligarchy, put the chivalry *hors de combat,* and swallow all the fire-eaters with a wink. Grant, who whipped Bragg at Missionary Ridge; who took Vicksburg and Pemberton, with Pemberton's army, all Pemberton's bacon, flour, sugar, rice, beans, and potatoes; who got whipped at Shiloh, and was saved next day by Buell; who, with eighty-four regiments at Donelson, beat ten regiments of Kentucky Home-Guards, aided by a few Virginians and Tennesseans, after a battle of three days and four nights;—Grant is the warrior whose prowess and fortune are to plant the eagle's victory upon every peak of the Alleghanies; upon each bluff of the Mississippi; around the entire Gulf and Ocean coasts, and upon every Capitol of the insurgent States. To do all this, Grant is trammelled with but one single order—"subdue the rebellion;" and furnished with an authority over the entire military force of his nation never before possessed by any general, except when that general was an absolute sovereign in the field.

Strange to say, the South regards the appointment of Grant to supreme command with a sort of satisfaction. They believe this favorite Yankee general to be nothing else than what is called, in homely phrase, a *humbug.* They consider him formidable only in the fact that, having the confidence of the Yankees, and the support of their Government, he may bring together larger military forces and employ more unlimited military resources than any general of less celebrity among his countrymen. Neither our army, our generals, nor our people entertain much respect for the military capacity of this officer, who has won reputation solely by the follies and faults of Jefferson Davis. But they do hold him in respect by virtue of the formidable numbers that always attend his standard, and which will now be controlled by him more than ever before.

This opposite appreciation of Grant by the two belligerents is characteristic of both peoples. The North admires success; the South, merit. The fault and folly of the Yankees is their overweening admiration for mere success, without regard to means;—whether it be in generalship, statesmanship, fortune-making, pulpitizing, impudence, insolence, vulgarity, or any other pursuit or characteristic, reputable or disreputable. Grant as a general, Seward as a politician, Lincoln as an unworthy winner of the Presidency by lottery, Barnum as the prince of humbug-mongers, Beecher as the cleverest of religious hypocrites, Heenan as a scientific bruiser, Law and Vanderbilt as millionaires by infinite frauds, Butler as model pilferer and despot,—these are the sort of worthies whose lives some Yankee Fuller will write for the admiration of remote Yankee generations.

The South is never imposed upon by base metal; her people look for merit and genius; and they bestow admiration only where these are found to be real and genuine. They look upon Grant as a hero by circumstance, accident, and Confederate folly; and they hold him in no sort of awe, except in regard to the formidable forces which he is always allowed to accumulate under his command. In the present campaign, the reputation which he enjoys at the North will enure to the profit of the Confederacy; for its generals will only have to ascertain where Grant intends to operate in person, to prepare to beat him by a corresponding concentration of their own forces. That point is no longer uncertain.

The mere appointment carries no danger in it to the South. The danger lies in the large accumulation of forces which is permitted to this general alone. With respect to the mass of troops which he will concentrate against Richmond, he is formidable; and the South must expect and prepare for the most formidable invasion, under his lead, that has yet been precipitated upon her. Grant's generalship she may afford to defy, but Grant's army she must prepare to resist, here, in Virginia, if anywhere with success.

APRIL 8, 1864.

HUMILIATION, fasting, and prayer are suitable to these days The shuffling recognition of that felonious Major-General Butler as a military commissioner treating with this Government—the practical withdrawal of that public, solemn proclamation denouncing him as a thief and murderer, outside "the pale of military respectability;" the kind and gracious message (reported by a contemporary) sent by the felon, through Commissioner Ould, to the President, to the effect that Major-General Butler is now satisfied with him, and that he, the Major-General, is proud to belong to the "Democratic party," and cherishes a sincere admiration and esteem for Jefferson Davis; these things promote, in a salutary manner, that chastening of the heart which properly prepares us for fasting and humiliation on this appointed Friday.

Nothing is wanting to this humbling lesson. We declare that we will not receive such a criminal under the safeguard of a flag of truce, nor treat with him in any manner. He knows what Confederate proclamations are made of: he does not coax or flatter us by any means; he does not come up to City Point to see whether he will be received or not: he simply establishes himself in our Virginian Fortress Monroe, and says, when you are quite ready, chivalrous Confederates, you may come *to me*, under flag of truce, and perhaps I may receive *you:*—and we go; and are benevolently received; for Butler would not break the bruised reed: he even sends back an indulgent and encouraging message, lest we be too much cast down.

Propitiated by our self-abasement, he condescends to enter upon negotiations with Commissioner Ould, and arranges a resumption of exchange under the cartel. But this is not all;—we learn by New York papers (not yet through our own official channels), that the body of Dahlgren, committed obscurely to the earth somewhere near this city, is to be exhumed as soon as possible and restored to the sorrowing parent of that dashing house-burner. Doubtless it will be delivered at Fortress Monroe with military honors, and under a salute of Confederate guns at the departure from hereabouts: for Dahlgren was a graduate of West Point; probably a member of the Democratic party, too; and how can simple civilians, or soldiers of a mere "provisional army," presume to say that a West-Pointer had not a perfect right to pelt us with oakum balls, and sprinkle us with turpentine? What can we know of the true principles of "military respectability?"

At any rate, humiliation is our cue this week. We can now point with the utmost confidence to at least one proclamation of the President, which was intended to be serious, and carried out to the very letter. Confederate proclamations, of a "proud," a "defiant," or menacing tone, do not perhaps now command much respect; but when the President announces humiliation, he means it. Mr. Davis has the reputation of unbending obstinacy and *hauteur;* but that is for his friends. When his own supporters and rightful counsellors, the men who created this Confederate movement, and elevated him to his great office, approach him with respectful advice or remonstrance, it may be that he is hard as flint; but let the public enemy command him at his peril, to eat his own words and come down from his high ground, and who so politic or "reasonable" as he? His stern self-will is for us, his confederates; his gracious gentleness for our foes. Triumph and gratified pride are for them; for us, fasting, humiliation, and prayer.

Thus we prepare ourselves, and we trust our readers also, to meet in fitting frame of mind, the services of Friday, the 8th of April. Let us fast on this day, as only Confederates can. Let us clothe our souls in the sackcloth and ashes of humility: and let us pray, saying: "From all privy conspiracy and hugger-mugger—from canting and re-canting, and all other shuffling sin—from the crafts and assaults of the devil, and Yankee democrats—Good Lord deliver us!"

APRIL 20, 1864.

IF the Government of the old United States was indeed "the best the world ever saw," it is we who have it and hold it. If it was a light to lighten the nations, it is we, who kindled the Pharos at first, that keep the light burning there still. As to "civilization," in its high and true meaning, we trust that there is no comparison whatever between us. The abandoned people whom we have cast out, are quickly losing all sense of that higher meaning which indeed, they never were sufficiently advanced to comprehend;—they think that civilization means gas and steam, printing presses and rapid railroads—no matter what pollution those presses pour forth, no matter on what base errand men rush so fast along their iron roads. Of the development of those faculties and sentiments which fit us to live as members of a political community and a cultivated society, they are rapidly losing all thought, all care. They are forgetting the use of their mother-tongue, which is not only itself an evil, but the sure sign of much other and deeper evil.

In our respective relations to the negro race, the contrast between us is most satisfactory of all. There can be no longer any question which of us two, the Confederate or the Yankee, is the real friend and protector of the black; the most feeble-minded of our once doubting people, has only to consider the fate of those of our poor slaves who have tasted the tender mercies of abolition; the weltering, festering masses of filth and disease, where multitudes of negro women, children, and old men are perishing miserably, while the able-bodied men are goaded forward by bayonets to take the first volleys, and make a breastwork with their bodies for their philanthropic protectors. If any one doubt what is in store for those poor creatures, let him read the proceedings of a meeting which revealed the desperate struggle for life amongst the whites themselves in that northern country. Competition of black people with them is simply out of the question: and what then remains for the black people? Death: death, slow but sure; in negro-pens and pest-houses; on public works and fortifications, where contractors will understand that they accomplish a patriotic duty in starving and slaving them to death. Many do and will escape from the fatal toils, and come back to search for their masters; but the majority will perish miserably; death alone will set them free. "These are the bones of slaves," in the words of tuneful Longfellow; bones which will long cry out to heaven "We are the witnesses!" Witnesses, indeed, of the savage philanthropy of Yankees in the nineteenth century.

So the progress of events makes our Confederate cause ever plainer to our minds, and dearer to our hearts. Freedom, civilization, and humanity are all with us; all against our enemies.

APRIL 22, 1864.

WASHINGTON, SCOTT, GRANT; these three names, the only ones that have ever been dignified with the title of lieutenant-general, in the United States, mark three widely different epochs, and sum up the rapid degradation of a people. In the political hierarchy, the names of Washington and Lincoln express a still more complete degeneracy, though broken by more intervening gradations.

Upon the illustrious Virginian, who, in the early days of the Republic, first bore the title of lieutenant-general, and served the Government which his native State had the principal part in establishing, mankind has set the seal of undying fame. Even the mongrel hordes against whom, if his lot had been cast in the present age, he would have now been defending his native soil with the same spirit with which he fought for it against the arms of George the Third, are forced to feign admiration of a virtue they are incapable of comprehending, and to claim the honor of a common country with him to whom they would have been the most alien and repulsive of mortals.

The second on the list, also a Virginian, is a proper emblem of a declining period. Not deficient in military talent, but void of the loftier qualities which make up the complete warrior-statesman, he played his part with sufficient credit in ordinary times. His ridiculous foibles were overlooked by an indulgent country, and his egregious vanity could hardly be condemned with severity by a people of which the larger division was the most vainglorious of communities, and the most blatant of boasters. Unfortunately for himself, he lived long enough to witness a crisis demanding higher purpose and more exalted generosity than he possessed. His present ignominy is the result.

The last of the lieutenant-generals, who at present commands the well-thrashed Army of the Potomac, is a worthy type of the Yankee nation, now that it is thrown upon its own unaided resources for the production of heroes. His capture of Vicksburg, after the fruitless attempt of a year, by a species of lucky *coup de main* and with an overwhelming force, would scarcely suffice to establish his military fame, no matter of how great advantage it might prove in the general progress of the war. But in a contest where they can scarcely boast of a single victory upon a fair field, and where successive heroes have been raised up—young Napoleons and all—only to be shivered to pieces like the toys of a capricious child, or the idols of a savage tribe whose prayers have not been granted, it is pardonable that the Yankees should make the most of a victory without examining too closely into its nature, and should extol a successful general without minutely scrutinizing his merits. " In the country of the blind," says the French proverb, " the one-eyed man is king." In the country of the McClellans, the Burnsides, and the Hookers, Grant may be fairly entitled to supremacy.

Whether his countrymen appreciate his relative merits justly, or not, is a question for themselves. The honors which they shower upon him are certainly characteristic of them, and are marked by the taste which is peculiar to the Yankee. The title of lieutenant-general suggests the image of the first of that rank. Imagine Washington mounted upon a sofa in the White House in order to receive the plaudits of swindling Yankee contractors, boorish politicians, and sallow, sharp-visaged, over-dressed, "miscegenating" women. Fancy Seward exhibiting the conquering hero, like a tamed lion, to the gazing audience. Picture him the centre of attraction to the gorging multitude of a mammoth *table d'hôte*, and think what immense strides we must make in order to comprehend the three degrees of comparison, from the first to the last of the lieutenant-generals.

But it is not only in empty applause that his countrymen testify their admiration. With that barbaric love of show which has displayed itself so frequently in their conduct, they have just presented their chosen chieftain with a sword worthy of the Great Mogul. Diamonds and precious stones of a wonderful value ornament this magnificent weapon, and recall to our mind the example of Asiatic potentates, who, in conflict with simpler warriors, have so often learned the pregnant truth that iron can always command gold. It is not by jewelled swords or splendid truncheons of command that Lee is to be vanquished. Pæans of victory before the commencement of the battle, and anticipated glorification of their commander, will not suffice to make the Yankee army superior to that which has so often overcome it.

MAY 4, 1864.

THAT the war "is still characterized by the barbarities with which it has heretofore been conducted by the enemy;" that foreign governments "*persist* in countenancing, if not in aiding" that enemy; that "in disregard of duty and treaty obligations" those foreign governments persist in refusing to recognize our independence; that there is nothing satisfactory to report touching exchange of prisoners, inasmuch as "the Government of the United States *persists* in failure to execute the terms of the cartel;"—these things are certainly sad to contemplate. No wonder it gives our President pain to notice, yet once more, the distressing facts. That persons, nay, whole Governments, enjoying the full blaze of Christian civilization, and living in the nineteenth century, should not only resort to wicked courses and derelictions of duty, but persist in the same, after the impropriety of their conduct has been duly expounded to them, is nothing short of sinning against the light. What could we have done, it may be asked, that we have not already done, to bring our invaders and the outside nations to a sense of their duty? As to the barbarities of the war, we have heretofore, in several executive messages, and even special proclamations, charged their cruelty straight home to the hard-hearted Yankees; we have gone the length of threatening to return barbarity for barbarity, but our enemy knew that we were too religious and chivalrous for that; we have macerated ourselves with fasting and prayer, and more especially with humiliation, and they have wished us joy of it. To convince and convert foreign nations to a recognition of our cause, we have spared no labor, no expense. Swarms of "agents," known to our Secretary of State, in the Grand Hotel du Louvre, judge and decide, with gnostic palate, the merit of the vintages of Chambertin (whereof each glass costs us about three pounds of cotton), and it would not be too much to assert that we have devoted the whole Hebrew talent of the Parish of Plaquemines—a learned parish in Louisiana—to the task of enlightening Europe. An eloquent Liverpool factor, named Spence, is also paid in present gold, and a hope of noble contracts, to make promises for us to enlightened Europe. What more could we do in that department?

In the matter of the cartel and the exchange of prisoners, we have gone even greater lengths to soothe and flatter our enemies in fulfilling their agreement. Our Commissioner has sneaked humbly to Fortress Monroe, and, under flag of truce, has sought an interview with Major-General Butler; who condescended indeed to receive him, and even gave him hope of resuming the exchange under the terms settled by the cartel; yet still there is nothing satisfactory to report: at rare intervals, a few disabled Confederate prisoners do come, who may, it is thought, be more properly fed and nursed in the Confederacy than abroad; but on the whole something seems still wanting to ensure to us the speedy restoration of those fifteen thousand muskets promised. We think we know what it is; and, until this needful form shall have been complied with, our Government cannot say that it has done *all* it could do to put the exchange on an easy footing; General Butler wants, in order to satisfy his wounded dignity, a formal and written disavowal of the President's proclamation which denounced him as a felon, and of Mr. Ould's letter placing him "out of the pale of military respectability." On receiving a short paper of this kind — mere matter of form—it is understood that General Butler would at once begin sending us our fifteen thousand prisoners—unless some other valid obstacle should arise.

On the whole, however, here are three matters of very considerable importance, upon all which the message of the President presents us with a quite unfavorable report. With regard to the brutalities committed by the enemy upon our defenceless old men, women and children, the President thinks there is a mode of redress and eventual reparation. "Sooner or later," he says, "Christendom must mete out to them the condemnation which such brutality deserves." We doubt this: we should like to have a better security. Christendom loves successful and unpunished atrocities: it is only those for which vengeance is exacted—you may remark—that Christendom condemns. Perhaps there is some more immediate and efficient remedy which might suggest itself to the President, in his capacity of military commander-in-chief, if he would apply to it the energies of his powerful mind.

Perhaps we have gone the wrong way to work also with the Powers of Europe. Possibly the statesmen of that continent, contrary to all expectation, have not been deeply impressed by the diplomatic talent of Plaquemines Parish, whether of the circumcision or of the uncircumcision. One might, perhaps, venture to suggest—as the first step in the right direction—that all our emissaries be suddenly recalled, that they may cease to solicit unavailing interviews with clerks of secretaries of ministers, who heartily wish they were all dead.

To rectify the difficulty about exchange of prisoners, we should not, after all, recommend that Butler be really propitiated by the written apology and retraction which he requires. Of one thing the public may be well assured, that there will be no regular exchange under the cartel until there is an excess of prisoners in our hands. Another matter may be set down as equally certain, that we may as well drop the appeals to "humanity," and that "Christendom" will not help us at all.

MAY 12, 1864.

A BRAVE man struggling with adversity presents human nature in its grandest form. This has been accepted in ancient and in modern times. The storm which develops danger, magnifies the value of the skill and courage that rides through it. Fear betrays like treason. The courage which holds at even work moderate abilities, is of far more value in troubled times than the higher intellect agitated and paralyzed by fear. A calm, steady temper exhibited by those in conspicuous positions, soon communicates its influence to all the land. The courage that will carry us through the present crisis, is the steady determination that fastens each individual to the part of the great plan to which he has been assigned. We want no spasmodic effort to accomplish what cannot be done. Flurry and excitement accomplish nothing except to disorganize all rational exertion. They spring out of fear and they generate fear. They will do where spectacles are exhibited for amusement, but not where examples are needed for action.

Our civil authorities have just now a great part to play before the country. If they abandon in cold cowardice the post of duty, of course the contagion of a bad example spreads. But a regular, constant, brave industry, addressed to the duties of their position, will be of infinite value in the reassuring influences disseminated everywhere. This is the part which Congress must perform or abandon. It must run from its duties, and, to the extent of its influence, spread panic abroad, or it must, with unexcited energy, perform its great duties, and give to the whole country the encouraging example of duty performed calmly, bravely, and efficiently.

The country has work for this Congress to do. The Congressman who can find no legislative work to perform, with advantage to the country, might, and ought, then, if the emergency presses, to have a musket in the ranks where his constituents serve, and where his personal influence would stir like a trumpet. But we would only advise this in the event that in the judgment of Congress the emergency becomes too great to admit the regular and proper discharge of legislative functions.

As a senator well remarked: "This is a Congressional Government." The great controlling powers are invested in Congress; and it is with regret, therefore, that we observe at this most important juncture of our affairs a movement already made to fix an early day for its adjournment.

MAY 19, 1864.

"WHAT did you do under the reign of terror?" "I lived," replied Sieyes. "The only philosophical utterance of the period," says a fellow-academician. It was no little feat to live then; it is no slight achievement to live now. Another series of battles, another array of hecatombs, another outburst of grief throughout the Confederacy, another occasion for self-congratulation to those whose duty did not call them to share the fate of the men whose carcasses fell in "The Wilderness." It will be a great thing to have lived through this struggle, provided the life has been such as the life ought to have been. If either of these conditions fail, unphilosophic as it may seem, it were better that the survivors of their liberty or their honor had failed in keeping their miserable souls and bodies together. It will be, in any event, a sad thing for any man that has a spark of native nobility in his soul to have crept through this war a witness but not a participant of the great agony; none but those who have fulfilled in their own persons the conditions of earthly happiness, "a bad heart and a good digestion," will be content in after times to say: The war cost me nothing: I lost no blood, I lost no sleep, I took mine ease, I watched the markets, I laid the foundation of an immense fortune. Pessimists tell us that all this will be forgotten; that, in the third generation, the descendants of the blockade-runner, the quartermaster and the hospital steward will be the magnates of the land, and that the children of the men who fought for our independence will hold but a poor position. We hope not. The bitter memories of this war will not die out so easily. The roll of honor will not fade away so soon. The heritage of shame or of glory shall indeed be a heritage. Memory, vindictive or grateful, shall keep alive the deeds and misdeeds of the men who have passed through the struggle; and the best advice which we can give to many sinners is, that they go and have themselves killed now, "while it is called to-day," as existence will hardly be tolerable to them at a future time. As "for the wretched souls of those who have lived thus far without infamy and without praise," their day of grace is not yet over, they are not yet within the gates of the *Inferno;* let them redeem themselves by some heroic effort, some great sacrifice, in this last stadium of the war.

MAY 20, 1864.

HOOKER, Burnside, Meade; anybody could keep a large army well in camp on the Rappahannock. From Grant another work is expected; and, to do him justice, he has, up to this moment, evinced a strong alacrity for trying, at least, to perform that work. But we shall not either attempt to foresee the events of to-morrow, or calculate the chance or consequence which attend them. The problem of the campaign is fairly stated, and every day, every hour is working it out so rapidly, that speculation as to the result seems, and is, superfluous. Scarcely is the editorial ink dry, when a new telegram announces a new stage of the process, and the divination which ought to anticipate the end, comes halting in behind the announcement of some accomplished fact. The *modus operandi* of whale-fishing is simple enough; yet the most confident theorist would not venture to predict, in any particular case, whether the huge creature will get off with the harpoon in his back, or upset the boat in his dying flurry, or run his hard head against the ship itself. Grant, like the whale, is no contemptible antagonist. We may believe him doomed: still he is dangerous. He has had the nerve to face the question with a directness which we find in no other Northern general. His assumptions are wrong; but he does not shrink from the legitimate consequences of the first step in the process. He has not tumbled back in dismay, as Burnside did at Fredericksburg; he has not lost his head, as did Hooker, at Chancellorsville. He has deliberately counted on "depletion," and a fearful depletion, too,—fearful to any man of less obstinacy and less selfishness. If he can effect, with every assault on our lines, not an equal, but a proportionate depletion of our ranks, then the satisfactory solution of the problem is, from his point of view, a mere question of arithmetic; a mere matter of time. He would coolly throw away a hundred thousand of his men, if, by that means, he could put fifty thousand of ours *hors de combat.* He believes that we are on our last legs, and, though those legs are sturdy and vivacious in the extreme, he thinks that certainly they are our last legs, and, once hamstrung, good-night to the Southern Confederacy. He is mistaken, profoundly mistaken; but this scientific fanaticism is exceedingly pertinacious. If a man is once convinced that he has squared the circle, rely upon it, that he will never retract. If a man fancies that perpetual motion may be made a reality, or that the philosopher's stone is something more than the fabled stone of Sisyphus, be sure that he will spend all his time, and waste all his substance in the endeavor to carry out his schemes. So Grant will not yield till he is fairly exhausted; and he means more than most Yankee generals do by their bravado, when he declares that he will not recross the river while he has a man left.

MAY 24, 1864.

The Northern journals certainly do keep up their game wonderfully well. They persist to the last in the noisy lie, the flagrant imposture, the palpable sophism, the vulgar boast, demanded by their master at Washington with unabated vigor and pertinacity. On the news of this movement of General Lee towards the Junction, they will, of course, raise the yell of triumph louder than ever. The retreat of Lee! The flight of the Confederates! Have they not abandoned Spottsylvania Court-House? Is not the Junction twenty miles nearer Richmond? What an amount of gaseous nonsense and truculent blackguardism will be expended on these themes! We suppose that people have sense in New York and London as elsewhere; and it will be difficult to make them believe that the Confederate army is flying, when it moves from a position which its adversary has abandoned, to place itself full before him across the new road on which he has determined to travel.

When General Lee moves his army after a lost battle, for the purpose of getting away from his antagonist, because he finds himself unable to maintain a struggle of brute force with him, he will have retreated. But if either party has done that, it is certainly Grant. Lee followed him from the Wilderness; he is now the last to move, and is pursuer, not pursued, from Spottsylvania. It is true that by both movements these armies have been brought nearer to Richmond; but for Lee, it was rendered necessary by the configuration of the soil and the lines of those rivers which he had resolved to defend—they have their sources remote from the city, approach it in their course, and empty their waters in the neighboring York. But for Grant it was choice. He is where he now is, because he could not pass over the road of his first and second selections. He might have come to Spottsylvania by travelling along the straight road from Washington to Fredericksburg, through Stafford, without firing a shot or losing a man. He might have arrived at Milford, from Port Royal, on the Rappahannock River, without the slaughter of his troops in the Wilderness or at the Court-House. He might have come still nearer—he might have come to the Piping Tree, within eleven miles of Richmond, without an engagement with General Lee. He might have come up the Peninsula, perhaps to Fair Oaks, and joined hands with Butler on the Southside, as some still expect him to do; and this he will doubtless proclaim, in the end, to have been the object of all his circuitous route. By each of these ways of advance he would have brought General Lee from the Rapid Ann nearer to Richmond. He did not take them because there were dangers and defeats. He preferred the first and the second before the third, and this before the fourth. That he abandoned, after trial, the two first, is due to two clear defeats in battle.

So far from losing ground, Lee has gained manifest advantages by each change of the lines. It is easier to defend that portion of his line which is near to Richmond, than that which was far removed from it. He is far better situated now than at Spottsylvania Court-House, and that was better than the Wilderness. In either place, his stores and reinforcements had to come up from Richmond. No reflecting man can doubt that the general situation is very much improved since the day when Grant crossed the Rapid Ann and Butler landed at Bermuda Hundreds. That was, indeed, a critical moment. The Confederate Government had been well warned of the concentration against Richmond. It was half convinced of its reality. But it was only half belief; an idea rather theoretical than practical.

But the ship had an original strength sufficient to stand the the shock when it came. Lee's thin army beat the chief force of the enemy; the second blow was deadened by the fortifications near Drewry. Every moment since has been gain to us. Time was all we wanted to bring up BEAUREGARD from the siege of Charleston, and we got time. When he forced the enemy from his intrenchments and reopened communications; and when Lee had given a final answer to the question whether he was able to stand up against the full weight of Grant; the chief danger, the danger of being crushed under the rush of an avalanche, ceased to exist. It is true, that the *chance of battle* may yet, some day, fall against us; but it is certainly far less probable now than then; and, therefore, we think there is convincing solid reason to believe that the military situation at this moment is much more favorable to us than when Grant crossed the Rapid Ann.

JUNE 2, 1864.

THE Yankee nation is too sharp for us—impossible to escape the penetration of that smart people. They have found us out. By the capture of a "rebel mail," and perusal of the letters therein, they have at length been enabled to see how we fare in the Confederacy; they can look into our meagre larders and see us sitting down to our daily meal. The revelation amuses them excessively, and no doubt encourages them too. Some of those unsuspecting correspondents, not writing per flag of truce boat, but speaking in the full confidence of privacy by this contraband mail, have even given their bills of fare: "One of the writers states that he purchases breakfast as follows: one loaf of bread, one dollar; four onions, two dollars; one egg, fifty cents; total, three dollars and fifty cents; *and with this meal he was satisfied until the next day!*" Our well-informed enemies, having intelligent spies in Richmond, have even discovered how very small that same dollar loaf has become; and can calculate by its rapid rate of shrinking in size, how soon it will arrive at about the dimensions of a pigeon's egg. Their newspapers of the more jocular turn, have an infinity of little jokes upon this matter; and undoubtedly the Confederate baker coming to your door, and not giving the trouble of opening it, but just inserting the family's bread for the day through the keyhole, is at this moment furnishing subjects for the lively artists of New York pictorials. "One lady," writing also, it seems, through the contraband mail, "states that she could do without another dress if she could but get one pound of tea." No wonder this picture of the Confederate table is exhilarating to those who have undertaken to "starve out the rebellion;" because they can now approximately determine about what time the four onions will come down to one, the egg will disappear altogether, the whole family will be subsisting all day upon the one dollar loaf—which can go through a keyhole—moistened with water,—the spirit of the Confederate mother, brave as she is, will sink and break as she looks upon her delicately nurtured children, to whom once she never denied a comfort or a delicacy, pining and whitening from day to day with the cruel hunger; until at last all hearts will turn with love and devotion to the "Old Flag," which symbolizes steaming kitchens and porterhouse steaks.

It is not surely, that our Northern brethren delight in human misery, or joy in the pangs even of hardened "rebels," when they dwell with satisfaction upon these things. But it has been their painful duty to convince us, by sore chastisement, that we can no more exist without the Union than without the boons of Nature and Providence—that in the Union alone we live, and move, and have our being—and that, if we would live and not die, we must pray to the Union, Give us each day our daily bread. We were to be taught that—as General Sherman says,—" it was not *we* who created the land;" it was the Union that created it; and the said Union is the supreme ruler and disposer of that land, with all that grows and lives thereon. Our teaching has been hard and stern, but they now hope it is nearly complete, if they know any thing of the human heart. Perhaps it is the human stomach they are thinking of—merely a mistake of one intestine for another. How much the stomach can digest, they probably *do* know, but what the heart of a man can dare and endure they have yet to learn.

If it were, indeed, true, that we Confederates are suffering the privations they announce, and if Yankee nature could understand the significance of the phenomenon, those philosophers would perceive that it is quite impossible to conquer a people who submit cheerfully to such trials for the sake of freedom; that it must be because of our extreme need to be rid of *them* forever that we thus face death, in every form, slow or swift, on battle-field, in hospital, or in beggared and desolate homes. If they could but understand this, they would see something grand in our one poor meal a day. This is not their ideal of grandeur; they would say, if it be grand to eat one meal a day, then to devour six meals a day is exactly six times as grand. What! are the rules of arithmetic, and "the whole greater than its part," to be subverted? Is it not as certain that six pounds of pork are better than one pound of pork, as that twenty millions of people must conquer five millions? There is no use in reasoning with such a people as this, and only one way of dealing with them. Be it known to them, however, that the atrocious calculation on which they now carry on their "war," as they call it, upon women and children as well as fighting men, only makes us more thankful to God for having cut them off from our society for all time, and more resolute to fight them to the death. Our one meal shall dwindle to an infinitesimal dose—our daily allowance of bread shall not go through a keyhole, but pass through the eye of a needle, before we call *them* fellow-citizens, to say nothing of calling them masters.

JUNE 3, 1864.

THAT wonderful dispatch to a Northern paper from the "Headquarters in the Saddle," which we published yesterday, certainly shows a most cheerful buoyancy of disposition in the Yankee nation. Once more, as if nothing of the sort had ever happened before, it is announced that "*On to Richmond* is now the watchword and reply." "Whole army again in motion," as if it had never been in motion before; and "By night we will be within four hours' march of Richmond!" Why, they have been ere now within two hours' march of Richmond, yet somehow failed to arrive there. Lee, also, the same dispatch affirms, "is *again* out-generalled "—by that masterly movement, namely, from the Rapid Ann to the Pamunkey, at a cost of seventy thousand men, which might have been accomplished without the loss of one. Nothing could be more cheery than the jolly strategy of this saddle-correspondent. He says playfully, "Once getting Lee snugly ensconced in his works, *away we go* around his flanks and into his rear." Capital fun!

Nor is it the saddle-correspondent alone who is so jovial. Secretary Stanton also announces a dispatch from Grant, "that every thing comes on finely;" and another dispatch from Washington says, "There are the best possible spirits to-night in official circles." Those most mercurial and irrepressible official circles were in just as high spirits on the same night gone two years ago. Then, also, *On to Richmond* was the watchword and reply; and the yet unconquered Young Napoleon had reached, without the slaughter of seventy thousand of his troops, a position quite as close to his "predestined prey." It is now announced, and received doubtless with jubilation throughout all the North, that "every cannon fired the last week has been heard in Richmond;" as if Richmond had never heard any cannon before. Marvellous, indeed, is that Yankee mind. Crush it to the earth a dozen times—sink it over and over in the very depths of despondency, still it springs up again as merry as ever, singing out, Who's afraid? Victory is in our grasp at last! Once this, or once that, point gained, and "*away we go!*"

One would almost begin to fancy that the enemy is really persuaded, this time, that he is indeed on the eve of the capture of Richmond, but for the one trifling circumstance that gold has risen to one hundred and eighty-eight. This proves to our mind that those at the North who know best, and have the most immediate interest in the matter, do not believe that the Yankee army is ever to come on to Richmond at all :—which is also decidedly the opinion of Richmond herself. If those highly excited official circles of Washington and delighted newspaper readers of New York and Boston could but see the tranquil serenity of these embowered streets at this day —how peacefully our people go about their daily business; how quietly they buy and sell, or even marry and are given in marriage, as in the day when Noe entered into the ark. It is true they know that a mighty power has gathered countless hosts around this place commissioned to raze it utterly and leave not one stone upon another: true, they know that accurate plans of the "Doomed City," multiplied by the hundred thousand, point out this very moment every approach to their peaceful homes, and indicate each most advantageous method of crushing, sacking and burning the place, drenching these leafy shades with blood, and strewing them with mangled bones and spattered brains. True, also, that they feel in their souls how much more blessed on that day of doom, if it should ever dawn upon them, would be the mangled dead than the landless, houseless living; they *do* hear every day—the Yankee acoustics are correct— the roar of cannon flaming in front and flank of that enormous host, advancing "with a celerity never known before;" they are well aware that this very night, before the stars shine out—if only one obstacle were removed—there might be a hundred thousand brigands in blue swarming in every street, rampant in every house, until the work of slaughter and rapine were done; and then, in a pyramid of fire, the city of their pride and love would rush skyward, with all its pleasant dwellings, with the hearths at which its old people have sat and the cradles in which its children have been rocked. Its murmuring river, reddened with flame and blood, would flow hereafter past mounds of gore-clotted cinders, which should stand for generations a monument of Yankee vengeance. Yes, they know all this; yet to-night they will lie down peacefully to rest, trusting in Providence that the morning sun will shine as serenely into their windows, through the whispering trees, as on any morning of the last hundred years.

It is not that our people are boastful, or presumptuous, or unconscious of danger, or insensible to the unutterable evils and curses which would come in a moment upon them and theirs in case of the enemy's success. They know well that the fortune of battle is doubtful, and that each instant of time may bring on the great arbitrament. But they are not demonstrative, nor by any means histrionic. The roll of the great artillery is in their ears; but they only set their teeth within closed lips :—they have done all they can; they have sent forth their bravest and their dearest to stem that roaring tide of fell foes, and can but await the awards of a just God in Heaven They feel, too, in every fibre of their hearts, that, in the very best event which can befall, many a gallant gentleman will lie low in the dust, whose single life could not be paid by a thousand of the base rabble-rout he holds at bay. Yet, after all, it is felt that this Richmond is our city; and that no living creature must be permitted to enter it against our will—and that if an enemy do come in, it cannot be save over our dead bodies; and that now, even as in old times, it is honorable and even delightful, (both *dulce* and *decorum*), to die for our country.

What a contrast is this we have sketched between the spirit and attitude of the two people now in presence upon this soil! The one race crazy with greediness, and intoxicated with a sense of brute power in their numbers and material resources, furiously striving to crush out of existence a people who have never wronged them, and exulting with loud, senseless glee in the near approach of the day that will crown with success the foulest national crime in history:—on the other side, a community of high-spirited freemen, seeking nothing in the world that is not theirs, doing and aiming to do neither hurt nor harm to any fellow-creature, standing up in defence of their own hearths and homes, sternly silent in the simple might of their own manhood, with the antique heroism that in all ages have impelled brave men to endure and dare all things for country and honor. Looking upon which contrast, and deeply penetrated with its significance, let every man say with all his heart, May God defend the Right!

JUNE 4, 1864.

One of the greatest compliments that the Yankees can pay us is their thankfulness for the small favors which they receive at our hands. Of course, a real success makes them delirious, but any kind of success is welcome. A hay-stack reduced, a corn-bin shelled out, a water-tank forced to evacuate, a pig-sty compelled to surrender unconditionally, a few yards of railway routed, the centre of a bridge broken, libraries gutted, plate-boxes emptied, furniture ground into its ultimate atoms; any kind, every kind of devastation and plunder; any thing, every thing, seems as a matter of rejoicing, as a theme for future Thanksgiving Dinner orations. However, these are exploits more to the taste of the genuine Yankee than the rude work of actual combat, and we do them wrong in depreciating the achievements, which, of all others, they will remember with most satisfaction in after years. And well they may; for, besides stolen spoons, pilfered pictures, and confiscated books, they will have little to show in their own country for the oceans of blood and the mint of money which they have lavished on their grand speculation, their great South Land Bubble; and they will hardly choose to come to our blood-stained soil, to our desolated fields, in order to revive the memories of Manassas and Chickahominy, of the Wilderness and the Southside.

Yet this same Southside has been the scene of one of those infinitesimal successes which the Yankee calculus has enabled them to comprehend—one of those trifling favors for which the grateful heart of Yankeedom overflows with thankfulness. Heartily rejoiced at his own escape from danger (for whenever Confederates are in the neighborhood there is danger), the Yankee reporter of the memorable affair of that memorable Monday, puts a fresh wit into his patent pen-holder, and proceeds to sum up the Federal gains and the Confederate losses. "Our gains are the developing the enemy's strength in our front, and compelling him to retain a large army in a position of little value in the real struggle." To the latter clause we are constrained to demur. Compelling a large Confederate army to remain in a position of little value is a feat which neither Butler nor Grant will be able to perform, so long as Beauregard and Lee are in actual command of our armies. That gain is altogether visionary—an Alnaschar day-dream. But to the first gain we have nothing to say; we hang our heads abashed, "veil our proud stomachs," and acknowledge with shame and confusion of face, that it is even so. Nay, we will go further, and admit that this same kind of success has attended the Yankees with remarkable uniformity during the whole war; that most of their gains have consisted in developing our strength in their front, and that from the time they cracked their skulls against the Stonewall brigade at Manassas, down to the last chapter of this eventful history, we have persisted in making the same blunder, and giving the Yankees the same advantage. After all the lessons which Lee has received, he, too, seems to be no wiser than Beauregard; he, too, is incorrigible—wherever Grant goes, across the Rapid Ann, across the North Anna, across the Pamunkey, he has the same great strategic success over his rebel rival; he still develops our strength in his front, and we are very much mistaken if the war does not end with the key-note which was sounded in the beginning.

What a result! Tens of thousands of lives sacrificed; hundreds of thousands of bodies maimed; millions reduced to poverty, overshadowed by sorrow, blackened by crime. Liberty, national credit, national honor, nay, every thing that distinguishes a nation from a band of robbers, a gang of galley-slaves, a den of harlots, every thing that is worth living for, gone. And all for what? To satisfy themselves that we intended to resist them stoutly, to resist them to the death, or, in military language, in order "to develop the enemy's strength in our front." Keep at it if you think it worth the while. In good time we will ourselves develop our strength in your rear.

JUNE 7, 1864.

SHORTLY after the Confederate Government was removed to Richmond, a bill was attempted in the Provisional Congress, to give the President a large sum, covering the expense of transporting his horses all the way from Mississippi in box-cars. This proposed appropriation of the public money was defeated by the fearless patriotism of another Davis, now, we believe, no longer a member of Congress. But the idea has not been forgotten; and, in this agony of the nation, a "joint resolution" suddenly sprouts up, and is whirled through the House with incredible alacrity, giving additional compensation and emolument to this functionary, under the name of "lights and fuel for the Presidential mansion," and forage in the Presidential stables for four horses during the war.

The joint resolution of Congress strikes in the teeth of the Confederate Constitution, which expressly stipulates that the President shall receive *a compensation which shall neither be increased nor diminished during the period* for which he has been elected. It is enough to declare that fact, as it is to state that two and two make four—it would be as foolish to argue the truth of one proposition as of the other. But the "President cannot live on his salary." Then let him resign, and live as other people do, without it. He has the best house in Richmond, furnished, and twenty-five thousand a year. If he cannot live on that, who can live in the Southern Confederacy? It is also said that similar "helps" were given to the President of the United States under the old Government. So they were, and it was the unspeakable corruption and villainy which came of this and other not more lawless expenditures of the nation's money, which overthrew the old Government. We make this war to get rid of the precedents and practices of the old Government. Would to God we might also get rid of all the detestable politicians, who made, by slow degrees and, many such precedents as this, all that corruption and all this war! It is said that this is a "*small matter;*" that opposition to it is faction, &c. But we say, OBSTA PRINCIPIIS—resist evil while it is small and can be resisted. If this small end of the wedge gets in, all the rest follows easily. It will become a precedent for another like it, and that for many others. If Congress can give the President this, it can give him millions. To-day one thing, to-morrow another; and who will stand up and draw on himself all the disfavor and evil turnings, all the malice and revenge of an Executive incumbent, by raising his voice in opposition to bills in which so powerful a functionary is *personally* interested? If a thing so "small" cannot be resisted, how shall its sequel be prevented? Here is a door which opens on the universe of corruption.

JUNE 8, 1864.

IN the war-chariot of old there were no supernumeraries; the driver and the fighter, and no more. We want no supernumeraries now—no men to act as a dead weight on our bloody progress through the ranks of a besieging foe, to be paraded hereafter in the triumphal chariot as the heroes of a contest which they only served to complicate, of a victory which they only helped to retard.

If the Southern community realized the fact that Bragg had his hand on the reins, a loud and stern protest would rise from every quarter of the land; a protest so loud and so stern that it would be impossible for the deafest ear not to hear, or the stiffest neck to keep from bending. As it is, everybody is dissatisfied with the provision which the President has thought fit to make for his favorites. Will nothing serve but to have these unlucky men in Richmond? The Catholic Church has bishops *in partibus infidelium*—bishops who never administer the rites of their religion to the soul of their cure; who never even behold the dioceses from which they derive their titles. Nova Zembla is too cold, Timbuctoo is too hot, the Cochin Chinese are too obstreperous, the Feejeeans too partial to the persons of their visitors. Why cannot we have generals *in partibus?* Is there no outlying territory, which we can claim, and only claim? Is not Delaware a Southern State? Does not Ohio belong to Virginia? Let us erect two departments of this sort—departments in which there is nothing to do, or, still better, in which nothing can possibly be done, and let us give them incontinently in charge to these men, with their head-quarters at some Fiddler's Green or Fool's Paradise. True, we cannot very well afford sinecures in our present circumstances, but we can still less afford to have two birds of ill omen haunting our capital at a time like this, when the pressure from without is so great that it is silly, nay, criminal, to do any thing that might have the least tendency to dampen the spirits of those who stand between the city and the foe, or to weigh down the buoyant hope of those whose all is entrusted to the keeping of such brave defenders. As we have said, time after time, it is hardly worth while to argue the matter. We believe Mr. Orr to be perfectly right in his estimate of General Bragg, and we hold that General Johnston's dispatches have fully demonstrated the calibre of Pemberton. Others may not go as far as we do. Some may think that Bragg would make a tolerable brigadier, and Pemberton a fair captain of artillery. But everybody outside of flunkeydom, deplores or execrates, according to his temperament, the appointment of these men to service at this place and at this time—of all other time sand places. The Yankees have brought their great success of the West to cope with our great success of the East; they have brought Grant and his myrmidons to meet Lee of Arlington and his unconquered veterans. We hope yet to make Grant deserve his nickname a second time, and in a different way, but we could not encourage our assailant and his army more than has been done, than by setting up in his front as kittles to be bowled down by slow balls or fast balls, whichever may seem best, such personages as Grant's old antagonists of Lookout Mountain and Vicksburg. As for the effect on our own men, it is doubtless true that the mass of the army cannot believe that their glorious commanders are actually the subordinates of any jack-in-office, and nothing except defeat could make them realize that they are following Bragg and not Lee. And yet it would be better, far better, even for our army, if there were no such external position as exists at present, and beyond measure desirable for the citizens of our capital and State. An official *démenti* has been given to the report that General Bragg ordered the evacuation of Petersburg. Granted that the report was false, was it as wholly unfounded? Put a man of known characteristics in any prominent position, and people will straightway begin to prophesy, and it cannot be said that their predictions are without foundation. The evacuation of Petersburg, like the recall of the general who whipped Sigel from the Valley of Virginia, would have been exceedingly natural things for General Bragg, and we do not wonder at the reports. In these points he may have suffered injustice only by anticipation. However, such anticipations are a more grievous injury to our cause than any anticipations can be to General Bragg's character for generalship; and we, in common with the rest of our countrymen, are more concerned for the salvation of the capital and the country than for the renown of any one man.

We are in no idle game. We fight not as men beating the air. We are driving the red battle car, and not a gilded coach, with room enough on the foot-board for uniformed *chasseurs* with marshal's batons. Cut behind! We are driving artillery into the fight. Get off the caissons! And horses accustomed to the flash of steel, to the roll of drums, to the waving of banners and the peal of cannon, have been known to start and shy at unfamiliar objects.

JULY 19, 1864.

THAT Confederate force which lately visited Maryland, has returned to Virginia. It has returned "safe;" the enemy has remained safe: its "losses are slight;" so are theirs. *Three ties*, however, of the railroad between Baltimore and Washington have been burnt near Beltsville.

One house was certainly burnt in the course of the expedition; let this comfort the tens of thousands of houseless Confederates whose homes have been destroyed by Yankee raiders! It is allowed each of them to say, "It is for *our* house that Bradford's was burnt." This is retaliation, not by gross, but by sample; not to hurt them, but, as it were, to bring home to their imaginations how they hurt others.

To Confederate troops the duty of retaliation is hard and odious; to retaliate every thing *in kind* indeed, would be altogether impossible for them; and no orders could make them outrage women or insult old men. Neither would any Confederate officer bring the dresses of Yankee women home as "trophies;" nor would Virginia girls like to wear such spoils. Retaliation, however, was a real and urgent duty, and the most essential business which our troops had in the enemy's country, if they had any business there at all.

If we recur so often to this tiresome subject of the treatment which we should give to our enemies, it is because this is no mere collateral and incidental question connected with the operations of the war; it is the very root of the matter; the heart and core of it; our whole national duty is involved in it, and our whole national destiny. These States claim to be sovereign States, vindicating an ancient independence; if our people are to be treated as rebels against their enemies, and thus visited with military execution, by fire and sword—and if we either cannot or will not, when we have it in our own power, pay slaughter with slaughter, pillage with pillage, conflagration with conflagration, then we fear that our doom is sealed.

JULY 22, 1864.

It is not generally known that the Japanese have a Commissioner in this country, for the especial purpose of reporting the progress of the war and the improvements in military science. Through the extreme courtesy of his highness Prince Dalgaku-Nokami, the Commissioner, we are permitted to lay before our readers the following extracts (kindly translated for us) from a report recently forwarded by him to his Imperial Master. From it our friends will learn in what high estimation our affairs are held by the Japanese officials:—

FROM THE GREAT CITY OF RICHMOND,
THE CAPITAL OF THE POWERFUL REPUBLIC
OF THE SOUTHERN BARBARIANS.

To the Tycoon, the High and Mighty Sovereign of the Empire of Japan, the Brother of the Sun, Moon, and the Stars, before whose glory all earthly Princes hide their faces:—

SIRE:—Your Commissioner having been sent to this great country of the Barbarians, charged by your Imperial Majesty with the duty of noting and reporting the events of the bloody war now being waged upon them by the powerful nation of Yankees, who dwell in the North, and live by thieving and deceit, humbles himself in the dust as he prepares to lay before your Imperial Majesty the results of his observations.

Your Commissioner, after encountering many difficulties and dangers by both sea and land, at last reached the great capital of the Barbarians.

Here, I lost no time in presenting my credentials to the Barbarian Government. Speaking the language of the country but imperfectly, I was fearful that I would experience some difficulty in making known to the officials the mission with which I am charged. Fortunately, I was informed by an officer of great respectability that the Chief Mandarin, who controls the intercourse of the Republic with other nations, had in his employ an official who could speak Japanese, and that he employed him some time since, in the hope that your Imperial Majesty would condescend to recognize the existence of his Government, when the official's abilities would prove useful.

The next day after my arrival was appointed for my reception by the Mandarin, whom the Barbarians call Benjamin. Accordingly I presented myself at the Palace of the official, which is a large, high building of white stone, containing many rooms, and was at once ushered into his presence. The Mandarin, a short, fat man, with a profusion of gold ornaments, received me with great delight. Had I permitted him to do so, he would have gotten down on his knees and kissed my feet. This honor I respectfully but firmly declined—your Imperial Majesty being entitled to it. He pressed upon me from the beginning of the interview his extreme admiration for the empire of Japan and its institutions, and extolled the advantages which would arise from a treaty between your Imperial Majesty and the Barbarian ruler. He also urged me to endeavor to persuade your Imperial Majesty to recognize the existence of his Government. He offered me every facility that it was in the power of his Government to bestow, and even went so far as to urge me to accept a position on the staff of the Barbarian general on duty at the capital. This is a mark of great distinction—a similar offer being made to every foreigner who arrives in the South. All do not accept it, or the Barbarian commander might soon have connected with his person a force sufficiently large to enable him to take the field. I great improvement upon the old system, under which the "Raiders" would have been shot or hung as soon as captured; and its advantages are so clear to every one, that I doubt not your Imperial Majesty will not hesitate to adopt it as soon as possible.

There are many persons among the Barbarians who violently oppose the conduct of the Tycoon; but they are bad and unpatriotic men, who are unwilling to lose their all that the Tycoon may have an opportunity of exhibiting his wonderful humanity, which is, indeed, the most remarkable ever exhibited by any earthly ruler. Nevertheless he has his reward. The people love him devotedly, for they feel that he has thrown around them the most ample protection, and will not hesitate to dare any thing to promote their safety.

* * * * * * * *

The Mandarin who has charge of the shipping showed me many attentions. The Barbarians have invented a new species of war steamer, which is plated with iron and is very formidable. These steamers cost immense sums of money and require many months in their construction. They are rarely used in actual conflict with the enemy. They are allowed to remain untouched for awhile, but are eventually blown up by their commanders. The Mandarin assured me that by destroying them thus the Barbarians impress their enemies with a sense of their desperation, and that each such destruction is equal to a victory. It also precludes all possibility of any Barbarian commander being forced to endure the humiliation of surrendering his vessel to an enemy. Should your Imperial Majesty desire to receive instruction in this new system, the Mandarin informed me that he is willing to order to Japan any or all of the officers who have thus distinguished themselves, and I am confident the people of this country would be delighted if such an arrangement could be effected.

* * * * * * * * *

Deserters from the enemy are encouraged to come in by being given employment in factories, arsenals, and workshops belonging to the Government. The natives of the country find it difficult to procure work of any description from the Government, but any one who has been connected with the enemy finds no difficulty in procuring such work as he may desire. This is a wise system and its advantages are every day seen; the Government constantly reaping great benefits from it in the satisfaction it affords the people and army.

* * * * * * * * *

Not long since the law-makers of the Barbarians enacted a law prohibiting, under severe penalties, any person from buying or selling "greenbacks," as the paper-money of the enemy is called. The Government of the Tycoon having use for the money of their enemies, set aside the law and appointed a class of men called "brokers," to act as agents for the purchase of the desired amount. Should your Imperial Majesty find it necessary or convenient to violate any of the laws of Japan, you will do well to employ a "broker" as your agent, for you may then violate the law with impunity and even with an appearance of innocence.

* * * * * * * * *

From what I have thus humbly and submissively laid before your Imperial Majesty, you will see that the Barbarians deserve great praise for their enlightenment and improvement in every thing attempted by them. They have given to the world many useful lessons by which it would do well to profit.

I shall forward to your Imperial Majesty another and a more detailed report at the earliest possible period.

With the prayer that your Imperial Majesty may live and reign prosperously for many years, I subscribe myself

Your Majesty's most faithful subject and slave,

DALGAKU-NOKAMI,
Prince of Suruga.

JULY 26, 1864.

For the first time we have the pleasure of heartily approving a State-paper of Abraham Lincoln. It is his letter addressed "To whom it may Concern." It concerns Messrs. Holcombe, C. C. Clay, and George N. Sanders, and, we would fondly believe, no other person or persons whomsoever. When officious individuals go creeping round by back-doors, asking interviews with Lincoln for "a full interchange of sentiments," it gives us sincere gratification to see them spurned, yes, kicked, from the said back-door. To Abraham we deliberately say, Bravo! or, if he likes it better, Bully! Think of an ex-Senator from Alabama and a Virginian member of Congress—for we say nothing of the third "negotiator"—exposing themselves gratuitously, idly, and unbidden, to receive such an ignominious rebuff at the hands of the truculent buffoon of Illinois.

The eccentric procedure of these two gentlemen has all the air of a device of the ingenious Sanders. He it was who, finding Mr. Clay and Mr. Holcombe travelling in Canada for their health, and sojourning at the Clifton House, bethought him of getting them into a correspondence about peace, and it was he who opened it himself by a letter to no less a person than Horace Greeley—asking him (Greeley) to procure a safe-conduct for the party to Washington, and thence to Richmond. It appears that Greeley, at first thinking this was a real embassy to offer submission, eagerly promised the safe-conduct in the President's name. They replied that they were not exactly and altogether plenipotentiaries; but had no doubt that, "if the circumstances disclosed in the correspondence" were communicated to Richmond, they, or somebody else, would be invested with full powers. And what were the circumstances disclosed? We learn this from a long letter of Messrs. Clay and Holcombe, written after their repulse; the circumstance disclosed was nothing in the world except Greeley's *unauthorized* offer of a safe-conduct. They say—and, in reading what they say, remember that it is two eminent Confederate gentlemen addressing a paltry abolitionist editor, not having the presumption to write to the Emperor Abraham himself—"exacting no condition but that we should be duly accredited from Richmond, as bearers of propositions looking to the establishment of peace, thus proposing a basis for a conference as comprehensive as we could desire, it seemed to us that *the President* opened a door which had previously been closed against the Confederate States, for a full interchange of sentiments, a free discussion of conflicting opinions, and an untrammelled effort to remove all causes of controversy by liberal negotiations." What right had they to even allude to "propositions looking to the establishment of peace?" Who commissioned them to "interchange sentiments" with Lincoln? And what do they mean by causes of controversy and *liberal* negotiations? If these officious gentlemen had been received at Washington, and had been accredited from Richmond, we should have felt very nervous on the subject of those liberal negotiations. However, Lincoln, so soon as he was informed that there were such people poking about that back-door, surmising that it was now partly open though "previously closed," and parleying with a New York editor in the hope of getting admittance,—shut up the door with a bang, right in their three noses, and warned them off by a notice "To whom it may Concern."

It is suggested that perhaps the cunning device of Mr. Sanders was only a contrivance for helping the peace-party in the enemy's country; that the answer of Mr. Lincoln was just the very kind of answer which the "many-counselled" George expected; and that it is to be used for the purpose of proving how ferociously and unrelentingly the present Yankee Administration is bent on war, and repulses the slightest hint of peace. As usual with such excessively cunning schemes, this one not only defeats itself, but helps the cause which it was, possibly, intended to damage. To exhibit an ex-Senator and member of Congress of the Confederate States thus timidly crawling by a roundabout way to the footstool of the emperor of the Yahoos, whining and snivelling about peace and "liberal negotiations," and haughtily refused admittance even to the sovereign presence, will serve not the peace, but the war, party; because it will be used to create the impression that the Confederacy must be in the agonies of death when two distinguished legislators make so pitiful an attempt to reach the ear of offended majesty. If such was the idea, then, in this case, as in the other, "those whom it may concern" have got what they deserve.

Has any one seen "the Reverend Colonel Jacques" and one Edward Kirk. What are the detectives about? Here have been two spies, manifestly spies, "at the Spottswood Hotel, Richmond, on a secret mission;" and now, instead of being in Castle Thunder, Kirk and the Rev. Colonel are again in their own country, giving mysterious hints to the Washington correspondents about their three days' elegant entertainment in Richmond, and about "two interviews" which they say they had with Mr. Davis. They cannot disclose, "for the present,—those deep diplomats—what passed at those interviews; but "it is intimated," and here is truly a startling fact—"that Mr. Davis would consent to nothing short of recognition of the Southern Confederacy." Of course these two Yankees were spies; or else they wanted to sell something in Richmond which they had run through the lines; or probably they combined the two objects. Our passport system, we fear, affords us but little protection; and the detectives are not sufficiently vigilant.

Howsoever that may be, there is now certainly a renewal of those vague whisperings of peace which have several times before circulated through society. Many think that peace is in the air. Peace, and rumors of peace, float around us; and men dream of peace at night. We have seen how unauthorized and officious persons, both Yankee and Confederate, repair respectively North and South about the same moment, as it were snuffing peace as horses snuff water in the desert. If gold declines a little in New York, even in the teeth of military disaster, a newspaper says it is because there is a kind of instinctive feeling that we are on the eve of peace. This is not unnatural : the plain avowals of the enemy's press, four months ago, that this year's campaign must be the final one,—the near end of Lincoln's bloody term—the financial crisis imminent in the United States—all combine to produce not so much a conviction as a presentiment that we are soon to have peace.

And it may be so. Peace may be nearer to us than we think, and may come suddenly, though one cannot see precisely how. One thing, however, is clear,—so desirable an event cannot be hastened by amateur negotiators, "exchanging sentiments" with Mr. Lincoln; nor by blockade-runners, thrusting "interviews" upon Mr. Davis; nor by any possible or conceivable correspondence between George Sanders and Horace Greeley.

AUGUST 2, 1864.

MR. DAVIS, in conversation with a Yankee spy, named Edward Kirk, is reported by said spy to have said, "We are not fighting for slavery; we are fighting for independence." This is true; and is a truth that has not sufficiently been dwelt upon. It would have been very much to be desired that this functionary had developed the idea in some message, or some other State paper, which would have carried it round the world, and repeated it in all languages of civilized nations, instead of leaving it to be promulgated through the doubtful report of an impudent blockade-runner, who ought to have been put in Castle Thunder. The sentiment is true, and should be publicly uttered and kept conspicuously in view ; because our enemies have diligently labored to make all mankind believe that the people of these States have set up a pretended State sovereignty, and based themselves upon that ostensibly, while their real object has been only to preserve to themselves the property in so many negroes, worth so many millions of dollars. The direct reverse is the truth. The question of slavery is only one of the minor issues; and the cause of the war, the whole cause, on our part, is the maintenance of the sovereign independence of these States.

At the beginning of the struggle, and even now, to a great extent, our enemies had, and have, the ear of the world; and they have very dexterously labored to represent us as rushing into a dreadful war on a paltry question of dollars. In the crusade they were about to make upon us, they have shown the utmost solicitude to gain for themselves, in advance, the sympathies of foreign nations, especially of England and France; and, of course, their chief means of gaining this point, consisted in representing that we had no higher or nobler cause to fight for than the possession of a certain quantity of serviceable negro flesh. Thus they knew that not only all the prevailing cants would be canted on their side, but also that a war waged to break up a free and beneficent government upon such a mean issue, would revolt all statesmen, publicists, and thinkers of high mark in every country, who have the true sentiment of national dignity, and can appreciate the loftier and purer springs of human actions on the grand scale. The Yankee knew he might boldly claim the good wishes of civilized communities, so long as he could make it be believed that the only thought and care of the South was that she might keep still on her plantations so many slave hands, raising each year —— bales per hand.

The whole cause of our resistance was and is, the pretension and full determination of the Northern States to use their preponderance in the Federal representation, in order to govern the Southern States for their profit, just as Austria governs Venetia, Russia governs Poland, or England governs Ireland. Slavery was the immediate occasion—carefully made so by them—it was not the cause. The tariff, which almost brought about the disruption some years ago, would have much more accurately represented, though it did not cover, or exhaust, the real cause of the quarrel. Yet neither tariffs nor slavery, nor both together, could ever have been truly called the cause of the secession and the war. We refuse to accept for a cause any thing lower, meaner, smaller, than that truly announced, namely, the sovereign independence of our States. This, indeed, includes both those minor questions, as well as many others yet graver and higher. It includes full power to regulate our trade for our *own* profit, and also complete jurisdiction over our own social and domestic institutions; but it further involves all the nobler attributes of national, and even of individual life and character. A community which once submits to be schooled, dictated to, legislated for, by any other, soon grows poor in spirit; it becomes at last incapable of producing a high style of men: its very soul withers within in it: in it no genius, no art, can have its home. If they arise within its borders, they migrate to the dominant country, and seek there their career and their reward: its citizens, become a kind of halfmen, feel that they have hardly a right to walk in the sun; take the lowest seats at the world's tables, and there is no man to say, Friend, go up higher.

And the people of Virginia do not choose to accept that position for themselves and for their children. They choose rather to die. They own a noble country, which their fathers created, exalted, and transmitted to them with all its treasures of high names and great deeds; with all its native wealth of untamable manhood. That inheritance we intend to own while we live, and leave intact to those who are to come after us. It is ours from the centre of the earth up to the heavens, with all the minerals beneath it, and all the sky above it.

It is right to let foreign nations, and "those whom it may concern," understand this theory of our independence. Let them understand that, though we are "not fighting for slavery," we will not allow ourselves to be dictated to in regard to slavery or any other of our internal affairs, not because that would diminish our interest in any property, but because it touches our independence.

SEPTEMBER 5, 1864.

So much for the third removal of General Johnston. First, he was virtually removed by being deprived of power to direct his lieutenant, Pemberton; and the cost of that gratification to the feelings of Mr. Davis was the army of Vicksburg. Next, he was superseded by Bragg; and the organization of the second army was destroyed at Missionary Ridge. Thirdly, after restoring it, he was removed at the very moment when his knowledge, skill and energy were indispensable to the success and even to the safety of the campaign; superseded by Hood, a commander of division, notoriously incapable of managing any thing larger than a division. The result is disaster at Atlanta, in the very nick of time when such a victory alone could save the party of Lincoln from irretrievable ruin.

General Johnston is thought over-cautious; too reticent about his plans; disposed to be mysterious as to approaching events. He was removed because "he did not speak with *entire confidence* about holding Atlanta." But results prove that if he was cautious in movement, and chary of promises, it was for good reasons. It is evident that, in each case, he knew where he was, what material he had in hand, and the best use to make of it. Whatever else may be said, it cannot be said that he ever lost an army, or any considerable body of troops, or incurred any disaster, or even disadvantage, that obscured our prospects for a moment. If any man has been so great a fool as to question his military capacity, his courage, or his earnest patriotism, certainly these events vindicate him. But alas! of what interest is that? of what importance is that? of what consideration is a single reputation, if the country must be lost to justify it? Who cares now whether Johnston was right, or Jeff. Davis was right?

Yet we must think of these things, for these are the causes which produce the effects. It is manifestly absurd to put up and pull down a commander in the field according to the crude views or peevish fancies of a functionary in Richmond. Such conduct of Government would paralyze the greatest military genius, ruin the oldest army, and render success in war absolutely impossible. Now, is it not hard, is it not cruelly hard, that the struggle of eight millions, who sacrifice their lives, sacrifice their money, who groan in the excess of exertion, who wrench every muscle till the blood starts with the sweat—should come to naught—should end in the ruin of us all—in order that the predilections and antipathies, the pitiful personal feelings, of a single man may be indulged?

With the scanty information at hand it is impossible to estimate, the late affair in Georgia. It is certain that Atlanta has been abandoned by our troops. We do not know whether the guns were left or not. The loss of the place is otherwise without material importance. As a military post it had no value whatever. It was once important as the junction of railroads, but has ceased to be so since the railroads to the North were lost. Sherman could not hold it a week if the Confederate army in the neighborhood was in proper hands. But the moral effect of its loss, though it may be temporary, will be great. It will render incalculable assistance to the party of Lincoln, and obscures the prospect of peace, late so bright. It may enable him to execute his draft. It will also diffuse gloom over the South. This depression, however, may be speedily relieved, if the administration has a grain of real sense or a spark of unselfish patriotism. The reinstatement of Johnston, or the appointment of Beauregard, would at once restore the confidence of the country and of the army; and the genius of either would soon prove Sherman's advantage to be an illusion and an abortion. But the confidence either of the country or the army will scarcely survive the continuation of Hood in command, still less the reappearance of Bragg. It is easy to see the path of wisdom now; but it is difficult still to hope any thing wise, or magnanimous, or unselfish, from the administration.

NOVEMBER 8, 1864.

The writer of the message intended to be cautious, but has in several points written an indiscreet paper. That part which will attract most attention, is the passage relating to a suggested conscription of negroes for soldiers. This project originated with those who had not fully reflected on its character, and has been a matter of some publicity by others who delight in all things which make a sensation. The proposition has, in fact, made a considerable sensation both in the Northern and Southern sections. It has not hitherto been mentioned in these columns, because there was no possibility that it would become a practical measure of policy, and because it was a matter to provoke violent discord of feeling and speech at a period when such discussion was most undesirable. Both from its delicacy and from the fact that it has never been a subject of official deliberation, we are surprised to see it treated in the President's message. But since the question has been so introduced, its consideration can no longer be avoided.

It is a proposition which can be supported only on the ground that good soldiers can be made of the negroes. Now, what is the real value of the negro as a soldier? The enemy's actual experiment is not the only test which has been applied to the race. Since the conquest of Algiers, the French army has contained a considerable force of negroes. They constitute nearly the whole of the troops popularly called in France Turcos. It is generally supposed that these Turcos are Moors. There are some Moors among them, but most, even of these, are of the mixed blood. The mass of these troops are negroes, blacker than any of our slaves. They were employed in the Italian war of 1859, or, at least, they constituted a part of that army which Napoleon III. marched into Italy five years ago, and which gained the famous victories of Magenta and Solferino. Great expectations were entertained of the negro soldiers by the misinformed. Their appearance among the European troops was a novelty, and the people amused themselves with apochryphal tales of their ferocious valor in Africa, about to be newly illustrated on the Austrians. But in none of the battles which followed were the negroes prominent; and they were only heard of occasionally as the guards of Lombard regiments, who had thrown down their arms and surrendered as soon as they got an opportunity. These negro legions were, of course, commanded by white officers, and kept under severe discipline. The writer of this made inquiries of many among said officers as to their military worth. When any of them would give a definite reply, it was always to the effect—that they were good sometimes for a rush, but they could not be made to stand grape.

This answer is the truth, and the whole truth on the subject. The Yankees have taken great pains, and persevered in the effort, to make soldiers out of negroes. They have given them the best of every thing. Nothing has been left undone to create a martial spirit. Their courage has been carefully nursed. They have been kept near to many battles without being exposed to the fire, so that they might become accustomed to the sights and sounds of war without being unnerved by their own slaughter. But what has the enemy gained by them after two years' trial? They got them to make a "rush" at Port Hudson and Battery Gilmer; but they took neither. Those who know the negro never expected less, and will never look for more. That race is capable of blind, brute, contagious excitement, and while in that state it can make, not a charge, but a rush on points where the intelligence of a trained white soldier would show to him only death without the possibility of success. By such wild and senseless onslaught batteries are not taken, nor victories won; for their mob-like rush is not fighting, nor is the excitation which destroys the sense of danger by a frenzied bewilderment the courage which directs the aim of the rifle and the point of the sword.

It is sometimes said that the negroes would make better soldiers for us than for the Yankees, because they would fight under the eyes of their masters and friends. Such sentimental suppositions show a great ignorance of the negro's character; and, even if they were founded on some truth, attachment to his master would be no balance to his native fickleness and the strong incentives to desertion which the enemy would hold out to him. The fact is, the negro soldier costs far more than he is worth to Frenchman and Yankee, and to us he would be more troublesome than to either of the others.

Our enemy has raised its negro army, not as a military, but as a political measure—to have the cant of the world on its side—to procure the full and consistent support of the Abolitionist party. With his views and purposes, the creation of the negro soldier is consistent and natural.

But the existence of a negro soldier is totally inconsistent with our political aim, and with our social as well as political system. We surrender our position whenever we introduce the negro to arms. If a negro is fit to be a soldier, he is not fit to be a slave; and if any large portion of the race is fit for free labor—fit to live and be useful under the competitive system of labor—then the whole race is fit for it. The employment of negroes as soldiers in our armies, either with or without prospective emancipation, would be the first step, but a step which would involve all the rest, to universal abolition. It would be so understood and regarded by all the world. Our enemy would perceive that he had succeeded in his design to the point of moral subjugation, and would not doubt that our absolute submission was far removed. To our own hearts it would be a confession, not only of weakness, but of absolute inability to secure the object for which we undertook the war. It would be felt by all as a compromise to the abolitionism of the world, incompatible with that independence of action for which the South strives.

But the objections to this project are so manifest that it is unnecessary at present even to suggest them. The President opposed the introduction of negroes into the army as soldiers, but desires a corps of forty thousand, to be used in labor on fortifications, as engineers, as teamsters, and as sappers and miners. To a proposition of that sort no one could have the least objection, if he had not concluded with an obscure passage, which, if it means any thing, means that the forty thousand slaves so employed shall be set free at the end of the war as a reward for their service. Here, while refusing to employ the slaves under arms, he adopts the fatal principle of the original proposition to its fullest extent, and puts forth an idea, which, if admitted by the Southern people as a truth, renders their position on the matter of slavery utterly untenable. We hold that the negro is in his proper situation,—that is to say, in the condition which is the best for him; where he reaches his highest moral, intellectual, and physical development, and can enjoy the full sum of his natural happiness; in a word, that while living with the white man in the relation of slave, he is in a state superior and better for him than that of freedom. But the negro's freedom is to be given to him as a reward for his service to the country; his freedom, therefore, is a boon—it is a better state—a natural good of which our laws deprive him and keep him from. Now, that is the whole theory of the abolitionist; and we have the sorrow to think that if one portion of this Presidential message means any thing, it means that.

DECEMBER 21, 1864.

THE news from Tennessee is bad. The situation is bad; but it is far from being irremediable. The army in Tennessee has been terribly misused, and has suffered great injury: but it is not lost, and may be restored to full efficiency by the same hand which redeemed it after Missionary Ridge. But to change the fortune of the country, the Executive and the Legislature must change their character, and abandon the road to ruin hitherto systematically pursued by both.

The opening of this campaign found our two best men in real command, and in the two principal positions—Lee in Virginia, Johnston in Georgia. The military condition of the country was never so prosperous as it was at midsummer; for these two men had so done their work, that it was then morally certain that the last supreme effort of the enemy was going to fail; and had it failed, it is impossible to doubt that this year would have been the last of the war. The unexpected and inconsequent freak of the Executive, the removal of Johnston, permitted in silence by the country, has produced fruits such as inconsequence, folly and subserviency never produced before. Although great evils might have been and were apprehended at the time, the results have so much surpassed expectations that they assume the appearance of a judgment.

But let the past go. The best remedy for present evils is simply to stop the courses which have caused them. Let the Executive cease to interfere with the armies; send Johnston to the wreck of that army which he surrendered to Hood in such magnificent condition; give him *carte blanche* to do what he thinks proper for its salvation and for the defence of the country, with a guarantee that neither his commission nor his plans will any more be meddled with; give to Beauregard complete discretion of action on the coast; leave to Lee his whole army and full powers in Virginia,—and prosperity will return, good fortune will again befall the army of the South, and the great dangers which now menace the Confederacy will vanish like the clouds of the last rain.

But good sense, modesty, and justice, will never actuate the Executive while Congress abdicates its functions, and public opinion its rights. Nations will suffer just punishment whenever they intrust power to puny hands, puff up the conceit and encourage the passions of their rulers by fulsome flattery or silent submission. We have done so. The follies of the Government are manifest to all, but if any one who pays their cost proposes opposition, or even a remonstrance, the amiable majority cry "*Hush!* oh, hush, hush! we can't get rid of him; and he will do thus and so, all the more, if he is opposed. Don't say any thing. We must have concord—unanimity—and there must be no opposition to Government."—Therefore, the only voice which is heard at all is the voice of flatterers—the voice of those who have neither head nor heart, neither knowledge nor principle. Hence the Executive is encouraged to pursue its fancies; and although every military misfortune of the country is palpably and confessedly due to the personal interference of Mr. Davis, the Congress continues at each session to be his subservient tool, and to furnish new incentives to perversity, new means of mischief.

It will not be sufficient for the Executive to have lucid intervals. Congress and the Southern public must change their attitude, adopt a more distinct and manly tone, deal with their own affairs with more resolution, keep the Executive in the path of duty, and curb it with a peremptory hand when it interferes with things beyond its capacity. Great adversity has fallen upon us; but the power of the Southern States is not broken; their resources are enormous; and on no side is the breach irreparable. Of all external dangers, there is not one which cannot successfully be met. But a greater danger is within; folly vested with license, and flattery to encourage folly. No calamity which has happened is in itself ruinous; but what will ruin us is this—that the Government should go on to do, and continue to do, the identical acts which have made calamity by the necessary sequence of cause and effect. The more harmony, and the more concord, and the more self-abnegation, we do evince under such circumstances, the more rapid is our progress to destruction. Let us determine that the course of the ship shall be altered; with that determination will be found the means to compel the change.

DECEMBER 29, 1864.

SEVERAL persons have employed themselves lately in preparing statistical tables of the wealth, food, and fighting men, remaining in the Confederacy, subject to the command of the Government. They prove conclusively that the amount of all these things is still very great—enormous—sufficient to support far greater efforts than the Confederacy has yet made. To question the accuracy of their facts is far from our purpose; indeed their truth has been so long and so well known to all who have examined the subject, that the proof and tabular exposition seem to them quite superfluous, and even uninteresting. Material exhaustion is not yet felt by the mass of the nation; not felt in the slightest or most distant degree. It will never be felt. But the nation may soon suffer from moral exhaustion. The country will never be unable, if willing, to supply the wants of its Government, but it may easily become unwilling; and then no pressure of legislation will be of much value. Pressure will obtain only those few drops which trickle from the squeezed orange, and soon get nothing at all.

These Southern States are lands of Goshen.—A hot summer and a fertile soil will always produce a superabundance of bread and meat. They contain five millions of the most fighting people in the world, and can always supply three hundred thousand arms-bearing men in the prime of life. The extent of their territory is so great, that its real occupation by the armed forces of two or three such nations as that we are fighting is inconceivable. The enemy is perfectly aware of the fact, and does not base his hope of subjugation on the practical application of main strength, but upon the submission of the will, and consequent inability, to contend to the last extremity, which he expects to see at some time spread over the land.

That is, in fact, the only contingency on which the subjugation of the South is possible. The Southern States are in no danger so long as the spirit of the people is what it has hitherto been. But let us not be blind to the truth, that there is such a thing possible as a decay of national confidence and a death of national spirit. There is such a thing as *heart-break* for nations as for individuals. There are such things as hopelessness and despair, lethargy and apathy. A conviction that all that it will do must come to naught, all sacrifices it can make be rendered vain by an irremediable cause,—a conviction resting on rational grounds, both of reflection and experiment, will produce this state of feeling in any nation, however heroic and however obstinate.

No people have ever or anywhere displayed more patient courage, more constancy in misfortune, or a greater magnanimity toward its Government than the Southern people. Neither Sidney Johnston's evacuation of Nashville, nor Lovell's of New Orleans; neither Murfreesboro', or Missionary Ridge, or Vicksburg were sufficient to damp their energy or their hope. Armies lost have been replaced by other armies. Resources squandered have been only the signal for the production of new treasures. No single calamity will dishearten them, nor twenty, nor a hundred, if, by any ingenuity, they can persuade themselves that they are the chances of war and accident, and not the necessary consequences of unfailing causes which must produce the like again and again forever. But it is impossible to bear up under such a weight as that painful conviction; and the conduct of the Government is likely enough to produce it in the end. The unparalleled absurdity of that management which sent Hood to Nashville and Sherman to Savannah, has produced a certain gloomy impression upon the public mind, too deep and strong to be removed by an ordinary anodyne. Words are now useless. Eloquent appeals, manifestoes, high-spirited resolutions, theories, nostrums of all kinds, will now be thrown away. Nothing will remove the cloud—or rather, the lurid, ill-omened light—which now rests on the future, but measures that touch the root of our evil.

Such a measure there is. A remedy for all discontent has suggested itself to the mind of every man who thinks, and has been advised by a thousand mouths in the same breath. It is the creation of a new officer—a commander-in-chief—who shall exercise supreme control over the armies and military affairs of the Confederacy; and the appointment of General Lee to be that officer. Such an act, if made in good faith, and solidly guarded against counteracting influences, would restore public confidence, and give the country heart for a new effort equal to that which it has hitherto made. It would do more to bring down the price of gold and restore faith in the currency, than any law that the Secretary can devise, however wise in principle, and however ingenious in detail. The people would be satisfied that their means are not thrown away; that the best use of their blood and property would be made that could be made. The adoption of such a measure would be the new birth of the Southern Confederacy. But it must be a real, substantial measure, guaranteed by the representatives of the nation; not a sham—not a duplex general order, creating another Beauregard or Johnston "Department under the control of the President." And it must be adopted in time—that is to say, now. We utter the general opinion, but confess that we see little encouragement to suppose that this present Congress has the decision of character necessary to give it force.

MEMOIR.

JOHN MONCURE DANIEL was born October 24, 1825, in Stafford County, Virginia. His early youth was marked by a fondness for books; being of a serious nature, inclined rather to shun than to enjoy the pastimes usual to one of his age. His father, Dr. John Moncure Daniel, took especial care to instruct him in the several branches of school education; and of this instruction he availed himself to the fullest extent, conscious as he was of the impossibility of going to a college or university, and of the necessity under which he would be to earn his own livelihood. It was remarked that his extraordinary passion for reading was not the silly mania of holding volumes before the eyes in order to be accounted a reader, but arose from an earnest desire to acquire knowledge that might be useful to him in the future; that whatever might temporarily distract his attention, he would ever hasten to resume his studies. One who had him constantly in view at that age, relates that "he was a very bright, handsome boy, giving promise to be of an unusual character." Before leaving his native county, he had ransacked all the libraries within his reach in the neighborhood, and had annotated the margins of their volumes, as the same authority further relates, "with many observations, frequently remarkable, always critical." At the age of fifteen he was sent to Richmond, in order to continue his education, sojourning in that city several years. On their expiration, law was fixed upon as a profession for him, and, accordingly, he studied that science in the office of Judge Lomax, in Fredericksburg. Before completing the ordinary course of reading, the sudden death of his father no longer permitting him to pursue the career chosen, which, for the rest, had never possessed any special attractions in his eyes, he returned, in 1845, to Richmond, to seek a support. After repeated researches and much disappointment, he finally succeeded in obtaining, through friendly recommendation, the task of superintending a small public library in Richmond, the fulfilment of which fetched him a mere pittance of money. With eagerness and alacrity he undertook the duties of the office, regarding it as a fair bargain, thanks to the books which would thus be under his control, and to the leisure time that would be at his disposal in which to read them. In this new position he labored incessantly to advance himself in knowledge, so much so as to incur friendly reproach and demand in regard to the requirements of health. At this epoch of his life he kept a diary, in which was commenced to be noted acts and occurrences; but these being very rare and few, the diary soon became changed into a register of meditations and criticisms upon miscellaneous topics, notably, religious and literary. His inclination for the pen being thus displayed, it was suggested to him by an intimate friend to write contributions for the newspapers; and the same friend volunteered to procure his debut in the press. This, it was thought, might bring him an increase of means. No sooner was this suggestion made than it was accepted. The contributions were submitted, published, attracted attention, and very soon afterwards there was made to the contributor an offer of the editorship of a monthly agricultural magazine, entitled *The Southern Planter*. This periodical he conducted for a short while, infusing a new tone into its pages. Propositions being made to him by one of the Richmond editorial corps to write for a new Democratic paper, then only recently established, entitled *Richmond Semi-Weekly Examiner*, they were at once accepted; the editorial chair of the *Planter* was assumed by another, and the following announcement appeared in the *Examiner:* "John M. Daniel, Esq., is connected with the editorial department of this paper." In a few months he became editor-in-chief and part proprietor of the *Examiner*, thenceforward exercising entire control over it.

In those days, as may be recollected, all men and all things belonged to the Democratic party or to the Whig party—at least in Virginia. Our enemies the Whigs; our friends the Democrats, and reversely; these were the watchwords of the two camps into which the State was drawn up in battle-array: a miniature war of words, in anticipation of the huge war of the sword which was fast approaching, unseen. The Democracy had all the prestige of success; they ruled at Washington, and they ruled in Virginia. But Richmond was confessedly a Whig city, and the publication of a new Democratic organ in the citadel of Whiggery met with no slight opposition. Hence, the *Examiner*, during the first stage of its existence, encountered many enemies, mostly political, not a few personal, owing to the style in which it was conducted. Everybody in the city read the new paper, while few citizens were disposed to assist it by subscriptions and advertisements.

Democracy had been a tradition in Mr. Daniel's family. He himself had been duly imbued with and instructed in the tenets of the true faith; and with all the enthusiasm of youth, and the consciousness of his journalistical powers, he enlisted under its banner, confident of being on the high road to promotion. Nor was it false confidence. Under the regime of the constitution then existing in Virginia, he was readily elected a member of the Council of State; and, on taking charge of the *Examiner* he at once attacked the Whigs wherever they were to be found, and especially those ensconced in the stronghold of Richmond City, fighting them with improved weapons, dealing stout blows, and neither asking nor giving quarter. The effect of such a violently offensive system was to enhance the prospects of the party and of the paper, but also, as well, to create for the editor a host of personal enemies, some of whom, suffering from the incurable wounds produced by his ridicule and sarcasm, entertained towards him an intense and bitter animosity as long as he lived. The attacks being made right and left, embracing some of the most prominent and powerful men of the city and of the

State, it was a matter of course that the columns of the *Examiner* should have been continually filled with exciting quarrels in regard to the politics of the day, and that the editor should frequently have been personally called to account for his public utterances, as was the case. However, coming unscathed out of all his troubles, and the several political and bodily struggles which befell him, having obtained by his course no slight influence and eminence throughout Virginia, he was forthwith promoted and accepted to be one of the leaders of the ever triumphant, great and glorious Democracy, and the *Examiner* recognized as its champion. He contended for the Democratic doctrines with zeal, believing them to be for the general welfare; but his zeal was not fanatical in the least. Party men and measures were examined, and rejected or accepted at will. Calhoun and Jackson he regarded as the only two Americans of latter days' celebrity who could claim his admiration. Depth and precision of thought in the one, strength of character, force of nerve in the other, had a fascination in his eyes, and he ever looked up to them with a feeling of satisfaction, as being strong men, an honor to any country. The lamentation he uttered after the death of Stonewall, and at a critical juncture of the war: "Oh, for the dead Dundee! Oh, for an hour of Jackson," possessed truly a double meaning.

In its quality of a semi-weekly sheet, the *Examiner* had few employees or reporters. It was the custom of the editor to furnish both original and selected "copy." Enjoying the society of a few chosen friends, who were all clever gentlemen, he induced some of them to write for his columns, and they eventually became regular contributors thereto, and writers of distinction. One of the marked features of the paper consisted in its literary reviews, all new books being unsparingly dissected. Edgar A. Poe was induced to revise his principal poems for special publication in the *Examiner*, and, at the time of his death, was under an engagement to furnish literary articles to its editor, who regarded him as the poet of America. Another feature of the paper, which was very effective with the Richmond public, was the treatment bestowed on personages of local celebrity, and the application to them of epithets, full of point and ridicule. Many of these epithets, because so happily coined and distributed, are remembered to-day all over Virginia.

The question of slavery was being agitated by the Levellers. These were engaged in the task of adding fuel to the flame destined to consume the edifice raised by Washington. Thus, Southern institutions being the theme of universal discussion, particularly in the press, the *Examiner* was not slow to descend into the arena to defend them against all comers. It singled out the *N. Y. Tribune*, as the recognized champion of the abolitionists, for a general argumentation of the exciting topic. Always on the offensive, it attacked the creed and practices of the abolitionists, as the sum of all villanies and hypocrisies, adducing unanswerable logic in explanation and justification of the course which the Southern people had thought fit and best to follow; against all of which the *Tribune* invariably returned to the charge, with repeated doses of its sentimental humanitarianism, abolitionism, fanaticism, and its renowned budget of crude theories.

Such an active participation in the political arena, such an efficient support of the Democratic party, extended the reputation of the *Examiner*, and during the Presidential campaign of 1852, it wielded a powerful influence in behalf of the Democratic candidate. On the inauguration of Mr. Pierce, he appointed its editor Chargé d'Affaires near the Court of Turin. Mr. Daniel thereupon sold his paper—reserving, however, the right to repurchase it on his return to the United States—and in the summer of 1853 left Richmond to enter upon the duties of his mission.* Scarcely had he reached New York, on the way, when he was arrested; not by order of the Government, however, but by the machinations of a Yankee pedler. This pedler had been severely criticised in the *Examiner;* denounced as a swindler, for attempting to palm off certain counterfeit wares upon people in the South. Consequently, keeping a sharp lookout for Mr. Daniel's arrival in Northern borders, with a view to picking up a penny, the said pedler brought suit against him for damages, and caused his arrest as soon as he put foot on New York soil. Bail being given, Mr. Daniel was allowed to proceed on his journey, and the suit was left to be the prey of contending lawyers. After many months of trouble, correspondence, and judicial postponements, decision was had in the case, and it need scarcely be added that the Southerner was mulcted.

American diplomatists labor under great disadvantages compared with those of Europe. Chief among these disadvantages, as being the one of most practical effect, is the question of languages: foreign idioms are not their specialty. It is clear that a President may appoint ambassadors in a twinkling; but it cannot come to pass that he should display equal facility in endowing them with a knowledge of the languages of the countries whither they are to be sent. In general, not one American in a thousand can speak French, the language of diplomacy, or any other foreign tongue, in an intelligible manner. There are the best of reasons for this. In the first place, the smattering of the living languages acquired at certain hours of the day in American schools and colleges, or in "private lessons," amounts to nothing, for the most part because promptly forgotten; and that little it occasionally does signify could never anywhere be entitled "speaking and writing," not to mention "speaking and writing correctly," according to authority. Languages are acquired only in the countries or localities where they reign supreme—and even then it is not given to all to become sufficiently acquainted with them. In a country where English alone is needed, and whose inhabitants are hurriedly and continually engaged in felling forests, building roads, digging canals, uprooting stumps in order to plough the soil, founding cities, and amassing material interests from the cradle to the grave—as must be the case in a new country,—little time is found, and less inclination, to meddle

* The writer accompanied him, and was his secretary during his residence in Turin.

with grammars and literature at large. Not needed, for instance, precisely on account of the situation of this country, they are not cared for. Whereas it would be quite different if the United States were placed similarly in position as any one of the countries in Europe, where each State adjoins half-a-dozen others possessing separate languages, and where hourly intercourse across frontiers leads those various languages to become generally known. Hence, there is ample ground of disadvantage for American diplomatists to labor under at the courts to which they are sent, as it were, to school, and where they remain, during their stay, as scholars learning the A B C of the country's language. Although this failure on the part of our representatives to express themselves with correctness and elegance, may be impossible of avoidance, though it may be apparently termed insignificant, it is nevertheless and in reality an immense drawback for the ambassador, personally, and might become one for his country. Jabbering in any language, or wretched blunders and errors, must ever excite to ridicule, to say the least.

In this respect, then, the comparison between the diplomats of the old and new worlds is wholly in disfavor of those of the latter. Diplomacy in Europe being a life-long career, all who embrace it must be thoroughly prepared therefor by long years of practical training; mastery of languages being the first requisite. But in other respects, also, though not in essentials, the difference between the two systems is immense: a difference from republicanism to imperialism. According to our system, a lucky blacksmith who climbs into notice, may get himself appointed a representative abroad, but with the certainty of being obliged in turn to cede his luck to another who will be anxious to enjoy the same high honor. Thus while the several diplomatic servants of "their Majesties" are arrayed in brilliant decorations, high titles, splendid equipments, furnished with princely salaries and dwelling in superb palaces belonging to their respective governments,—the agents of the State Department are always remarkable for simplicity—of some kind— which springs from necessity, of some kind, seeing that republics, for their part, are only disposed to allow their servants the plain comforts without any of the luxuries of life, lest at any time a contrary practice might serve to their detriment either in pocket or dignity. For the rest, the United States have often sent to Europe eminent and clever men clothed with the ambassadorial character; never a diplomat in the proper or European acceptation of the term.

Mr. Daniel was not only a diplomatist of the American school through necessity, but was by nature entirely unadapted to become an adept in the art of the Talleyrands and the Metternichs. On leaving his country, he was probably better informed of European history and customs than the generality of agents sent out from Washington;—as to languages, he spoke French as Americans and Englishmen only can. But though enabled to perfect his acquaintance with the French while in the diplomatic service abroad, under two administrations, it was not his aim, in accepting the appointment conferred on him by Mr. Pierce, to become a diplomatist or a linguist. He went to Turin with the special purpose of observing the European world and of travelling over it: and in this point of view his mission was successful, being particularly beneficial to himself, and possessing no signification or importance in the nature of things. Mr. Marcy and Mr. Cass had as little business of a political character to transact with the kingdom of Sardinia as with the man in the moon.

In pursuance of instruction, Mr. Daniel proceeded without delay to Turin, his predecessor having already left the Legation vacant. Besides this, the new chargé d'affaires received one other instruction from the State Department. Mr. Marcy had imagined that his agents should not be required to dress otherwise in attending foreign courts than they would in visiting the President of the United States, and, accordingly, had issued a circular, prescribing a plain suit of black as the only uniform for American ministers—a circular which forthwith produced innumerable disputes and vexations at all the courts. It was given to Mr. Daniel for his guidance. He observed it strictly, and never appeared "in the uniform of his charge" before the king of Sardinia, though such a proceeding at first met with polite objections on the part of the court officials. On arriving at his post, he took possession of the Legation and presented his letter of credit to General Dabormida, the minister of foreign affairs, who, finding it in good and due form, procured him an audience of the king, Victor Emmanuel II. The usual interchange of speeches friendly and to the point having passed, the ceremony of presentation was over. It was three years after this that Mr. Daniel received, in accordance with Act of Congress, the promotion in rank to be minister resident near this sovereign.

In 1853, Italy was subdivided into seven little principalities or kingdoms. Sardinia was one of the smaller ones, but it attracted greater attention and was considered more important, viewed politically, than all the others combined, since it could boast of a constitutional government. Turin, its capital, had just entered upon the most famous stage of its existence; in the duration of which the dynasty of the Dukes of Savoy was to pass from an insignificant rule over five millions of subjects to that over twenty-five millions: transforming itself into Italian royalty, and accomplishing the dream of many centuries—the cherished aim of the great Dante, or the formation of Italy into one State. Thanks to Cavour and Napoleon III. Never was there a more brilliant period, perhaps for any country; certainly one replete with instruction to an attentive eye-witness, and extremely interesting.

Turin itself was receiving celebrity, becoming the theme of all Europe and the asylum of distinguished and oppressed patriots. Cavour had initiated the "Italian Question" or clamor against Austrian tyranny in the Peninsula. Victor Emmanuel had not then met with the family bereavements—the death of his wife, child, and brother occurring in the short space of a few weeks—

which obscured the lustre of subsequent ceremonies, and consequently the court was gay. Operas, theatres, balls, &c., &c., where attended royalty, with all its concomitants of parade, etiquette, finery, and foolery, were in full blast.

Into participation of all such festivities and ceremonies Mr. Daniel was brought by his official character. But soon an occurrence, most unfortunate for one in his position, deprived him, of his own will, of many of the prevailing enjoyments. During the first few months of his sojourn in Turin he had written a letter to one of his former companions in Virginia, criticising very sharply the society and customs of the country in which he found himself, and, in particular, his colleagues of the diplomatic corps. It was a disparaging letter of that kind which are penned and returned to their homes by curious travellers, suddenly struck with the difference existing between their own and the countries they visit, excepting that it was written with greater strength of terms than is usually the case. It contained rough truths in regard to Piedmont and the Piedmontese; but it was marked "strictly private and confidential," and was not in the least intended to receive publicity. Through some inattention on the part of the receiver of the said letter, it was allowed to go out of his keeping into the columns of a newspaper. Of course, translated immediately and circulated in the European journals, it went the rounds all over the Continent as a specimen of American diplomacy in actual practice. Mr. Daniel had written and mailed the letter: it had been forgotten by him. Had a miracle been accomplished before his eyes, it would not, perhaps, have caused him greater astonishment than did one fine morning the perusal of his views in print, in regard to " garlick," Turinese "counts," and "empty-headed diplomats, with titles as long as a flagstaff." It would be difficult to describe the effects of this publication at Turin, in an old and illustrious court highly mounted on etiquette, where a look, a gesture, a movement, in any way opposed to the received routine, were wont to be construed of the utmost importance. With the citizens, the uproar produced by its reception was such as if a small-sized Vesuvius had been transported for forty-eight hours into the capital of Piedmont. It must be said, however, that the newspapers and good folks of that plain but comfortable city overlooked the affair after the first outbreak of indignation, with a generous facility. The only action had in the matter was taken by a club composed of the *élite* of the nobility and the entire diplomatic corps. Mr. Daniel had up to the time been a constant frequenter of this club, where he had especially enjoyed the companionship of Chevalier Bunsen, the Prussian representative and son of the celebrated writer; but, though not severing his membership, he discontinued his visits there after the occurrence related. A very polite letter was addressed to him by the President of the club, informing him of the "unpleasant effect which a certain letter, said to have been written by you, sir," had caused, and stating that "the association has directed me to request of you, sir, any explanation that it may please you to furnish." In satisfaction of this request,

Mr. Daniel made a frank statement, announcing his regret that what had been only written in the strictest confidence should have been spread before the public gaze; offering to hold himself in readiness to give any honorable satisfaction that the club, collectively, might deem due to itself, or that any of its members, individually, might choose to demand. The club's reply was to the effect that this explanation was considered entirely satisfactory to all concerned, and no further steps were taken on any side afterwards. The letter, as published, was as follows:

"Apropos, we take the liberty of publishing extracts from one of Mr. Daniel's recent letters of private correspondence, which will furnish answers to the daily inquiries which are so kindly made, by letter as well as orally, concerning his health and his opinions of Europe.

"'It may be strange, but it is nevertheless true, that I have been as really and truly homesick for the last three months, as ever was any little school-girl in her first quarter at the boarding-house. If you knew how much pleasanter a life of real work and study in the United States is than this nonsensical travel and idleness, you would not be so discontented. One will only learn by experience, however; and the best thing I expect to get, personally, out of this mission, is just this: that I will be satisfied when I get back, and never again be haunted by those intolerable longings for Europe which tormented me in the years gone by.

"'The pleasure of actually seeing celebrated places is small. It is all anticipation. The real comforts of Europe don't compare with those of the United States.' [An exaggeration, as is well known, drawn at first sight.] 'The people are nowhere as good as ours. The women are uglier; the men have fewer ideas. I intended to write a book about it all; and I thought, when I left the United States, that I would have to stretch the blanket a good deal to make out our superiority. But there is no need. The meanness, the filthy life, the stupidities of all the countries I have seen, surpass all I expected and all I hoped.

"'Here, in Turin, which is the most beautiful city I have seen, I am busily learning to speak French, and studying what is popularly, but most falsely, termed the "great world" and "polite society." I have dined with dukes, jabbered bad grammar to countesses, and am sponged on for seats in my opera-box by counts who stink of garlick, as does the whole country.' [Rather garlicky, in truth.] 'I receive visits from diplomats with titles as long as a flagstaff, and heads as empty as their hearts, and find the whole concern more trashy than I had ever imagined. I must, however, keep up their miserable acquaintance, for that is the only way of seeing the elephant of European life. So I dance the dance of fools, like the rest of them, and return their visits sedulously.

"'The pictures, the operas, the ballets of Europe are good things; the people, the governments, the society, more contemptible than can be conceived.' [A rash judgment in the first days of discontented residence; one partly reversed by subsequent residence.]

"'I have not yet got altogether well of my dreadful attack of last July. Till shortly after I got here, I was troubled with a chronic irritation—the remains of the epidemic, which annoyed me excessively. I was cured of it by a physician who is the cleverest person I have seen.' [Dr. Giacinto Pacchiotti—a remarkable linguist, speaking English perfectly, without ever having set foot out of Italy, and discoursing upon Scott and Bulwer, Dickens and Thackeray, even as any other; his practice consisting in administration of doses of talk extracted from the authors mentioned, to the English and Americans with unfailing curative effects, at 2 fr. a visit.] 'He gave me a decoction of tamarinds and poppies, a tumblerful every three hours, and a hot bath every morning. In some things I think better of European medical practice than our own. I find the idea current among them which I have often broached to you, that chemistry is not competent to extract all the essential components of natural productions.

"'You ask about the court-dress. I will wear no court-dress, having made good my point with the authorities on that subject.'"

Mr. Daniel offered his resignation o
the administration at Washington; but, on a full investigation of all
the circumstances, it was decided by the American authorities to
decline accepting it, and advice was consequently sent to him to remain where he was. This he was more than disposed to do, and
precisely in order that it should not appear as if he sought to avoid
the consequences of his incautious correspondence. But, naturally
enough, his subsequent intercourse, quite restricted with all those
people about whom he had written so freely, was robbed of cordiality, for his own part, and constant vexation in regard to this affair
never left him. His remaining pleasure consisted in continual travel
and in the observations he was thus enabled to make of the various
European countries. The fair skies of Italy and the mechanical duties of a sinecure office had at last but a very slender fascination for
one of his active temperament, and under all the circumstances. Yet
he did not resign because preferring as more advantageous the position of minister to that of editor—even though he congratulated him-.
self upon having already passed the ordeal of the "snapping village
curs," as he informed a friend in the United States who besought him
to resume his duties as a journalist. Whenever remaining at his
post in Turin he suffered from ennui in its fullest measure, which was
only partially gotten rid of by hard study and literary entertainment.
He was at all times a constant reader. Moments passed in visiting
places of note, and inspecting famous objects of art also furnished occupation quite suited to his tastes. In his quality of prospective editor,
moreover, he kept well posted in general politics; American newspapers being always far more welcome at the Legation than American
visitors, who were mostly of the importunate and inquisitive class.

Mr. Daniel had intended in the beginning of his diplomatic service to make a short stay out of the United States, and to gather
while absent material wherewith to write a book. He soon found,
however, that such a purpose was untenable; that every thing had
been said about Europe, over and over again, and he was not inclined to write what he would consider as trash, or to make mere
repetition. Many friends from home wrote to him suggesting and
urging the "propriety" of his writing a book at all hazards; but he
replied, after mentioning the circumstances, that he did intend to
write *one*, namely, a political history of the United States. He had
firmly resolved to execute this intention whenever he should return
home. Undoubtedly he might have composed a work in regard to
the European system, either a political treatise or a romance replete
with portraiture from living models — models rare and piquant —
which would have sold well in the great American literary trash
market. His early debut in politics, perhaps more than the bent of
his disposition, prevented him from becoming a sensational novelist.
Book-making in any shape he never attempted. He often stated that
he knew exactly what he was adapted to do best, and that was to
exercise his powers in the open field of journalism; and certainly,
"know thyself" was not an unobserved maxim with him.

In the mean while he displayed an industrious research in collecting antique coins, books, &c., and came to be regarded a connoisseur by the antiquarians in all the principal Italian cities. Often individuals in sad plight arrived at the Legation, who, about to be refused admittance as belonging to the vast tribe of beggars which in that country most do congregate—and elsewhere than on the Rialto —would immediately exhibit a rusty image of one of the twelve Cæsars; a passport invariably recognized. Copies of the celebrated paintings in the daub condition he despised; and those worthy of the originals were only to be obtained through great expenditure of money; much to his regret, for he appreciated the works of high art and desired to procure a collection of them both for himself and for others.

The duties at the Legation were light, belonging chiefly to the category of red tape routine indulged in so profusely by the diplomatic profession. One of the most important affairs that came under Mr. Daniel's consideration was that of an Italian who had been naturalized in the United States and who afterwards visited Sardinia, the place of his birth. The authorities there, disregarding the doctrine of expatriation and naturalization cherished by the American Government, held him to perform his duties to the crown just as any other subject: a practice prevailing with all the European powers, and one involving war for the United States or a surrender of their claims. This man was conscripted for service in the army of Victor Emmanuel, and thereupon made the usual complaint to the Legation at Turin. Mr. Daniel, acting upon the avowed principles and policy of the Washington Government, considering that every naturalized citizen should in reality receive full protection and all the privileges accorded to native Americans in return for his allegiance, took the case in hand and demanded his release of the Sardinian authorities. They refused the demand, whereupon Mr. Daniel protested against their action, and referred the matter to Washington. He fully expected that the case would necessitate a rupture of the diplomatic relations existing between the two countries; but, instead of this, there came a dispatch from Mr. Marcy,—one of that kind showing the difference between buncombe and solid realities,—approving the correspondence and course pursued, but simply deciding that the case had better be dropped.

Many of that class of petty difficulties into which Americans entangle themselves while abroad, and from which they expect their representatives, in the teeth of all national propriety and international usage, to extricate them, were brought to the notice of Mr. Daniel, and were mostly by him disregarded, excepting in so much as to return a curt refusal to mix in the same. He always endeavored to protect American commercial interests whenever the officers of mercantile vessels fell under ban in Sardinian ports, which was frequent on account of their imprudence or ignorance. His intercession saved many of these from heavy fines, and many cargoes from confiscation by the revenue officials, who otherwise would have eagerly siezed upon an easy prey.

During the Crimean and Italian wars, in which Piedmont took

an active part, Count Cavour displayed his genius to the world, and to his own people his faculty of absorbing power. He was the whole Government within himself. All diplomatic affairs and business of all kinds were personally attended to by him. In all Mr. Daniel's negotiations with him, the Count exhibited a frankness and liberality of dealing, for which he was ever distinguished in official transactions. His promptness to satisfy the importunate exigencies put forward by Americans was remarkable; at last his kindness was so often taxed by these people desirous of witnessing the operations of war during the campaign of 1859, that Mr. Daniel decided to decline presenting their petitions to the Ministry of Foreign Affairs.

In January, 1859, Prince Napoleon was sent by the Emperor Napoleon to Turin, to contract a matrimonial alliance with Victor Emmanuel's daughter, Princess Clotilda. On this occasion the ceremonial followed was pompous. Upstarts were being received into one of the most illustrious families of Europe—the House of Savoy—and with considerable murmuring on the part of the high old indigenous nobles. The festivities were prolonged; as a matter of course, his royal Majesty gave a magnificent ball in honor of the event; and to this ball all the diplomats of the corps were invited. Mr. Daniel attended, escorting a cousin of the Napoleons—the Countess Marie de Solms. Notwithstanding the fact that this lady was a grand-daughter of Lucien Bonaparte, and his own cousin, Napoleon III. had seen fit to exile her from France when the second empire was established, because of her republican ideas and mocking disposition towards the new empire. Taking up her abode in Savoy, within the dominions and under the protection of Victor Emmanuel, she established herself as an authoress without difficulty, being remarkably intelligent and accomplished. She wrote books giving the history of her banishment and her correspondence with distinguished characters; she abused the empire; and she published a literary magazine. In fine, both she and her cousin seemed to have reproduced for effect the admirable parts formerly played by the first emperor and Madame de Staël. Visiting the literary home—Coppet style—she had created in Savoy, were to be found some of the most eminent authors and writers of France,—among whom were Eugene Sue, Ponsard, Girardin, &c.,—all republicans and all ardent haters of Bonapartism. With this highly-gifted lady Mr. Daniel became acquainted, and found in her salon this cultivated and clever society to be the most congenial and charming he had yet met with in Europe. On the occasion alluded to, the lady was advised by her friends to attend the ball, in order to bring about a reconciliation with her puissant imperial relatives, and Mr. Daniel was called upon to afford his friendly assistance for that end. Her appearance at the court grievously displeased several of the high officials, who were almost walking on their knees in order to show zeal in behalf of the "Man of the Second December." To Mr. Daniel remark was politely made by the king's prefect, upon the informality of presenting a lady at the palace who had not received a special invitation—although she had often before been presented at court. With that the affair was ended at Turin. But Count Cavour, being especially in need of the good graces of the master reigning at Paris, in view of the outbreak of his long-sought and much-nursed Italian war, conceived the idea of writing a private letter to his representative at Washington,—with instruction to report its contents *verbally* to the American authorities,—advancing charges that Mr. Daniel had disregarded the rules of the court, and thereby given offence. This proceeding, according to the practice of Italian finesse, was effected without the least sign of change in the noble count's mood or manners towards the Legation. Through the courtesy of the Secretary of State, Mr. Cass, the contents of this letter were made known to Mr. Daniel's friends, who immediately informed him of the occurrence, and he at once returned a statement in regard to the case so reported, as was entirely satisfactory to President Buchanan. A few years afterwards Napoleon's cousin-authoress married Signor Ratazzi, until within the last months prime minister of the king Victor Emmanuel, and by far the most able Italian statesman since Cavour's death. Thus it may be presumed that she never encountered any further difficulties in attending court balls at the royal palace of Victor Emmanuel, king of ITALY, " Cyprus and Jerusalem,"—or in ruling as the recognized head of court society in the present capital, Florence. As Madame Ratazzi she has recently created quite a little war among the personages of celebrity in Florentine circles, thanks to her keen French wit and fine-pointed pen. Several of her books upon the said society have had the fortune to draw general attention on the Continent, owing to the "flood of light" which they throw upon the doings of the *great world*.

During the excitement that prevailed in Piedmont when the moment arrived for putting into execution Count Cavour's bargain, made at Plombières with the emperor, viz., the annexation of Savoy and Nice to the empire, a laughable incident connected therewith was brought to Mr. Daniel's notice. The enthusiastic and eccentric Garibaldi was bitterly opposed to the said annexation; he was a Nicean, and hated Napoleon III. What must he bethink himself to do, therefore, but hasten to Turin, and make the most singular appeal that, perhaps, was ever addressed to a minister. He went to the Legation, and simply told Mr. Daniel that he had come to ask him to annex Nice to the American Republic by throwing over it the " powerful protection of the American Banner ! " He stated that he made the request because he himself was proud to be a citizen of the United States, and because his " fellow-citizens of Nice loathed the French." The flattering offer was declined, owing to the exigencies of the Monroe doctrine—duly explained,—and only on that account, of course; otherwise the tri-color might have met the stars and stripes in the streets of Nice.

In regard to the political fortunes of Italy, Mr. Daniel kept the Government at Washington constantly well posted, receiving high compliments both from Mr. Marcy and Mr. Cass upon his dispatches. One of his friends at home, thinking to do him a service and friendly act, wrote to him, stating his determination to have the said dispatches "called for in the Senate, that they may appear before the world." To this the following reply was sent:—

"* * * That idea is so unlike you, that I cannot conceive how it ever entered your mind. Surely it must have been suggested by another person. Certainly, if I have a rancorous enemy, who wishes to do me the greatest possible harm in the most intelligent manner, he would resort to that course. He would force the Government to publish all my official correspondence—*written not to be published*—on topics that concern the present welfare and excite the most violent and most sensitive passions of millions, and so place me up with hands tied in a great pillory, for all the villains of two worlds to throw dirt on. What John Daniel might say, when a private individual would pass unnoticed; but a minister represents a nation, and he might compromise both it and himself by a single public word. Now I was instructed and encouraged to write true accounts of the politics of Italy for the information of the State Department. To be exact, I was obliged to say many words which would grate so harshly on the public ear and be so disagreeable to the Government here, that my position would be wholly untenable the moment they were printed. I am sure, my dear friend, that you have never read my dispatches; you have not the time; they will be printed without your knowing what is in them, and no one will be so much surprised and grieved as yourself, when you are waked up some morning by the uproar they can produce.

"Soon after I left Virginia I found that a strange malady, an insane rage for publishing other people's letters had attacked all my young associates there. If I wrote a friendly letter to anybody, I got the smiling reply that they had just published some of it, or were just going to do it, or that they thought it would be quite well to publish this and that passage;—as if the greatest happiness, benefit, delight and honor that could possibly befall me was to be printed in a newspaper! They evidently thought that I would be pleased—while every such intimation caused me pain. Finding that my friends were so infected by this disease that they had become oblivious of the first social law, I ceased to write letters to any of them, and confined my correspondence to * * * and the United States Government. But are the printers and the public to intervene even then? If there is any thing which should be left to a man's own action, it should be the publication of his own manuscript, the utterance of his own words. It is he alone that must be responsible—he alone must pay for them; and he alone can judge of the effect they will produce. Can it be supposed that if I wrote any thing for the public, I could not have it printed?

"Do not take it ill if my words seem warm. I am sure that you will not be offended, if you will for a moment change places, in thought, with me, and imagine yourself in a position always delicate, and rendered doubly difficult by a previous publication. If you will then suppose the anxiety you would suffer if told that a voluminous correspondence, written in perfect security, most unsuitable to publication, and even gravely compromising, was to be printed for your benefit, but without your consent, and long before you could intercept or explain by word or sign, you would certainly then find this letter but a faint reflex of what your own sensations would be. Seven of the years which ought to have been the best and brightest of my life, have been spoilt and poisoned by an adventure similar to this; and if now, when my ills seem to have nearly ended, when fortune is once more in my favor, I should for the second time fall on the same strange and inconceivable mischance, it would be cause of sore vexation and chagrin to me."

The threatened publicity was not given to the documents in question, and Mr. Daniel remained quietly at Turin until December, 1860. At that date he was informed of South Carolina's hasty steps to break the Union; and no sooner heard than he remarked: "It has got to come to this at last, and the sooner the better." Without delay he obtained leave to quit his post, and returned home to take part in the fortunes of Virginia, to which he was ever sincerely attached.

On resuming the editorial control, and taking possession of the

Examiner, he found that Mr. Jefferson Davis had placed himself at the head of the revolutionary movement of the South, and, what was of greater significance, had been accepted as Chief of the new Government then just inaugurated at Montgomery. Mr. Daniel from the first perceived the necessity of prompt and united action on the part of the South, as also of the unswerving and unfaltering energy requisite to carry the movement to a successful issue, whether by peaceable or forcible means. Accordingly he fell into line, and contended vigorously in his columns for secession in general, and for the secession of Virginia in particular. The latter event having placed the South apparently in a united, determined attitude towards her enemies, the *Examiner* quickly called upon the new Government to come to the front at Richmond—the real capital—estimating the effect of Mr. Davis's presence in Virginia to be an equivalent of fifty thousand troops, such was the prestige of his name at the time and the value placed on him, not only by his friends and admirers, but by the people generally. The new President came; but at a very early date afterwards, the *Examiner* announced its belief that mismanagement had accompanied him, and soon reached a decided conclusion, that the accepted Chief was not the right man to guide the Confederacy. The reasons, causes, motives for this conclusion are herein recorded: it may only be remarked that they constitute the best possible commentary on the struggle itself, in that its very nature admitted and tolerated such a ruler and such criticisms to meet face to face.

His course during the war is well known: his whole heart and soul were placed in the maintenance of Southern Rights. He was one of those few who sought eagerly, definitely, and uncompromisingly for the sovereign independence of the South as a separate nation. And not alone with the pen did he strive to advance this purpose, but by service in the field as well, though entirely unfitted for such service through lack of health and strength. Appointed a major in the staff service, he campaigned a short while with General Floyd, in Western Virginia; and subsequently, during the battles before Richmond, he was wounded in the arm at the fight of Mechanicsville, while serving on the staff of General A. P. Hill. This wound requiring him to leave the field, he resumed the conduct of his paper. Later, in 1864, he was again wounded in a duel which he fought with the Treasurer of the Confederate States.

From early youth he had shunned society, preferring to enclose himself within a small circle of intimate friends with whom he could associate more agreeably to his tastes. Judged by this course he was called by some a misanthrope. Yet this preference was not prompted by any hatred of men, but was the simple result of appreciating men and things and time at their true value. Never extravagant in any thing, he always kept about him—according to the inclination of a prominent and very tenacious character—a goodly amount of strong, stern common sense which guided him as well in his actions as in his opinions and judgments, enabling him to look beyond the surface. He early established for himself the rule to follow evenly the dictates of right; and, while it need scarcely be added that he had his faults and committed faults, it may undoubtedly be asserted that he sincerely endeavored both to write and to act justly. His writings were influential only because they were dictated by a sincere and correct judgment, however plainly and harshly worded to the ears of authority, of the parasites of authority, and of the vast band of mutual admirers engaged in varnishing over the truth and each other. The brusqueness of manner and of speech which was natural with him was often taxed as being impoliteness; whereas he entertained high regard for " civility ;"—just as a certain stiffness in personal appearance was erroneously taken by some to be mere haughtiness. It is true, he was entirely opposed, through a fastidious temperament, to that pellmell system peculiar to the very mixed society of America which fosters the living and leaning together of everybody, the ferreting and prying into others' affairs by the inquisitive. Such a code of manners he regarded as being strictly apart from and unauthorized by the creed of the illustrious Democratic party and the immortal Declaration of Independence. Born, so to speak, a critic, he was eminently fitted for the profession which he adopted. At times his artistic leanings would outcrop, but they were of a passing kind. Always particular about every thing that concerned him, he was especially so in regard to his paper, with which he would now and then artistically experiment, when one day the *Examiner* would appear with a "head" and then without. No one was ever more convinced than himself of the importance due to all those outward trifles that go to make up "style" in a newspaper, and in general, and which please or strike more or less according as they are observed or neglected. It was one of his chief endeavors to write simple, plain Anglo-Saxon, and his constant advice to others was: "write plain English : it is good enough to convey all that you should have to say." And, in effect, his style was smooth, while strong and direct, sinning never against taste, only against grammar —but according to the permission and authorization of the laws of euphony. Good taste, sarcasm that partook of biting acrity, brilliancy allied to strong sense, were his natural gifts. His public writing, generally serious and augumentative, was unappropriate to the ornament of wit, of which his private correspondence gave always evidence,— a wit consisting in ingenious thoughts naturally and happily turned, not in that worst sort of false wit, puns, points, and intolerable affectations.

Early in the beginning of 1865, Mr. Daniel, who had always been delicate of health, and who had been apprised of his tendency to consumption by physicians in Paris,—in whose declarations, however, he refused to place faith,—was attacked first by pneumonia, of which he was relieved; then by acute phthisis, which rapidly extinguished life. He died on the 30th March, 1865, only three days before the utter collapse of the Confederacy that he had predicted from his bed of illness, and the last number of the *Examiner*, printed on the day preceding the evacuation of Richmond, contained the announcement of his death. The *Examiner* shared the fate of the Confederacy—it was destroyed in the conflagration of Richmond.

E 487 .D18 1970

DEC 1 9 1991